THE BROKEN VOICE

The Broken Voice

Reading Post-Holocaust Literature

ROBERT EAGLESTONE

OXFORD
UNIVERSITY PRESS

Great Clarendon Street, Oxford, OX2 6DP,
United Kingdom

Oxford University Press is a department of the University of Oxford.
It furthers the University's objective of excellence in research, scholarship,
and education by publishing worldwide. Oxford is a registered trade mark of
Oxford University Press in the UK and in certain other countries

© Robert Eaglestone 2017

The moral rights of the author have been asserted

First Edition published in 2017

Impression: 1

Published in the United States of America by Oxford University Press
198 Madison Avenue, New York, NY 10016, United States of America

British Library Cataloguing in Publication Data
Data available

Library of Congress Control Number: 2016955972

ISBN 978–0–19–877836–3

Printed and bound by
CPI Group (UK) Ltd, Croydon, CR0 4YY

Acknowledgements

I have many acknowledgements. Perhaps foremost I'd like to thank my colleagues and students in the Holocaust Research Centre at Royal Holloway, primarily Dan Stone whose scholarship and intellectual generosity are nonpareil: I owe him a special debt of gratitude, as I do Barry Langford and the late David Cesarani, who are both present in these pages. I'm also grateful to graduate students past and present—Lia Deromedi, Dan O'Gorman, Deborah Lilley, James Milton, Oliver Paynel Natalie Woodward, and to Imogen Dalziel and Simone Gigliotti.

My colleagues at Royal Holloway have been a great support, including Tim Armstrong, Andrew Bowie, Douglas Cowie, Máire Davies, Colin Davis, Judith Hawley, Jennifer Neville, Adam Roberts, Laura Shoulder, and Debbie Wheeler among many others.

I also want to thank Jenni Adams, Eva Aldea, Gina and Laidon Alexander (although I am aware I haven't answered some of their penetrating questions), Elleke Boehmer, Lucy Bond, Matthew Boswell, Peter Boxall, Arthur Bradley, Matthew Broadbent, Gert Buelens, Robert Burns, Bryan Cheyette, Pie and Mel Corbett, Jo Cotrell, Stef Craps, Penny Crawford, Holly Crocker, Tommy Crocker, Richard Crownshaw, Jerome De Groot, Sarah Dimmerlow, Brian Docherty, Sam Durant, William and Jadwiga Eaglestone, Caroline Edwards, Martin Eve, Patrick Finney, Malcolm and Jane Geere, Paul Ging, Simon Glendenning, Geraldine Glennon, Hannah Gruy, Judith Hawley, Nick Hoare, Ann Hobbes, Katy Iddiols, Betty Jay, Jane Kilby, Martin McQuillan, Gail Marshall, Hanna Meretoja, Stephen Morton, Jennifer Neville, Zoe Norridge, Jessica Rapson, Anthony Rowland, Danielle Sands, Jo Sockett, R. Clifton Spargo, Gavin Stewart, Richard Tennant, Sarah Tennant, Paul Thimont, Julian Thomas, Liz Thompson, Sue Vice, Robert Vilain, Lucie Wenigerova, and Angie Wilson.

I'd like to thank the library staff at Royal Holloway, University of London, Senate House, the Wiener Library, and the British Library (especially in Humanities 2). At Oxford University Press I'd like to thank Sophie Goldsworthy, Jacqueline Norton, and Eleanor Collins for their support and encouragement, and the other staff at the press. I'd also like to thank Darren Almond for permission to use his *Bus Stop (2 Bus Shelters)* for the cover of this book. I especially want to thank Brian North for copyediting with painstaking care and excellent judgement.

I am also grateful to the anonymous readers of the manuscript for their interventions, which I have attempted to follow. All errors are my own.

I am especially grateful for a Research Fellowship from Leverhulme Trust and a grant from the AHRC, as well as sabbatical terms granted me by Royal Holloway. Material was given in lectures at the Imperial War Museum, and at the universities of Cambridge, Cardiff, Ghent, Helsinki, Lancaster, Leeds; at the Institute of Germanic & Romance Studies at University of London; and at the universities of Manchester, Porto, Ružomberok, St Andrews, Salford, Sheffield, Southampton, Sussex, Turku, York, and Zaragoza, as well as at various MLA and ACLA conventions, and I appreciate the discussions that arose on those occasions.

Earlier versions of parts of some chapters have appeared elsewhere: aspects of Chapter 1 appear in *The Future of Testimony*, ed. Jane Kilby and Antony Rowland (London: Routledge, 2014) and of Chapter 4 in *After Representation? The Holocaust, Literature, and Culture*, ed. R. Clifton Spargo and Robert Ehrenreich (New Brunswick, NJ: Rutgers University Press, 2010). Some ideas from Chapter 2 were aired in 'Avoiding Evil in Perpetrator Fiction', *Holocaust Studies* 17 (2011), 13–26 and from Chapter 5 in '"You would not add to my suffering if you knew what I have seen": Holocaust Testimony and Contemporary African Trauma Literature', *Studies in the Novel* 40.1–2 (2008), 72–85.

Finally, I would like to thank my partner, Poppy Corbett, and my children, Alex and Isabella Eaglestone, for their love and forbearance: I dedicate this book to them.

Contents

Introduction

Between Meaning and Truth

'Which writer today is not a writer of the Holocaust?' asked Imre Kertész, Hungarian survivor and novelist, in his Nobel acceptance lecture. He continued: one 'does not have to choose the Holocaust as one's subject to detect the broken voice that has dominated modern European art for decades'.[1] The aim of this book is to attend to this broken voice in literature in order to think about the meaning of the Holocaust in the contemporary world.

The idea of meaning is not straightforward, nor is its relationship to literature. Hannah Arendt famously wrote that 'storytelling reveals meaning without committing the error of defining it'.[2] As with so much in her work, this seemingly simple sentence draws its force from a deep engagement with the history of Western thought, and is illuminated by the contrast she develops in her final, incomplete work *The Life of the Mind* between the idea of meaning and the idea of truth. *The Life of the Mind* is one in a long line of philosophical attempts, starting with book VI of Aristotle's *Nicomachean Ethics*, which seek to illuminate distinctions between different forms of knowledge. Arendt argues that thinking 'is not inspired by the quest for truth but the quest for meaning. And truth and meaning are not the same. The basic fallacy . . . is to interpret meaning on the model of truth'.[3] She finds this contrast between meaning and truth in Plato, Aristotle, Leibniz, Heidegger, and others. In Kant, centrally, she finds the distinction between *Vernunft* (reason) and *Verstand* (intellect, the faculty of cognition) (57): 'intellect desires to grasp what is given to the senses, but reason wishes to understand its meaning' (57). Truths are given to the senses, 'factual truths', 'cognition or knowing' (54), provable or

---

[1] Imre Kertész, 'Heureka!' *PMLA*, 118:3 (2003), 604–14, p. 607.
[2] Hannah Arendt, *Reflections on Literature and Culture* (Stanford: Stanford University Press, 2007), p. 270.
[3] Hannah Arendt, *The Life of the Mind* (London: Harcourt, 1978), p. 15. Further page references to this volume are given in parentheses in the text.

disprovable. Truths arise from the world of appearances and are the sort of things scientists seek, which arise from the world of appearances. In the process of the discovery of knowledge, 'thinking' is only a means to an end (that is, when someone searching after truth 'thinks', it is for the concrete purpose of finding better methods or approaches, or new ways of framing and so understanding evidence). The success of science and the impact of modernity have led us to take this to be the paradigm of all intellectual work, and so to downplay or even ridicule 'thinking'.

In contrast, meaning arises from reason and from speech. Indeed, 'thinking beings have an urge to speak, speaking beings have an urge to think' (99). Arendt argues that the quest for meaning is 'implicit in the urge to speak' (99) because meaning originates in the straightforward requirement to make meaningful sentences (these need not be true: 'a prayer ... is a logos, but neither true nor false' (99)) and grows into the need for people to 'give an account ... of whatever there may be or may have occurred' (100).[4] While our desire to know generates a 'growing treasury' (62) of facts, our thinking, our desire for meaning leaves nothing tangible ('and the need to think can therefore never be stilled by the insights of "wise men"' (62)). This 'intangibility' is, of course, another reason to distrust 'thinking' in capitalist modernity, or to find it idle or foolish.

Meaning and truth have a complex interrelationship. From an Arendtian perspective, the core intellectual debates of the last century or so are really about the interactions or confusions of truth and meaning. However, nowhere is this relationship more complex and challenging, I believe, than in thinking about the past and in the discipline of history because these draw on both a positivist 'quest for truth' and the intangible thinking activity that Arendt discusses. To simplify, it is the interpretation of the 'facts', including the interpretative decision of what counts as a 'fact' or as evidence, rather than the discovery of 'new' facts that is most frequently the cause of disagreement between historians and others. The understanding of the past is shaped not by evidence but by the meaning to which that evidence is put, and this, crucially, depends on aspects of thinking that do not arise from the historical study of the past. Yet, all thinking arises from the experience of the past: for Arendt, all thought 'is an after-thought', re-membered. She sums up: 'all thought arises out of experience, but no experience yields any meaning without undergoing the operations of imagining and thinking' (87). This everyday but complex interaction is

---

[4] Meaning, for Arendt, is close to metaphysics, especially if we take A. W. Moore's definition that metaphysics is 'the most general attempt to make sense of things': *The Evolution of Modern Metaphysics: Making Sense of Things* (Cambridge: Cambridge University Press, 2012), p. 1.

especially clear in Holocaust historiography, precisely because the extremity of the events so obviously pose existential questions, which demand 'thinking' in Arendt's terms, in tandem with matters of fact: intangible questions of meaning as much as more straightforward provable or disprovable claims. (This is perhaps one source of the feeling which sometimes steals across many Holocaust scholars that, despite a life of work on the destruction of the European Jews, nothing of significance has been understood.) Meaning and truth are not opposed to each other, but in the study of history, while meaning without truth is empty, truth without meaning is hollow. This is why Bernard Williams writes (echoing Macaulay) that with 'history... every statement... can be true and it can still tell the wrong story'.[5]

This interaction between meaning and truth is clear in Arendt's own work which undertakes two linked tasks. She explicitly seeks the meaning of the past, rather than only claiming to describe 'what actually happened'. But in addition, her work also seeks to understand the ways in which this might change how we form meaning. Like Adorno in this, she believes that after Auschwitz, the 'mutual indifference of temporality and eternal ideas is no longer tenable' and metaphysics—how we make sense of things—has to change.[6] This is clear in her discussions of the idea of evil, for example.

Art and culture play a fundamental role in this process. For Arendt, thinking, insofar 'as thinking is an activity... can be translated into products, into such things as poems or music or paintings... thought-objects... inspired by some human need and want'.[7] Fiction, testimony and memoir: forms of storytelling, which, as Arendt suggests reveal meaning, 'thought-things' (62) which give an account. As works of thought, they enframe and shape meaning. Fiction can initiate or disclose new categories or concepts through which the Holocaust can be seen and understood, or can refine and elucidate what we already know or take for granted, and, in so doing, go further than the licence given to the discipline of history. The past is too important to be left solely to historians and becoming attuned to these texts, we come to understand the meaning of the past.

---

[5] Bernard Williams, *Truth and Truthfulness* (Princeton: Princeton University Press, 2002), p. 244.

[6] Theodor Adorno, *Negative Dialectics*, trans. E. B. Ashton (London: Routledge, 1973), p. 361. See also: Lars Rensmann and Samir Gandesha (eds.), *Arendt and Adorno: Political and Philosophical Investigations* (Stanford: Stanford University Press, 2012).

[7] Hannah Arendt, *Responsibility and Judgement*, ed. Jerome Kohn (New York: Schocken Books, 2003), p. 97.

However, at the same time, art and fiction—works of culture—are inexorably involved with the world of appearances, and so with the quest for truth. Indeed, culture in this sense is the shuttle between meaning and truth, responding to the demands of both but fully of neither. (A novel, for example, may more or less profoundly shape meaning, but also makes assertions about the world that can be judged correct or incorrect in terms of truth: London is or is not the capital of the UK.) Significantly, our most active form of engagement with memory is through stories and culture which not only recall the past but assign meaning to it and so shape the present. This is why, despite using the metaphor of the voice in his Nobel acceptance lecture, Kertész finds writing and culture so significant. In contrast to the widespread fears that the memory of the horrors will be lost with the generation of survivors, he argues that the Holocaust will 'remain through culture, which is really the vessel of memory'.[8]

However, the idea of 'remaining through culture' is not straightforward, for several reasons. First, if facts are hard to establish, meaning is always, perhaps rightly, a source of controversy and argument (it stems from speech, after all). Second, the passage of time changes how we understand events. As actions they pass from the saeculum of living memory into history: they may not be forgotten but they do undergo a sea change ('Nothing of him that doth fade / But doth suffer a sea-change' sings Ariel in *The Tempest*). Different questions and problems, different responses, emerge, dominate, and recede over time. This is clear from the shifting tides of Holocaust history and historiography, and, in literary studies, the emergence of new ways of thinking about Holocaust writing.[9] More widely, for example, the way the Holocaust underlies fears about genetics or biopower today would be incomprehensible—or at best, science fiction—to those just after the war concerned with the power of the state, race, or war crimes. Even how we understand evil and complicity, which are not new in themselves, has changed, as I suggest in the first three chapters.

Third, in Raymond Williams' famous remark, culture is 'one of the two or three most complicated words in the English language'.[10] It is a truism to say that 'culture' is not one thing: it speaks not in one single, monologic voice but is a site of conversation and contest over space as well as time.

[8] Imre Kertész, *The Holocaust as Culture*, trans. Thomas Cooper (London: Seagull, 2011), p. 42.

[9] See, for examples in historiography and in criticism: Dan Stone, *Histories of the Holocaust* (Oxford: Oxford University Press, 2010); Jenni Adams, 'New Directions in Holocaust Literary Studies', in Jenni Adams (ed.), *The Bloomsbury Companion to Holocaust Studies* (London: Bloomsbury, 2014), pp. 237–63.

[10] Raymond Williams, *Keywords* (London: Fontana Press, 1988), p. 87.

This multivocal complexity is audible in the stories by which the Holocaust is remembered. Different communities, shaped by different pasts and frameworks of memory, are interwoven in different ways: 'memories are mobile; histories are implicated in each other'.[11] In a postcolonial and globalized era, the relationship between the Holocaust, the legacy of empire, other genocides, and cultures has been complex and often fraught. I discuss this in Chapters 4 and 5.

Finally, 'remaining in culture' is hard in this specific case because as the late David Cesarani maintained, the Holocaust has 'never been so ubiquitous . . . never been studied so extensively, taught so widely or taken with such frequency as a subject for novels and films'.[12] The Holocaust is clearly present in the political and cultural world: in 2005, the UN took the anniversary of the liberation of Auschwitz by the Red Army, 27th January, as International Holocaust Memorial Day. Tony Judt's magisterial account of post-1945 European history, *Postwar*, concludes with a meditation on how the now omnipresent memory of the Holocaust shapes the future of a Europe 'bound together by the signs and symbols of its terrible past'.[13] Philippe Lacoue-Labarthe suggests that National Socialism 'never ceases to haunt modern consciousness as a sort of endlessly latent "potentiality", both stored away and yet constantly at hand within our societies'.[14] Jacques Derrida declared that '"Auschwitz" has obsessed everything that I have ever been able to think'.[15] And the Holocaust, as well as the Second World War, underlies the 'latency' which is the subject of Hans Ulrich Gumbrecht's remarkable philosophical investigation-cum-memoir *After 1945*.[16] And, to the ridiculous, in 2012, the *OED* admitted the term 'Godwin's Law': 'a facetious aphorism', named after Mike Godwin, the US lawyer and author who formulated it, he claims as satire, 'maintaining that as an online debate increases in length, it becomes inevitable that someone will eventually compare someone or something to Adolf Hitler or the Nazis' (*OED*).

---

[11] Michael Rothberg, *Multidirectional Memory: Remembering the Holocaust in the Age of Decolonisation* (Stanford: Stanford University Press, 2009), p. 313.

[12] David Cesarani, *The Final Solution: The Fate of the Jews 1933–1949* (London: Palgrave Macmillan, 2016), p. xvii.

[13] Tony Judt, *Postwar* (London: William Heinemann, 2005), p. 831.

[14] Philippe Lacoue-Labarthe, *Heidegger, Art and Politics: The Fiction of the Political*, trans. Chris Turner (Oxford: Blackwell, 1990), p. 77.

[15] Jacques Derrida, 'Canons and Metonymies: An Interview with Jacques Derrida', in *Logomachia: The Contest of the Faculties*, ed. Richard Rand (Lincoln: University of Nebraska Press, 1992), 195–218, pp. 211–12.

[16] Hans Ulrich Gumbrecht, *After 1945: Latency as the Origin of the Present* (Stanford: Stanford University Press, 2013).

But this ubiquity of 'Holocaust consciousness' is not unproblematic: survivors, historians, and those most involved with the memory of the Holocaust are often troubled by how the Holocaust is used and misused in culture, finding forgetfulness linked with trivialization. As long ago as 1967, survivor and philosopher Emmanuel Levinas wrote that 'too many novels, too much suffering transformed on paper, too many sociological explanations and too many new worries' have dulled 'the acuity of the apocalyptic experience lived between 1933 and 1945'.[17] In 1986, Primo Levi wrote of the 'gap that exists and grows wider each year between things as they were down there and things as they are represented by the current imagination fed by approximate books, films and myths': for Levi, these slid 'fatally towards simplification and stereotype'.[18] And both these declarations, with nearly twenty years between them, predate the current period of widespread interest in the Holocaust. Cesarani argued that there is a 'yawning gulf' between popular understanding and the 'current scholarship': this is, he writes, 'hardly surprising given that most people acquire their knowledge of the Nazi past and the fate of the Jews through novels, films or earnest but ill-informed lessons at schools which frequently rely on fiction for young adults or their filmic versions'.[19] For Cesarani, that gulf is created by the divergence between the representation of events in fiction and the versions provided by historians. I am less convinced by this, and agree with Saul Friedländer who valued artworks because they can present the 'reality of the past in a way that sometimes reveals previously unsuspected aspects'.[20] But Cesarani is also right that some Holocaust representations are misleading factually and present, explicitly or latently, very questionable or even facile accounts of what the Holocaust means. They can responsibly be described in such terms, and Chapter 6 discusses new examples of Holocaust kitsch.

For the Holocaust to 'remain through culture' involves not only the conservation and memorialization of texts, as if these would preserve the victims, but it also calls for analysis, for new or renewed concepts.[21] These should grow out of the analyses of texts and, in turn, shape that analysis. This book develops five concepts for listening to the 'broken

---

[17] Emmanuel Levinas, *Alterity and Transcendence*, trans. Michel B. Smith (London: Athlone Press, 1999), p. 84.

[18] Levi, Primo, *The Drowned and the Saved*, trans. Raymond Rosenthal (London: Abacus, 1988), p. 129.

[19] Cesarani, *The Final Solution*, p. xvii: this last refers to John Boyne's novel *The Boy in the Striped Pyjamas* and its film adaptation, which I discuss in Chapter 6.

[20] Saul Friedländer, *Reflections on Nazism: An Essay on Kitsch and Death*, trans. Thomas Weyr (Bloomington: Indiana University Press, revised edn. 1993), p. 12.

[21] Amy Hungerford's *The Holocaust of Texts: Genocide, Literature and Personification* (Chicago: University of Chicago Press, 2003) warns against conflating texts with people.

voice' of the Holocaust today: the public secret, evil, stasis, disorientalism, and kitsch. These are not an exhaustive or programmatic list, but ways to understand the complexity of the meaning of the Holocaust in culture. Chapter 1 focuses on how the 'public secret' shaped the subjective experience of Germans during the 'years of destruction'. In order to do this—precisely because this subjective experience is so elusive—it examines Kazuo Ishiguro's *Never Let Me Go* (2005), a novel not about the Holocaust but clearly inspired by it. The novel reveals the structure of complicity and how this works to deform communities and individuals. Chapter 2 discusses the question of how evil is to be understood. After analysing Hannah Arendt's developing theories of evil, this chapter turns first to a series of accounts by and about perpetrators, and then to many of the contemporary fictions about perpetrators, focusing on Jonathan Littell's *The Kindly Ones*. Chapter 3, 'Stasis', examines how the post-Holocaust era engages with the idea of 'working through' the past. Drawing on the origin of working through as resistance in Freud, it juxtaposes two forms of 'stasis-as-resistance': Imre Kertész's post-Holocaust stoicism, stemming in part from his experience as a survivor living in post-war Hungary, and the problematic forms of memory resistance in the tropes and narrative strategies of W. G. Sebald's work. The conclusion contrasts these two with the complex temporality of Otto Dov Kulka's recent memoir *Landscapes of the Metropolis of Death*. Chapter 4, 'Disorientalism', takes its title from the etymological coincidence of 'the orient' and what Blanchot calls 'the disaster' and places together, as a handful of critics are beginning to do, the Holocaust and the colonial and postcolonial past. To explore these associations, and using what has been learned about the representation of genocide from Holocaust writing, I offer a newly inflected reading of Conrad's *Heart of Darkness* as a novella set in and about a genocide. Memories meet and shape each other in many ways: some of these encounters are problematic or assimilative. This concern frames Chapter 5, 'Disorientalism Today', which explores the same sort of reading process, drawing Holocaust studies and postcolonial studies together, but with an eye to complications and difficulties. It tentatively draws positive and negative distinctions between contemporary narratives of genocide and atrocity in Africa and Holocaust testimony. Chapter 6 analyses post-Holocaust kitsch in order to see what it reveals about our contemporary relationship to the Holocaust.

Finally, as is already clear, this book turns often to the work of Hannah Arendt. Seyla Benhabib finds in her work a power which redeems 'the memory of the dead, the defeated and the vanquished by making present to us once more their failed hopes, their untrodden paths and unfulfilled dreams'.[22] For Agnes Heller, it is 'a vehicle of political interventions' which does not 'merely tell readers something philosophical about political actions . . . but also instructs them that there is the possibility to act'.[23] Lisa Jane Disch finds in her work resources for 'marginal critical theory'.[24] I have found a slightly different aspect. The Jewish philosopher and survivor Emmanuel Levinas wrote that the cries of the victims of the Holocaust 'are inextinguishable: they echo and re-echo across eternity. What we must do is listen to the *thought* that they contain' (my italics).[25] I have found the work of Arendt invaluable in trying to follow the spirit of this injunction, in trying to attend to the thought of this broken voice in literature: here, at least, Levinas and Arendt are complementary.[26] This does not mean that her ideas, which develop over her career and embody the Western philosophical canon, are unproblematic, but that they seem to begin a conversation which is attuned both to the past and to the present.

---

[22] Seyla Benhabib, 'Hannah Arendt and the Redemptive Power of Narrative', *Social Research* 57 (1990), 167–96, p. 196.

[23] Agnes Heller, 'Hannah Arendt on Tradition and New Beginnings', in Steven Ascheim (ed.), *Hannah Arendt in Jerusalem* (Berkeley: University of California Press, 2001), 19–32, p. 27.

[24] Lisa Jane Disch, *Hannah Arendt and the Limits of Philosophy* (Ithaca: Cornell University Press, 1994), p. 9. See also David Luban, 'Explaining Dark Times: Hannah Arendt's Theory of Theory', *Social Research* 50:1 (1983), 215–48; Seyla Benhabib, *The Reluctant Modernism of Hannah Arendt* (London: Sage, 1996).

[25] Emmanuel Levinas, 'Loving the Torah more than God', in Zvi Kolitz, *Yosl Rakover Talks to God*, trans. Carol Brown Janeway (London: Jonathan Cape, 1999), 79–88, p. 81.

[26] While a superficial overview of their biographies might suggest that Arendt and Levinas had much in common (both philosophers, both early students of Heidegger, and both their oeuvres are marked by an agonistic struggle with his thought; both were diasporic Jews with intellectual investments in the Diaspora; both were involved in the Holocaust, Arendt as a refugee, while Levinas had been in a POW camp for French Jewish soldiers) there are marked and profound differences: where Arendt's focus is on the political and historical, Levinas' focus is on ethics and religion. Moreover, Levinas' biographer suggests that there was, from Levinas' side at least, a sense of rivalry over their interpretations of Heidegger, as well as an animus over her views on Israel and the US (see Marie-Anne Lescourret, *Emmanuel Levinas* (Paris: Flammarion, 1994), pp. 289–90).

1

The Public Secret

The knowledge of the murder of the European Jews was a public secret in
the Third Reich. What is a 'public secret'? How is it experienced? What
does it mean? How does it shape or reshape a society? The answers to these
questions are important in understanding the Holocaust, many other
genocides and atrocities, and our present. However, the public secret is
elusive because of its nature: when it is at its most socially and culturally
powerful, it cannot be explicitly discussed, or only at great risk; when the
secret no longer holds such power, people deny their knowledge of its
content and their complicity with any concealment. One result of this is
that both the subjective experience of the public secret and its wider
meaning are beyond the limits of the discipline of history and both are
better elucidated through a work of fiction: in this case Kazuo Ishiguro's
Never Let Me Go, a novel which reflects on the past and present in the way
historians cannot. Significantly—and this is also revealed by Ishiguro's
work—the public secret and consequences of complicity which accom-
pany it are important concepts for understanding the post-Holocaust
world, too. In this way, *Never Let Me Go* is a post-Holocaust fiction
which is engaged with a crucial but obscurely understood aspect of the
'Final Solution' and its legacy.

'WHICH OF US DID YOU MURDER?'

In his letter of 19 March 1947, Karl Jaspers commented on a draft preface
by Hannah Arendt in which she had written, 'what, after all, has in the
meantime become more natural and obvious than to ask every German
we meet: Which of us did you murder?'[1] Jaspers suggested that most
Germans,

---

[1] Hannah Arendt and Karl Jaspers, *Correspondence, 1926–1969*, ed. Lotte Kohler and
Hans Saner, trans. Robert and Rita Kimber (New York: Harcourt Brace Jovanovich,
1992), p. 704 (letter 54, footnote 1). Further page references to this volume are given in
parentheses in the text.

99.9%, did not commit such murders, not even in their thoughts. However, as we sometime experience here, the fact that so many of the 0.1% are still among us can lead us, when we are physically face to face with an unfamiliar person, to ask that hidden question. (75)[2]

In her reply, Arendt picks this up, characteristically moving from the abstract to the concrete:

> You say 0.1% at most. Perhaps I am completely mistaken, but that strikes me as a very small percentage and would correspond to 70,000 people. What seems more important to me is this: regardless of how many were directly involved, this in any case small percentage was no longer limited, as it was until 1942, to the convinced Nazis and carefully selected SS troops. Regular troop units, which represent a cross section of people, could be and were employed for these purposes.... Then, too, it is said over and over again today, now that the entire population knows all the facts (and it is said not only by newspaper correspondents or propagandists but by many people, indeed, by everyone who returns from Germany), that the percentage of those who even today would, let us say, cheer Hitler has if anything grown larger than it was in 1943... that can only mean that all these people, who are estimated... to make up 60–70% of the population, would consciously tolerate murder. (84)

Defeated on this point, Jaspers replied that Arendt was 'probably right about what you say about the percentage of "murderers" and probably about the mass of the population too' (88).

As this exchange from 1947 begins to demonstrate, the question of how much the German population knew about the genocide of the European Jews was to become vitally important for understanding the Holocaust. It is intrinsically linked to many others: for example, to questions of civic cowardice or to the question of why support for Hitler remained strong even as the war was being lost and, indeed, even immediately after the war; to questions about anti-Semitism, whether 'redemptive' (Friedländer) or 'elimationist' (Goldhagen); and to questions of guilt (central for Jaspers). More, 'how much the Germans knew' has much wider implications for

---

[2] This feeling has a mirror, but not an equivalent: imprisoned in Israel, awaiting trial, Eichmann wrote:

> In the five years I spent underground, living as a 'mole', it became second nature to me, whenever I saw a new face, to ask myself a few questions, like: Do you know his face? Does this person look like he has seen you before? Is he trying to recall when he might have met you? And during these years, the fear never left me that someone could come up behind me and suddenly cry: 'Eichmann!' (Bettina Stangneth, *Eichmann before Jerusalem*, trans. Ruth Martin (London: Bodley Head, 2014), p. xii)

understanding other genocides and atrocities: it changes how we understand perpetrators and their world views and it questions the plausibility— or even perhaps the possibility—of being simply a 'bystander', and so makes it important to rethink these categories.

It is also a question that is at or beyond the limit point of historical study, both philosophically and practically. Philosophically because, as Ian Kershaw remarks in his important study on popular opinion in Bavaria, 'documentary evidence can hardly provide an adequate answer to the question: "how much did the Germans know?"'.[3] The question of 'what people know' is not clear cut (what, after all, counts as 'knowledge' in this context?): evidence here is effervescent, hard to pin down, much more a matter of judgement than a document. Practically, it is because many sources, even if they could be usefully consulted, were destroyed. This is also precisely the sort of issue about which people are unlikely to be honest if asked. However, there are a number of surviving archives to which historians have turned: among others, Nazi party Situation and Morale reports (the *Lage-* and *Stimmungberichte*), propaganda reports, local newspaper archives and court files, as well as reports smuggled out of the Reich to the German Socialist Party in exile.[4] These sources, and others, have helped challenge the scholarly and popular consensus, held for some decades after the war, which maintained that very little was generally known by 'ordinary Germans' about the extermination of the Jews in Germany during the period of the Reich, a consensus that led the sociologist Stanley Cohen to write that the 'Nazi period contributed two folk clichés to the lexicon of bystander denial: the "good German" and "we didn't know"'.[5]

The historian Frank Stern quotes a German mechanic on his memory of a Jewish boy at school, who says,

> [S]ometime or other, he suddenly was no longer around. I don't have the slightest idea what happened to him. We never heard anything after that. But when you'd ask, well, then you'd get those vague answers. Though, as I say, I don't know anyone personally who suffered persecution... if that kid... ended up in some camp, well, I don't know. He just disappeared one day, I don't know any more than that.

---

[3] Ian Kershaw, *Popular Opinion and Political Dissent in the Third Reich: Bavaria 1933–1945* (Oxford: Clarendon Press, 1983), p. 364.

[4] See Otto Dov Kulka, Eberhard Jackel, and William Templer, *The Jews in the Secret Nazi Reports on Popular Opinion in Germany 1933–1945* (New Haven: Yale University Press, 2010).

[5] Stanley Cohen, *States of Denial* (London: Polity, 2001), p. 12.

Stern also cites another school child, later a Nazi party member, to the effect that she didn't even know what *Der Stürmer*, the Nazi newspaper, was.[6] Historians have found this sort of account by ordinary Germans extremely suspect. Obviously, those directly involved with the extermination knew. So did those indirectly involved: Michael Burleigh writes of the secretaries in the T-4 Bureau who 'shared their offices with jars of foul-smelling teeth' taken from victims.[7] Other major studies have suggested that much of the population knew more, but this knowledge remained unspoken. Ian Kershaw focuses on what he calls the 'muddled majority'.[8] He argues, as others do, that there was no 'public opinion' in a real sense during the period of the Reich, because the public sphere was controlled by the party. There was, however, 'popular opinion' which, if not a place of dissent, certainly recorded 'grumbling' and from this it is possible to get some little sense of what Germans knew. There are occasional reports of people stating things publicly: a Catholic priest condemned the extermination of the Jews in February 1943; a middle-aged Munich woman was imprisoned in Autumn 1943 for discussing the same thing; an Augsburg man was indicted for calling Hitler a mass murderer in September 1944.[9] But these are very isolated incidents. Yet despite the lack of public discourse, Kershaw argues that there was a quite a high level of knowledge about the exterminations: he writes that 'there is incontrovertible evidence that knowledge of atrocities and mass shootings of Jews in the East was fairly widespread' and that knowledge 'of the systematic extermination of the Jews in the camps was more widely circulating than is apparent from surviving documentation'.[10] He describes this knowledge as 'passive complicity' and argues that ordinary Germans knew enough to know that they didn't want to know more.[11] Timothy Snyder is more forthright: he argues that it

> is not possible that many Germans did not know about the mass murder of Jews.... In the East...most people knew what was happening. Hundreds of thousands of Germans witnessed the killing, and millions of Germans on the eastern front knew about them. During the war, wives, and even children visited the killing sites: and soldiers, policemen and others wrote home to their families, sometimes with photographs, about the details.[12]

---

[6] Frank Stern, *The Whitewashing of the Yellow Badge: Anti-Semitism and Philosemitism in Postwar Germany*, trans. William Templer (Oxford: Pergamon, 1992), pp. 224, 221.
[7] Michael Burleigh, *Death and Deliverance* (London: Pan, 1994), p. 123.
[8] Kershaw, *Popular Opinion*, p. viii.
[9] Kershaw, *Popular Opinion*, pp. 365, 367.
[10] Kershaw, *Popular Opinion*, pp. 364, 367.
[11] Kershaw, *Popular Opinion*, p. 370.
[12] Timothy Snyder, *Black Earth: The Holocaust as History and Warning* (New York: Tim Duggan Books, 2015), pp. 207–8. Snyder suggests that while the many forms of mass

Hans Mommsen, too, discusses the 'vague consciousness of injustice' in relation to the genocide and goes on to state that, with qualifications, the 'majority of German adults at the time were probably aware... of various details of this state secret'.[13] Recent economic histories of the Reich have, too, revealed the wide and public extent of the resale of everyday goods and property stolen from deported German Jews: Mommsen notes the 'numerous requests for the yielding up of Jewish living quarters and furniture submitted to the authorities'.[14] This also strongly suggests that the ordinary population knew about what was happening but kept it in a 'peculiar atmosphere of semi-darkness'.[15] Mary Fulbrook focuses on these questions in some detail, through the figure of Udo Klausa, the administrator of Będzin. Drawing out useful differences in the commitments of 'ordinary Germans', and with both an appropriate degree of historical sympathy and a clear-eyed assessment of his post-war evasion, she acutely locates the situation of this mid-ranking Nazi official and suggests that while there is some evidence that he began to worry that he was, in his words '"innocently becoming guilty"', 'when the policies reached the point of deportation to death in Auschwitz', this made no significant difference to his behaviour.[16]

David Bankier speculates on the nature and reason for the secrecy maintained about this public knowledge. In the Germans' efforts to maintain a "normal life", he argues, 'the annihilation policy was a sort of taboo topic to be mentioned only in family circles or among friends': being heard to discuss the murders openly would lead to trouble.[17] More than this, Bankier stresses simply the sometimes near impossibility of believing such a thing (he cites one German who records in her diary in 1944, having read Vrba and Wetzler's report, 'is one to believe such a ghastly story? It simply cannot be true. Surely even the most brutal

killing were well known, the details of Auschwitz might have been less familiar. Yet, paradoxically, the elevation of Auschwitz to the core symbol of the Holocaust, for a range of post-war political reasons on all sides, means that much of the Holocaust, and the knowing complicity of so many with it, was conveniently 'excluded from history and commemoration' (p. 208).

[13] Hans Mommsen, 'What Did the Germans Know About the Genocide of the Jews?' in *November 1938: From 'Reichskristallnacht' to Genocide*, ed. Walter H. Pehle, trans. William Templer (New York/Oxford: Berg, 1990), 187–221, pp. 210, 221.

[14] Mommsen, 'What Did the Germans Know', p. 197. For accounts of the public taking of Jewish goods, see also Aly Götz, *Hitler's Beneficiaries: Plunder, Racial War and the Nazi Welfare State*, trans. Jefferson Chase (New York: Metropolitan Books, 2005).

[15] Mommsen, 'What Did the Germans Know', p. 220.

[16] Mary Fulbrook, *A Small Town near Auschwitz: Ordinary Nazis and the Holocaust* (Oxford: Oxford University Press, 2012), pp. 234, 354.

[17] David Bankier, *The Germans and the Final Solution: Public Opinion Under Nazism* (Oxford: Basil Blackwell, 1992), p. 106.

fanatics could not be so absolutely bestial'). Even some anti-Nazis, he suggests, found the events 'inconceivable'.[18] Nicholas Stargardt sums up even more recent research and argues that 'knowledge of the murder of the Jews was both widespread and detailed' and that, spread by rumour and word of mouth, unsupported by open propaganda from any state agencies, 'it was essentially private knowledge' and as such 'uncontrollable... people had to fall back on their own resources in order to work out what it meant'. He too describes the knowledge of what 'actually happened' as 'taboo'.[19]

Stargardt goes on to discuss the context or frame of this taboo: when the murders were discussed, it often went hand in hand with fear of Allied or Jewish retaliation: indeed, Martin Brozat and Saul Friedländer both suggest that the fear of Jewish revenge played no small part in keeping the Germans fighting even after the war was lost. This was also true at the highest level: in the spring and summer of 1944, Himmler gave speeches to high-ranking Nazi generals so that 'in the event of a military defeat, they would not be able to pretend they were unaware of the fact the murder of the European Jews was one of the regime's war aims'.[20] He had done the same the previous October, with his famous speeches at Posen to SS officers and Gauleiters, in which he told them on the record—literally, he recorded the speeches—what they already knew about the Final Solution and so made them 'formally' and, as it were, archivally, complicit with the murders. (As I will discuss in Chapter 2, it is no wonder that Albert Speer was so keen to prove his absence from the occasion of these speeches.) Stargardt argues that this makes a division between the view of the events taken by the perpetrators and a view taken by the victims: the secret was divisive and their 'respective positions were marked by huge asymmetries not only of power, but also of empathy and identification'.[21]

The historical record, then, shows that although this was in one way private knowledge, spread by rumour and known to be a secret, it was also public. Denied after the war, it was dangerous, indeed, even taboo to express knowledge about the murder of the Jews openly during the war. On the way to answering the question of 'how much the Germans knew',

---

[18] Ibid., pp. 114, 115.

[19] Nicholas Stargardt, 'Speaking in Public about the Murder of the Jews', in *Years of Persecution, Years of Extermination: Saul Friedlander and the Future of Holocaust Studies*, ed. Christian Wiese and Paul Betts (London: Continuum, 2010), 133–56, pp. 137, 139. See also Alon Confino, *World without Jews* (New Haven: Yale University Press, 2014), pp. 220–1.

[20] Peter Longerich, *Heinrich Himmler*, trans. Jeremy Noakes and Lesley Sharpe (Oxford: Oxford University Press, 2012), pp. 694–5.

[21] Stargardt, 'Speaking in Public', p. 150.

an odd and seemingly paradoxical idea has appeared: the public secret. What this is, what it means, and its wider impact cannot, as Kershaw suggests, be adequately answered with reference to the historical record. Because it lies within the discursive space of personal and communal subjectivity, works of literature may be better suited to explore it.

DEFINING THE PUBLIC SECRET

What, then, *is* the 'public secret'? In many ways, it is easier to say what it is not. It is not the making public, say through publication of historical records or through the work of investigative journalism or biography of something hidden. This is just, straightforwardly, a secret exposed. Nor, in this historical and political context, is it the external showing of some part of ourselves that is shared, but hidden culturally, socially, or psychologically: it is not the unconscious, or desire, or the fact that we all excrete but rarely discuss these bodily functions. These are not secrets but simply, and for complex reasons, seldom part of our everyday discourse. Nor do I mean that the 'public secret' is something like mid-twentieth century camp, something both hidden and revealed in public for those in the know.

Closer to what I mean, but not exactly, is what the anthropologist Michael Taussig discusses in his account of masks and unmasking, *Deface-ment*, inspired by Elias Canetti's dictum that 'secrecy lies at the very core of power'. As 'that which is generally known, but cannot be articulated' the content of the secret is both known and disavowed, both repeated and kept hidden.[22] Indeed, this simultaneous knowing and not knowing is, for Taussig, the central structuring feature of a society. In a long chapter on the Selk'nam people of Isla Grande in Tierra Del Fuego (wiped out by colonial genocide in the late nineteenth century), he describes the central functioning secret of their society: that spirits walked among them. Everyone knew that the spirits were men of the tribe, but acted as if they did not know. This sort of mutually agreed yet unspoken secrecy is, for Taussig, the grounds of both social power and the desire to resist or expose it: a taboo. He also cites numerous examples where the revelation of the secret of a taboo simply leads to the death of the exposer. In one terrible case, Christian missionaries unintentionally engineered the collapse of a whole social order by telling the indigenous people what they already knew, that the 'sacred noises' were simply flutes hidden by the men. This is closer to

---

[22] Michael T. Taussig, *Defacement: Public Secrecy and the Labor of the Negative* (Stanford: Stanford University Press, 1999), p. 5.

the sense I am trying to evoke (Stargardt and Bankier both refer to the knowledge of the Holocaust as a taboo). But in the cases Taussig discusses, the secrecy is imbricated with much longer-standing social structure, not a historical and contingent event. In these cases, the taboo is part of the formation of a society: it does not actively deform it.

I want to suggest that the public secret names something that is widely and publicly known, and yet is the object of a considered and collaborative act of secrecy. Stating the public secret openly can result in legal or social punishment because the secret is both information (the resettlement camps are really sites of murder) and more than information: it is a process or *structure of complicity* that draws people, wittingly or not, into collusion and, in so doing shapes and implicates them. To paraphrase Stanley Cavell, when the hearer takes on a public secret, they learn not just the secret, but who they are, as public: it is a 'form of life'.[23] Or, perhaps more accurately, a 'deforming of life'. Because of this shaping power, the public secret is highly powerful and dangerous. It has an effect even after its power and context have decayed, because generally people choose to deny they have been shaped by it.

Literature, in its play of empathy and identification, in its singular freedom and because it is in language and uses narrative which nearly everyone shares and uses every day, has a central role in what Meile Steele calls 'connecting public imagination to practical reason and history'.[24] In this case, because the effects of the public secret are in part beyond documentary evidence, because its structure always implicates and because it concerns both interior personal and shared communal subjectivity, the deformations and stresses of the public secret in the social, political, and personal spheres can most usefully be analysed and understood in closer and finer detail by looking at a work of fiction.

From his earliest novels *A Pale View of Hills* (1982) and *An Artist of the Floating World* (1986), Ishiguro's work has been concerned with national and communal history, guilt, and complicity.[25] His most recent novel,

---

[23] In 'learning language you learn not merely what the name of things are, but what a name is; not merely what the form of expression is for expressing a wish, but what expressing a wish is; not merely what the word for "father" is, but what a father is; not merely the word of "love", but what love is. In learning language, you do not merely learn the pronunciation of sounds, and their grammatical orders, but the "forms of life" which make those sound the words they are' (Stanley Cavell, *The Claim of Reason* (Oxford: Oxford University Press, 1979), p. 177).

[24] Meile Steele, *Hiding From History: Politics and the Public Imagination* (Cornell: Cornell University Press, 2005), p. 76.

[25] For useful overviews of Ishiguro, see Sean Matthews and Sebastian Groes (eds.), *Kasuo Ishiguro: Contemporary Critical Perspectives* (London: Continuum, 2009); *Novel* 40:3 (2007), special issue on Ishiguro.

The Buried Giant (2015), is a semi-allegorical fable which mediates on the benefits, the perils and, ultimately, the impossibility of a communal forgetfulness of violence and destruction. *Never Let Me Go* (2005) set in a fictional 'England, late 1990s' is, subtly about the victims of an ongoing atrocity: in fact, as I will argue, a genocide. However, the novel focuses less on the genocide itself and more on the public secrecy that both hides and empowers it. I am not suggesting that this complex novel maps easily onto Holocaust fiction or testimony: the clones are not Jews, nor the perpetrators Nazis. Rather, by analysing how the public secret circulates in the novel, it is possible to see how secrecy affectively forms (or, rather, deforms) individuals and the wider social structure.

THE PUBLIC SECRET IN *NEVER LET ME GO*

'My name is Kathy H. I'm thirty-one years old, and I've been a carer now for over eleven years. That sounds long enough I know, but actually they want me to go on for another eight months, until the end of this year.'[26] These first two sentences of *Never Let Me Go* encode the whole novel. Why 'H' and no full name? Reminiscent of Kafka's characters ('K') in *The Castle* and *The Trial*, trapped in frightening mad-yet-recognizable worlds, it also summons up the idea of a 'batch' number. The words also sound strange and euphemistic: 'carer' seems more than simply a job description. As the novel progresses, it will emerge that 'carer' and 'donor', 'student' and 'completed' are words in a deformation of everyday language. Much research has pointed out the oblique language of the Nazi perpetrators: resettlement camps, special measures, and so on. But Victor Klemperer also analysed the everyday language of the Third Reich, and showed how

> Nazism permeated the flesh and blood of the people through single words, idioms and sentence structures which were imposed on them in a million repetitions and taken on board mechanically and unconsciously.[27]

Not quite Orwellian 'Newspeak', the languages of the Reich and of the world of *Never Let Me Go* change or make euphemistic the meanings of words. More, in these opening sentences, the 'they' and the informal and conversational tags 'I know' and 'until the end of the year' fix us, the reader, as someone in conversation with Kathy, by giving us information that we know and share (it must be April, the cruellest month, when she is

---

[26] Kazuo Ishigoru, *Never Let Me Go* (London: Faber and Faber, 2005), p. 1.
[27] Victor Klemperer, *The Language of the Third Reich*, trans. Martin Brady (London: Continuum, 2000), p. 15.

talking to us, for example: eight months left until the end of the year) and information that we are obviously *supposed* to know, but do not. She clearly assumes that we know what 'long enough' means (long enough for what?) and who 'they' are. These phrases do more than 'unsettle the reader': as a manifestation of the public secret, they make us complicit, even though (as readers) we do not yet understand with what.[28] That is, the opening sentences tell us that there is a secret which is both known and not known—a public secret—with which we, the addressed and implied reader, are complicit. More, we have to orient ourselves in relation to this secret.

What is hidden and yet revealed by this is a medical-industrial mass murder on a huge national (and, we can infer, global) scale. The protagonist, Kathy, and her friends and peers are 'students' at what appears to be a strange arty school called Hailsham, run not by teachers but 'guardians' (another euphemism) including the head Miss Emily, the passionate Miss Lucy, and the mysterious Madame. However, the students are clones whose bodies are to be harvested for organs ('donations', but not really gifts at all). The entire 'genus' of the clones is marked for death because they are clones, 'only' a resource: they are forbidden to reproduce (indeed, perhaps they are genetically sterilized) and, as the novel makes clear, any cultural production of theirs is destroyed; thus, a genocide of beings created for genocide. In an efficient twist, resonant of what Levi described as the Nazi's 'most demonic crime', the creation of the *Sonderkommando*, the clones work as carers for the donors before becoming donors themselves. As Levi points out, the creation of the *Sonderkommando* was pragmatic, 'to economise on able men' and 'to impose on others the most atrocious tasks', but also had a more subtle point: an 'attempt to shift the burden of guilt on to others—specifically the victims—so that they were deprived of even the solace of innocence'.[29] The clones are complicit with the processes of their own destruction.

Never Let Me Go is structured a like a *Bildungsroman*, divided into three sections, each corresponding to a stage in Kathy's life: the 'school', Hailsham; the 'cottages' (the cheap and nasty accommodation where the clones stay between the age of sixteen and becoming carers); and her life as a carer. Yet, like much Holocaust testimony and fiction, it is an *anti-Bildungsroman*.[30] Instead of developing as an agent from a child's to an

---

[28] Anne Whitehead, 'Writing With Care: Kazuo Ishiguro's *Never Let Me Go*', *Contemporary Literature* 52:1 (2011), 54–83, p. 58.

[29] Primo Levi, *The Drowned and the Saved*, p. 37.

[30] Barbara Foley's 1982 essay is the clearest statement of this twist on a genre: 'Fact, Fiction, Fascism: Testimony and Mimesis in Holocaust Narratives', *Comparative Literature* 34 (1982), pp. 330–60.

adult's world, Kathy's world and agency are destroyed. Rather than become integrated into a community, she becomes more and more solitary as her friends are taken from her by the system and are then murdered for their organs. She learns, really, that she was never supposed to have any *Bildung* at all. In each section, the strangeness of the public secret, that which is known but not discussed, deforms society and human relations. The novel is obsessed by secrets and lies, their covering and uncovering.

At Hailsham, for example, the secrets and lies seem minor, almost appropriate to the genre of a school story novel. Tommy is teased by conspirators—'he doesn't suspect a thing'[31]—so that he loses his temper to general amusement; there are secret games of the imagination that create cliques, and students take roles as 'secret guards' (48) for the guardians; 'horrible stories' (50) circulate about secret activities in the woods. But even these relatively normal secrets have profounder significance: each of these little secrets is a symptom of the bigger secret with which Hailsham is involved. The origins of a pretty pencil case, belonging to Ruth, a friend of Kathy's, are mysterious. Ruth falsely gives out it was a gift from a guardian: Kathy thinks that 'the idea of a guardian giving a present like that was . . . beyond the bounds' (57) of the profound culturally created gulf between clones and human guardians. And whereas Ruth is grateful for the way Kathy covers up her lie, others are repelled. The secrets have ramifications and leave people feeling 'awful' and 'confused' (60); they deform social relationships. As the clones get older, the secrets and rumours change: they claim to have had sex, or that they are boyfriend and girlfriend. Stories circulate about the guardians ('Mr Chris, she said, looked at us girls in that way' (95)), or about students who do not become carers (the old Hailsham boy who, it is claimed, is a park keeper, for example (150)). Some clones claim to have seen their 'possibles', the source of their genetic material and, the clones believe, a key provider of insight into who they really are. The most significant of these secrets is the rumour about deferrals, which suggests that a clone couple in love can delay the moment at which they are summoned to become a carer or donor. The search for the truth of this secret motivates the rest of the novel, in which Kathy, Tommy and, for a while, Ruth, seek out the 'guardians' from Hailsham, long since closed down, to ask them for a deferral. They do finally meet them, and are told in private much about themselves that, oddly, they already know: this circularity is the motif of the novel and the structure of the public secret.

---

[31] Ishigoru, *Never Let Me Go*, p. 7. Further page references to this volume are given in parentheses in the text.

Commentators in the science fiction community did not like *Never Let Me Go*, even though it was shortlisted for the UK's annual science fiction prize in 2005. It was argued that it had no 'science'—no real or invented 'science facts'—in it and that the processes of cloning and so on were not explored: but this is to miss the point.[32] It is not a warning about cloning but an analysis of the past and present: it is about the experience of knowing and not knowing about a genocidal atrocity and what that means. The novel investigates how the creation of a public secret lets that atrocity happen, how it shapes and deforms individuals, ethics, and politics.

THE IMPACT OF THE PUBLIC SECRET

First, the public secret, known and accepted by everyone but never discussed, debated, or questioned, sets up an unbridgeable divide between the clones and the 'normal humans'. Kathy says that 'we certainly knew—though not in any deep sense—that we were different from our guardians, and also from the normal people outside' (69) but investigating this is not possible, in part because it is always already established, already known. Early on, at school, the clones realize that Madame, who visits three or four times a year, has a visceral fear of them ('she's scared of us' (33)). Because of this, they decide to play a trick on her. As she arrives on one occasion, they rush her:

> I can still see it now, the shudder she seemed to be suppressing, the real dread that one of us would accidentally brush against her . . . she was afraid of us in the same way someone might be afraid of spiders. We hadn't been ready for that. It had never occurred to us to wonder how we would feel, being seen like that, being the spiders. (35)

The impact of this moment on the clones is tremendous: Kathy says it's like 'walking past a mirror you've walked past every day of your life, and suddenly it shows you something else, something troubling and strange' (36). Their identity—tellingly, the metaphor is that of a mirror—is shaped by something they know but is also secret from them. The visceral revulsion of humans for clones occurs throughout the novel: much later Madame sees Kathy and Tommy and 'decided in a second what we were

---

[32] In her article, 'Science and the Cultural Imaginary: The Case of Kazuo Ishiguro's *Never Let Me Go*', *Textual Practice* 23:4 (2009), 645–63, Gabrielle Griffin argues against such myopia, stressing that the novel is 'critical science fiction' which intervenes in 'the history of the present' (p. 653).

because you could see her stiffen—as if a pair of large spiders was set to crawl towards her' (243). The only time a 'normal' human talks to them, in a second-hand shop in Norfolk, one clone remarks that 'if she'd known what we really were' (164) she wouldn't have talked to them, wouldn't have mistaken them for art students: they are 'passing' as human here. They are called 'creatures' (249, 267) and, of course, although Kathy says that 'carers aren't machines' (4) they are discussed as 'what', not 'who', by others and even by themselves.

In the final section, when Kathy is a carer, the political and social impact of this division is made even clearer. The clones have no or very little money. They have no privacy or right to belongings: possessions, like Kathy's tape on which the song 'Never Let Me Go' is recorded, are just taken from them (73). They are not allowed even basic freedoms: no smoking (67) and they are warned off sex. Clones are not supposed to visit other carers (148) or talk to others. Kathy complains of her solitude (203) and she always describes 'normal' human beings in a slightly odd way, often just as 'them' (211). No normal human is named by a clone without an honorific. The carers operate in a separate world, isolated from the rest of humanity, rarely meeting normal people. They move all over the country looking after donors in order, presumably, to stop them from making networks and contacts in one area, in case that led to solidarity and so resistance. (Slaves in ancient Rome were not uniformed for fear they would realize how large their numbers were, and so begin an uprising.) What contact they do have is clandestine, like camp inmates: Kathy sent a 'message . . . through a contact' (213); rumours spread quickly in unknown ways (211); Ruth 'ran a few risks' (229) to get Madame's address; Kathy spies on Madame (238) and others, and the final, climactic meeting is 'against regulations' (254).

Second, the public secret means that the clones are passive in the face of their own genocide. John Mullan movingly discusses Kathy's acceptance of her lot and the limit on her thought and expression.[33] These limitations in turn come from the specific deformation of the discourse of the public secret. The clones accept that being harvested for their organs is what they are for: 'it's what we're supposed to be doing, isn't it?' (223), they were 'created' for this 'purpose' (80). The euphemism 'to complete' for 'to die' (or: to be murdered, in fact) doesn't only cover up the genocide, but frames it within a teleological framework with religious overtones. The task of the gift givers, the donors, is 'completed': they are sacrificed. The clones have no position from which to resist, no roots from which to draw

---

[33] John Mullan, 'On First Reading *Never Let Me Go*', in *Kazuo Ishiguro*, ed. Sean Matthews and Sebastian Groes (London: Continuum, 2009), pp. 104–13.

sustenance or thought. Tommy's terrible rages—which seem to come from deep inside him—are not an expression of his unconscious but paradoxically of his conscious knowledge: 'you always knew', Kathy says to him. No wonder all the clones in the school watch, over and over, Steve McQueen's doomed motorcycle break-out in *The Great Escape* (87). It is their lives. But unlike Steve McQueen, Kathy can't escape and will never be rescued. Her war will never be over. They are habituated to the structure of knowing and not knowing: Ruth disposes of her collection of things—she asks if it can go to Oxfam, and hopes it does—but supposes that it's just dumped in a bin: tellingly, she says, 'at least I didn't have to know that' (129). Here, she accepts passively her own knowing and not knowing. Indeed, in the absence of any political hope, the best the clones have is their memories of Hailsham: but this, too, reveals something about the public secret. It is repeatedly held up as a wonderful place (a donor who hadn't been there wanted to 'remember' it (5); other clones think those from Hailsham have special knowledge). And indeed Hailsham, Miss Emily reveals, sheltered the clones. But she goes on: 'we kept things from you, lied to you. Yes, in many ways we fooled you' (263). *Hail Sham* indeed. The school turns out to have been no more than a better sort of concentration camp, or a place, like the Łódź Ghetto under Chaim Rumkowski where, for whatever reasons, the genocide is postponed for a short stay. Miss Emily's argument is a meliorist one: Hailsham, in its lie, made things a little better. But, on the other hand, she admits 'knowing what lay in store for each of you . . . you would have told us that it was all pointless, and how could we have argued with you?' (263). The very existence of Hailsham is a tool for 'fooling' the clones. Resistance is impossible; the 'old kind world' is forever destroyed by the more 'scientific, efficient . . . harsh, cruel world' (267). In the final climactic scene, Madame seems to realize that what Hailsham has done might be more cruel and she the more implicated as a perpetrator: 'Poor creatures. What did we do to you? With all our schemes and plans?' (249). Miss Emily, moments later, says that Tommy and Kathy have 'thought carefully . . . hoped carefully' (253) but that there are no deferrals, no escape.

Third, the public secret also deforms the clone's view of themselves and their own relationships. Ruth, in an outburst, reveals that she and other clones think that their genetic material—and their real self—is simply 'modelled from trash . . . if you want to look for possibles . . . then you look in the gutter. You look in the rubbish bins. Look down the toilet, that's where you'll find where we all came from' (164). More than this, the clones, especially as their time as a carer approaches are obsessed with keeping or revealing secrets. Ruth lies repeatedly to Kathy about Tommy and matters of sexuality. The secrecy also deforms their self-understanding.

Kathy seems to have a good sense of other people's motives but she is often blind to her own: 'even today, I'm puzzled by the sheer force of emotion that overtook me' (54) she says, hoping to understand the relationship between her genesis and her sexuality, which (wrongly) she feels is out of control. She is also blind, until the final pages, to the source of Tommy's rages. Whereas his girlfriend Ruth thinks Tommy is sort of 'semi-detached' from Hailsham, Tommy himself knows that his rages inchoately express his anger about being treated as a living vat of organs to be harvested.

A fourth consequence, from the victim's point of view, of the tension at the heart of the public secret—held between known and not known—is an incomprehension of a sort. The clones know about 'what's going to happen to us one day. Donations and that' (29), but whereas they 'knew a few things about ourselves', crucially, they 'hadn't understood what any of it meant' (36). That is, their world has complexities that they cannot resolve. They wonder if their head guardian, Miss Emily, is mad because during assemblies she would suddenly stop and exclaim 'What is it? What is it that thwarts us? Then she'd stand there, eyes closed, a frown on her face like she was trying to puzzle out the answer' (43). Even events in their world directly related to them are unknown—the successes in the 1970s of the movement to make people think differently about clones, the 'Morningdale scandal' and 'that awful television series' (259). All these things hide, as it were, in the plain sight of their knowing about the genocide.

This failure to make sense is clearest in their relationship with Miss Lucy, the only character in the novel to be given a first name and a surname, Lucy Wainright: she is also the only 'normal' human to hug a (non-infant) clone. Miss Lucy believes that the clones should be much more clearly informed about what is going to happen to them (Lucy means 'light': in the Christian tradition, St Lucy is the patron saint of the blind). In talking to Tommy about his artwork, for example, she is described as 'shaking with rage' (28) (although Tommy uncomprehending does not know with whom she is angry) because they are not 'taught enough' (41). She is prepared to explain why smoking is so wrong for the clones (68) and, during a significant discussion of Second World War camps, gives the tiniest revelation as to the real horrors of the genocide by letting drop that it is good that the fences at Hailsham are not electrified because 'you get terrible accidents sometimes' (77). Only Kathy wonders about what this means: the use of the present tense links the electrified camp fences at Nazi death camps and the camps the clones live in, so bringing together subtly the world of the novel and the world of the Holocaust. (Indeed, much of the power of this novel revolves around the use of tense.) It is Miss Lucy, unable to contain herself, who finally reveals to the clones and clearly to the readers the secret: 'you've been told and not told. You've been told but none of you really understand, and I dare say, some people are quite happy to leave it that way' (79).

> Your lives are set out for you. You'll become adults, then before you are old, before you are even middle-aged, you'll start to donate your vital organs. That's what each of you was created to do.... You were bought into this world for a purpose. And your futures, all of them, have been decided. (80)

Miss Lucy then disappears. Tommy suggests that this policy of being 'told and not told' was intentional (81) and even Kathy thinks there is something in this. The 'being told and not told' is the public secret: Kathy says that if 'we were keen to avoid certain topics, it was probably more because it embarrassed us. We hated the way our guardians, usually so on top of everything, became so awkward whenever we came near this territory' (69). If making sense of things is, at root, what metaphysics is, then the impossibility of making sense in this context demonstrates, in a tiny way, the damage to the most profound grounding of the social by genocide.

Fifth, art, too, is deformed by the public secret. At Hailsham, the clones produce all sorts of art: the best is picked for 'the gallery'. They are curious about why this is, but even Miss Lucy can only say that 'it's for a very good reason' (40). Early in the novel, Miss Lucy tells Tommy that it's alright for him not to be creative (23) but later withdraws this (105). Tommy recalls her telling him he 'should forget everything she told me before. That she'd done me a big disservice telling me not to worry about being creative' (105). Miss Lucy says the art was important 'not just because it's evidence. But for your own sake' (106). Kathy interrupts: 'Hold on. What did she mean, "evidence"?' (106). It emerges that the art is being used in a campaign for the amelioration of their conditions (but not the end of the genocide). In a repeated phrase, creative work is supposed to reveal 'what you were like inside' (173, 255), reveal the 'soul' (173, 255) of the clones. The art is used to reveal what the reader already knows from Kathy is there: the clones have a rich, human interior life and feeling, their 'soul'. Kathy, as the last shreds of her innocence are being torn away, is amazed that such a thing is even in question and plaintively asks: 'Did someone think we didn't have souls?' (255).

However, and sixth, perhaps the worst consequence is that the public secret makes Kathy and the clones actively complicit. As I have suggested, Kathy's resistance (passing messages, driving around to find and then spy on Madam, and so on) is unsurprisingly quite limited and her complicity, as a carer, assured. Towards the end of the novel she discusses what happens if a clone doesn't die ('complete') at their fourth operation ('donation'). The fourth and usually final donation is a moment of congratulations: 'white coats' (273), putting aside their revulsion, even shake the clones' hand. But, Kathy goes on, drawing the reader into complicity, too: 'You'll have heard the same talk' (274):

> How maybe, after the fourth donation, even if you've technically completed, you're still conscious in some sort of way; how then you find there are more donations, plenty of them, on the other side of that line; how there are no more recovery centres, no carers, no friends; how there is nothing to do except watch your remaining donations until they switch you off. It's horror movie stuff. And most of the time people don't want to think about it. Not the white coats, not the carers—and usually not the donors. (274)

Kathy, with her eleven years of caring, clearly knows this happens, but, as a 'good' carer in conversation with Tommy, the most intimate person in her life, describes this as 'rubbish' (274). Many critics have noted Kathy's clichéd way of talking and limited vocabulary. This exists in part, clearly, to prevent her and the other clones from talking to each other, and to themselves, and so from thinking deeply. But this is also tied (as Chapter 2 will suggest) to the structures of complicity. I've already discussed 'special words' within the diegetic of the novel which are markers of a public secret, but the novel's style is also contorted by the demands of secrecy and complicity. As I will suggest in Chapter 4, *Heart of Darkness* has a strange style that hides or covers up the relationship between genocide, complicity, and the secret at its core. The same occurs in *Never Let Me Go*, instantiated principally in matters of tense. Mark Currie cites two sentences from the novel and identifies not only three tenses (the past perfect, the simple past, and the present) but also six (!) 'temporal reference points'.[34] He discusses this as the 'proleptic past perfect', the 'recollection of anticipation' (358), which 'acts as a kind of restriction on information that helps the story to enact the process by which a total institution [the medical clone genocide] brings its inmates to the unacceptable' (358). The torsions of tense reflect the relationship between time and language, concealment, and admission of knowing and not knowing, in the ravelling and unravelling of the public secret.

CONCLUSION

Alon Corfino writes that his task, as a historian, is 'not to master the past but to find ways to account for the historical sensation of the period that shaped the event and the subjective experience of the contemporaries'.[35]

---

[34] Mark Currie, 'The Expansion of Tense', *Narrative* 17:3 (2009), 353–67, p. 358.
[35] Alon Confino, *Foundational Pasts: The Holocaust as Historical Understanding* (Cambridge: Cambridge University Press, 2012), p.14.

In this chapter, and in this case, I've tried to show that this is best done through a fiction. The public secret is not just about what is known or occulted. It has active, shaping effects. It divides clones and humans, prey and predators; in its universal acceptance, it creates a passivity in the victims; it deforms the lives of all caught in it; it covers up knowledge by 'hiding in plain sight'; it deforms creativity; and worse, it makes victims complicit with their own trucidation. The consequences of these deformations are severe. Unlike a shared collective memory, for example, the public secret creates not a community but an 'un-community', binding people in shame and secrecy. It creates a world of divisions: a symptom of this is that there is no easy or communal language that clones and normal people can share.

Historians have discussed what Dan Stone calls the 'voluntaristic turn' in Holocaust historiography, 'the claim that the Nazi regime was ruled less by terror than by consensus'.[36] The nature of the public secret is central to the nature of this consensus, binding people together in complicity. However, perhaps only works of fiction are able to give a fuller view of how the public secret works to deform societies and make un-communities. The deformation of self and community through complicity with the public secret marks the need to understand the social construction of more complex and shaded subject positions and categories beyond perpetrator, bystander, and victim.[37]

Further, these processes are not limited to the time of the Holocaust. Despite being demonized by populist politicians and media in in the UK, all over Europe and in the USA, the treatment of 'immigrants' both by the state and in wider society is rarely discussed outside moments of crisis. As a camp or holding centre, Hailsham House has corollaries throughout the UK, which have similarly innocuous-sounding British names: Brook House and Tinsley House at Gatwick, Campsfield House in Oxfordshire, Colnbrook and Harmondsworth near Heathrow in Middlesex, Dungavel House in South Lanarkshire, Larne House in Antrim, Morton Hall in Lincolnshire, Pennine House in Manchester, The Verne in Dorset, and Yarl's Wood in Bedfordshire. These are immigration detention centres, now called 'removal centres', where foreign nationals are held, although not guilty of any crime, while their asylum claims are being processed or while they are waiting to be deported. That people who are not criminals

---

[36] Dan Stone, *Histories of the Holocaust*, p. 4, also pp. 162, 285.

[37] See, for example, Michael Rothberg, 'Beyond Tancred and Clorinda: Trauma Studies for Implicated Subjects', in *The Future of Trauma Theory: Contemporary Literary and Cultural Criticism*, ed. Gert Buelens, Samuel Durrant, and Robert Eaglestone (London: Routledge, 2013), xi–xviii.

are deprived of their liberty is hardly ever discussed.[38] There are analogies, of course, worldwide. Public secrets and the complicity they create and demand may be more widely spread: reflecting on the meaning of the Holocaust, trying to listen to its broken voice, rightly draws our attention to them.

[38] For literary focused discussions of these matters, see *inter alia*: Agnes Woolley, *Contemporary Asylum Narratives: Representing Refugees in the Twenty-First Century* (Basingstoke: Palgrave Macmillan, 2014); Lyndsey Stonebridge, *The Judicial Imagination: Writing After Nuremberg* (Edinburgh: Edinburgh University Press, 2011).

2

Evil

Gitta Sereny, author of two major studies of Holocaust perpetrators, wrote that she felt 'it was essential . . . to penetrate the personality of at least one of the people who had been intimately associated with this total evil'.[1] There are many historical and biographical accounts of Holocaust perpetrators, and even some memoirs: there are growing numbers of serious fictions, too, which focus on perpetrators.[2] In these, what are we taught about evil? Yehuda Bauer writes that if 'we, at some future date, know the exact way the murder was implemented, what will that knowledge give us? We will know who, what, and when, but we will not have asked the really important question: Why?'[3] It is almost universally the case that these historical or fictional accounts do *not* seem to explain evil but leave our speech broken, with nothing to say. Why do they fail to 'penetrate the personality' of perpetrators, fail to answer the question 'why' satisfactorily? Even accounting for evasion and mendacity, and for some of the more mundane difficulties of communication, the accounts of perpetrators and their fictional counterparts seem shallow and unproductive.

This failure is important because evil, the memory and meaning of evil are inextricably part of the Holocaust's legacy. As early as 1945, Hannah Arendt wrote that the 'problem of evil will be the fundamental question of post-war Europe—as death became the fundamental problem after the last war'.[4] Evil is not only of literary, psychological, philosophical, or theological interest. Even very down-to-earth historians like Tony Judt, not much given to philosophical speculation, acknowledged that the Holocaust was 'more than just an undeniable fact':

---

[1] Gitta Sereny, *Into that Darkness* (London: Pimlico, 1974), p. 9.

[2] See, among many historical accounts, Robert Gerwarth, *Hitler's Hangman: The Life of Heydrich* (New Haven: Yale University Press, 2012); Catherine Epstein, *Model Nazi: Arthur Greiser and the Occupation of Western Poland* (Oxford: Oxford University Press, 2012); Claudia Koonz, *The Nazi Conscience* (Harvard: Harvard University Press, 2005).

[3] Yehuda Bauer, *Rethinking the Holocaust* (New Haven: Yale University Press, 2002), p. xiv.

[4] Hannah Arendt, *Essays in Understanding* (New York: Schocken Books, 1994), p. 134.

[as] Europe prepares to leave World War Two behind—as the last memorials are inaugurated, the last surviving combatants and victims honoured—the recovered memory of Europe's dead Jews has become the very definition and guarantee of the continent's restored humanity.[5]

The memory of evil underwrites what, at least for Judt, European humanity is or might be. Others have gone further: Daniel Levy and Nathan Sznaider argue that the Holocaust is the foundation of a 'new cosmopolitan memory... transcending ethnic and national boundaries' which, as a 'moral certainty... unites Europe and other parts of the world'.[6] For them, this universal shared, mediated memory can serve as a 'new epistemological vantage point', grounding present and future discussions of human rights.[7] Yet this ambitious claim in turn relies on the 'abstract nature of "good and evil" that symbolises the Holocaust' and understanding evil and its impact on what it means to be human is far from straightforward.[8]

The Nobel laureate William Golding wrote that that anyone who lived through the years of the Second World War 'without understanding that man produces evil as a bee produces honey, must have been blind or wrong in the head'.[9] But Arendt's work does not just draw attention to those evils, nor assume them to be, as Golding's metaphor does, simply natural. Instead, she advances the idea that the Nazi camps and the age of totalitarianism *changed* what was meant by evil by adding a new dimension to it. She wrote that after the war, morality 'suddenly stood revealed in the original meaning of the word', not transcendent but a 'set of mores, customs and manners, which could be exchanged for another with hardly more trouble than it would take to change the table manners of an individual or a people'.[10] Her subsequent engagement with the question of evil began, in the perspicacious words of Richard Bernstein, to 'expose and underscore a new and more horrifying form of evil' instantiated in the Nazi horrors.[11] So, in order to discover why testimonies and fictions about perpetrators seem to 'swerve' from explaining evil, this chapter begins by

---

[5] Judt, *Postwar*, p. 804.

[6] Daniel Levy and Nathan Sznaider, 'Memory Unbound: The Holocaust and the Formation of Cosmopolitan Memory', *European Journal of Social Theory* 5:1 (2002), 87–106, pp. 88, 93.

[7] Levy and Sznaider, 'Memory Unbound', p. 103.

[8] Levy and Sznaider, 'Memory Unbound', p. 102.

[9] William Golding, *The Hot Gates and Other Occasional Pieces* (London: Harvest/HBJ, 1985), p. 87.

[10] Arendt, *Responsibility and Judgement*, p. 50.

[11] Richard J. Bernstein, *Radical Evil: A Philosophical Interrogation* (Cambridge: Polity, 2002), p. 227. See also his excellent *Hannah Arendt and the Jewish Question* (Cambridge, MA: MIT Press, 1996), esp. chs. 7 and 8.

tracing Arendt's development of the idea of a new form of evil through her intellectual career, moving from 'radical evil' to the 'banality of evil' and then from 'superfluousness' to 'thoughtlessness'. Arendt's work seems to me to be the most powerful and insightful—if not unproblematic—account of the evil of the Holocaust. The chapter then turns first to perpetrator testimony and a new genre, the 'accusatory biography'—invented in its modern form by Arendt's book on Eichmann—to explore how these ideas are tested and borne out in writing by and on perpetrators. Then I turn to 'perpetrator fiction', a sub-genre of Holocaust fiction, and especially to Jonathan Littel's *The Kindly Ones*, in order to analyse how these fictions engage with the same series of ideas because, perpetrator fiction, too, is often motivated by the desire to 'penetrate' and 'explain' evil.

THE REALITY OF THE
NIGHTMARE: ARENDT ON EVIL

The 'reality is', Hannah Arendt wrote in a book review in 1945, that 'the Nazis are men like ourselves'. She goes on: 'the nightmare is that they have shown, have proven beyond doubt what man is capable of'.[12] This idea, that the Nazis are 'men like ourselves', was starting point of Arendt's lifelong reflection on evil—that the Holocaust was not committed (and, as suggested in Chapter 1, accepted and supported) by people who were, who had always been, monsters, but by seemingly ordinary people. Poignantly, in her 1964 lecture 'Personal Responsibility under Dictatorship', Arendt remarked that 'what disturbed us was the behaviour not of our enemies'—she meant the committed fascists, thugs, and criminals—'but our friends'.[13] In the 1940s, Arendt—and she was not alone in this—was struggling to come to terms with precisely this seemingly straightforward idea. She wrote in a letter to Jaspers that we 'are simply not equipped to deal, on a human, political level with a guilt that is beyond crime': she went on, in a later letter, to say that

> I realise completely that in the way I've expressed this up to now I come dangerously close to that 'satanic greatness' that I, like you, totally reject. But still, there is a difference between a man who sets out to murder his old aunt and people who without considering the economic usefulness of their actions . . . built factories to produce corpses. We have to combat all impulses to mythologize the horrible, and to the extent that I can't avoid such

---

[12] Arendt, *Essays in Understanding*, p. 134.
[13] Arendt, *Responsibility and Judgement*, p. 24.

formulations, I haven't understood what went on. Perhaps what is behind it all is only that individual human beings did not kill other individual human beings for human reasons, but that an organised attempt was made to eradicate the concept of the human being.[14]

It is clear that she was struggling to find a way of writing and thinking about what would be called the Holocaust which did not demonize the perpetrators: to do this would offer only a simplistic sort of evil, myth not politics. Instead, she is trying to understand how it is that ordinary people—even 'our friends'—could have become perpetrators.

This struggle to understand evil is at the core of *The Origins of Totalitarianism* (the first edition was published in 1951). Arendt suggested that it is

> inherent in our entire philosophical tradition that we cannot conceive of a 'radical evil', and this is true for both Christian theology, which conceded even to the devil himself a celestial origin, as well as for Kant, the only philosopher who, in the word he coined for it, must have suspected the existence of this evil even though he immediately rationalised it in the concept of a 'perverted ill will' that could be explained by comprehensible motives.[15]

And, while Kant's position on radical evil is complex and disputed, the point Arendt is making here is that we have many resources to contemplate 'normal' evil (selfishness, greed, ignorance, putting one's desires over the good of others) but 'we have nothing to fall back on in order to understand a phenomenon that nevertheless confronts us with its overpowering reality and breaks down all standards we know' (459).[16] Even if 'we have nothing to fall back on', Arendt is clear about how this phenomenon actually works and what it does: it is the totalitarian system 'in which all men have become equally superfluous' (459). This is one of the great and provocative themes of that book, the deep historical reasons for and methods by which human beings as human beings are made superfluous (the word is almost a technical term for Arendt). Indeed, the title is almost misleading: by 'origin' Arendt means something less like a positivist history and something more like an enquiry into the essence, or founding basis of totalitarianism. Her interest is not in the 'men of brutal deeds and active bestiality' (183), the sociopaths and the mad, but in the ways that whole systems of thought turn some ordinary people into victims (from

---

[14] Arendt and Jaspers, *Correspondence*, p. 69 (letter p. 50).
[15] Hannah Arendt, *The Origins of Totalitarianism* (London: Harvest, 1958), p. 459. Further page references to this volume are given in parentheses in the text.
[16] See, for a discussion of this and a line of argument, Gary Banham, *Kant's Practical Philosophy: From Critique to Doctrine* (Basingstoke: Palgrave Macmillan, 2003), esp. ch. 5. See also Peter Dews, *The Idea of Evil* (Oxford: Blackwell, 2008).

whom 'spontaneity'—for Arendt a quintessential human characteristic—was removed) and others into perpetrators 'beyond the pale of even solidarity in human sinfulness' (459). The end result, she writes, 'in either case is inanimate men, i.e. men who can no longer be psychologically understood' (441), a symptom of the destruction of what is human in humans.

What creates this destruction I have called elsewhere, influenced by Levinas, the 'metaphysics of comprehension'.[17] Arendt describes how an '-ism' or idea can explain everything to its adherents, what she describes as an ideology. For Arendt, ideology soon 'becomes independent of all experience' (470) and explains (or explains away) any and all events:

> Ideological thinking orders facts into an absolutely logical procedure which starts from an axiomatically accepted premise, deducing everything else from it. The deduction may proceed logically or dialectically; in either case, it involves a consistent process of argumentation which, because it thinks in terms of a process, is supposed to be able to comprehend the movement of the suprahuman, natural or historical processes ... Once it has established its premise, its point of departure, experiences no longer interfere with ideological thinking, nor can it be taught by reality. (471)

The form and shape of ideological thinking, once its starting premise has been accepted, is not special to ideological thinking but follows the same logical or dialectical processes as other forms of thought. But because of the premise and the inexorablility with which it is followed, ideology destroys the individual's ability to, as it were, experience experience, or to reflect on events. It destroys, that is, the faculty of judgement. Significantly, because reflection comes from dialogue with oneself or others, ideology in this sense both calcifies the ability to see things from another's perspective and deprives language of its communicative function. Ideology, for Arendt, is opposed to real thought.

Attending the Eichmann trial in 1961 gave Arendt the opportunity to extend and adapt this idea of evil as well as to explore its mechanisms in more detail: this is the core of her contentious *Eichmann in Jerusalem*. In trying to think of evil in relation to the 'terribly and terrifyingly normal' Eichmann, she famously writes not of radical evil but of the 'fearsome,

---

[17] See Robert Eaglestone, 'Against the Metaphysics of Comprehension', *The Cambridge Companion to Postmodernism*, ed. S. Connor (Cambridge: Cambridge University Press, 2004), pp. 182–95. On Levinas and Arendt, see Robert Eaglestone, 'The "Subterranean Stream of Western History": Arendt and Levinas after Heidegger', in *Hannah Arendt, Imperialism, and Genocide*, ed. Richard King and Dan Stone (Oxford/New York: Berghahn), pp. 205–16.

word-and-thought-defying banality of evil'.[18] The term 'banal' does not mean that evil is reduced to mundanity: rather, the 'banality' contrasts in part with the sense of 'demonic'. More, it summons up not the innocence of a perpetrator (as a 'cog in a machine', an argument Arendt dismissed) but the sheer chronological (and geographical) scale of the evil because, as Selya Benhabib suggests, a better phrase than the 'banality of evil' might have been the 'routinization of evil' or its *Alltäglichung* (everydayness).[19] Part of the point of the much criticized phrase was to warn that, given the structural and ideational circumstances, this sort of evil was *not*, as Eichmann was at his trial, boxed behind glass, not simply trapped in the past but involved with wider and more complex processes in our world as well as in the world of the Reich.

In the courtroom, beyond the accounts of atrocities and crimes, a very significant aspect of that evil was being made audible. Because Eichmann 'was genuinely incapable of uttering a single sentence that was not a cliché' (48), Arendt became acutely aware that

> evil is closely connected with an inability to *think*, namely, to think from the standpoint of somebody else. No communication was possible with him . . . because he was surrounded by the most reliable of safeguards against the words and the presence of others, and hence against reality as such (49).

This attack on Eichmann's inability to speak without cliché is not simply, as some have suggested, a form of (pre-war) snobbishness on Arendt's part, although that is perhaps present in *Eichmann in Jerusalem*. Rather it is an attentiveness to the fundamental importance of language in this context: for Arendt, real language, real communication with others and so with oneself opens up the reality of the world. Conversely, the language of Nazism, of cliché and evasion, is the vector through which ideology destroys or recasts experience and prevents thought. In a similar vein, Robert Lifton discusses the way 'totalistic ideology' involves 'loading' of language 'into definitive, through-terminating solutions for the most complex human problems'.[20] Again, in parallel, Victor Klemperer's *The Language of the Third Reich* shows over and over in a myriad of examples, both gargantuan and petty, how language itself was corrupted. Normal words began to have a particular meaning; new words were invented to shape or to limit thought; 'fanatical', 'duty', *artfremd* (alien), *deutschblütig* (of German blood), *niederrassig* (of inferior blood), *zerfasernder Intellekt*

---

[18] Hannah Arendt, *Eichmann in Jerusalem* (London: Penguin, 1994), pp. 252, 276. Further page references to this volume are given in parentheses in the text.
[19] Benhabib, 'Hannah Arendt and the Redemptive Power of Narrative', 167–96, p. 185.
[20] Robert Lifton, *The Nazi Doctors* (London: Papermac, 1987), p. 472.

(hair-splitting intellect) all took on new and menacing tones. For Klemperer, the Nazi use of *Weltanschauung* is an especially good example. He writes that what attracted the Nazis to this word was 'not the idea of it being a translation into German of the foreign word "philosophy"' but rather the fact that it expressed the

> all-important antithesis of philosophical activity... The requisite antithesis of clear thinking is not... to see properly... *schauen* [to see]; that would also get in the way of the constant Nazi Socialist rhetoric of deception and stupefaction. Instead it finds in the word *Weltanschauung* the insight [*das Schauen*], the vision [*das Schau*] of the mystic, i.e. the vision [*Sehen*] of the inner eye, the intuition and revelation of religious ecstasy.[21]

The word then denies dialogical thought and shared analysis and instead comes to present a single incontestable vision—an axiomatic premise—that is beyond argument. Klemperer's point (and Arendt's, and Orwell's, with 'Newspeak') is that the whole of language is reduced to cliché, so real communication becomes impossible. (Bakhtin's work can be read as a theorization of these same totalitarian linguistic processes.)

A major study of Eichmann by Bettina Stangneth appeared in 2011 which drew on some unknown conversations of Eichmann's recorded in Argentina by a circle of admirers—a real-life *Nazi Literature in the Americas*. It was claimed, by Stangneth and others, that many of the revelations in this book overthrew Arendt's views of Eichmann.[22] Stangneth suggests that Arendt named Eichmann's evil 'banal' because he portrayed himself as a bureaucratic desk-murderer at the trial, when, in fact, during and after the war he was a committed anti-Semite and Nazi, a 'cautious bureaucrat... attended by... a fanatical warrior' as Eichmann wrote of himself.[23] She argues that the post-war conversations display precisely his 'complete philosophy' and so his ability to think (266). But Stangneth has misunderstood Arendt: Stangneth goes on to say that it 'isn't the foundations of the argument that are missing... but the... willingness to criticize the structures of totalitarian thought' and its 'dogmatic approach' (267). But this lack of a dialogic interrogation of a position is *exactly* what Arendt means by Eichmann's inability to think: indeed, unwittingly supporting Arendt's claim, Stangneth comments on the 'monological structure' (231) of Eichmann's thought. The language used in these Argentinean conversations 'reflects the disconnection from civilized society'

---

[21] Klemperer, *The Language of the Third Reich*, p. 143.
[22] For a similar argument, see David Cesarani, *Eichmann: His Life and Crimes* (London: Heinemann, 2004).
[23] Stangneth, *Eichmann before Jerusalem*, p. 302. Further page references to this volume are given in parentheses in the text.

(267) of Eichmann's circle: again, this repeats Arendt's point about his insulation from real communication. Stangneth points out that mass murder is 'the result of a political philosophy that is perverted from the ground up' (267)—an insight akin precisely to Arendt's analysis of ideology I outlined earlier. The banality of evil is not to do with Eichmann's being 'deskbound' nor his evasive performance on trial but to do with his ideology and the impact that it has on his language and so his self-understanding. As Benhabib wrote in one of the many pieces discussing Stangneth's book, Eichmann 'was banal precisely because he was a fanatical anti-Semite, not despite it'.[24]

Battered, perhaps, by the storm around this book—and around the concept of the banality of evil, especially—Arendt returned to discuss evil in much more detail during the 1960s, and especially in her lecture courses at the New School in 1965–6, published as 'Some Questions of Moral Responsibility'. In these lectures, she develops further, and in more theoretical detail, her work on the relationship between evil and thought. She begins by reflecting that, almost overnight, in the Reich, 'morality collapsed . . . not with criminals but with ordinary people' (and ironically, bearing in mind her correspondence with Jaspers in the late 1940s, 'we must say we witnessed the total collapse of a moral order not once but twice' because with the Germans, 'Hitler's criminal morality was changed back again at a moment's notice, at the moment "history" had given notice of defeat').[25] In a way expanding on her comments to Jaspers about satanic evil, she turns to the great villains of literature (Iago, Claggart, and Milton's Satan) as resources for thinking through evil: there is in them, she argues, envy and despair but there is 'still some nobility in this despair-born envy, which we know to be utterly absent from the real thing' (74–5): 'the real evil is what causes us speechless horror, when all we can say is: this should never have happened' (75). For Arendt, fiction which is interested in 'satanic greatness' cannot encompass the evil of the Holocaust.

Turning to the philosophical tradition Arendt asks why Plato argues that it is better to suffer wrong than do wrong. Arendt writes that this is because each of us is a 'two-in-one' (90) and we are in constant, animated dialogue with ourselves. This dialogue 'of myself with myself' (92) is, simply, what she calls thinking. She continues:

---

[24] Seyla Benhabib 'Who's On Trial, Eichmann or Arendt?', 21 September 2014: http://opinionator.blogs.nytimes.com/2014/09/21/whos-on-trial-eichmann-or-anrendt/?_r=0. There is an insightful discussion of this 2014 controversy in Richard King, *Arendt and America* (Chicago: University of Chicago Press, 2015), pp. 297–318.

[25] Arendt, *Responsibility and Judgement*, p. 54. Further page references to this volume are given in parentheses in the text.

[if] I do wrong I am condemned to live together with a wrongdoer in an unbearable intimacy: I can never get rid of him . . . it is as though you are forced to live and have daily intercourse with your own enemy. No one can want that. (90, 91)

For Arendt, morality arises from thinking, from self-dialogue, for the following reason: thinking arises out of any occurrence ('an incident in the street' (93)) and even more strongly from 'something I have done myself' (94). Yet doing wrong spoils this ability because, precisely the 'safest way for the criminal never to be detected and to escape punishment' (94) is to forget that they ever did anything. 'No one' writes Arendt 'can remember what he has not thought through in talking about it with himself' (94). But if someone chooses instead thoughtlessness and forgetfulness, he or she forfeits 'the highest actualisation of the human capacity for speech' (94) and in *refusing to remember*, Arendt says, they would be ready to do anything. And this train of thought leads right back to Eichmann and to evil.

The greatest evildoers are those who don't remember because they have never given thought to the matter, and, without remembrance, nothing can hold them back. For human beings, thinking of past matters means moving in the dimension of depth, striking roots and thus stabilising themselves, so as not to be swept away by whatever may occur—the Zeitgeist or History or simple temptation. The greatest evil is not radical, it has no roots, and because it has no roots it has no limitations, it can go to unthinkable extremes and sweep over the whole world. (95)

Dialogue both grounds and is, in the form of self-dialogue, thinking: not to think and not to remember, not to attend to the past, is the source of the thoughtlessness which is, as she said of Eichmann, integral to the 'banality of evil'. This is not at all denying that he, or others, are responsible. Indeed, in her essay 'Personal Responsibility under Dictatorship' from around the same period, she makes it absolutely clear that even those who claim only to be small cogs in the machine of an evil regime are responsible for their actions. Rather, her view is an attempt to explain how this form of evil rises.

Arendt analyses the consequences of this lack of thought and memory which stems from an absence of internal and external dialogue by turning to the Western philosophical tradition. She cites a remark from Cicero: 'I'd much rather go astray with Plato than hold true views with these people' (110) and another from Meister Eckhart, who, in conversation with a beggar hears the view that 'I'd much rather be in hell with God and in heaven without Him' (111). For Arendt, both these remarks reveal that there 'comes a point where all objective standards—truth, rewards and punishment in the hereafter etc—yield precedence to the "subjective"

criterion of the kind of person I wish to be and to love together with'
(111). Arendt believed that we learned from examples more than rules.
'Reversed', as it were, in terms of the question of evil, this focuses attention
on the evil agent, the person and their qualities, rather than their acts.
Arendt then claims that the

> trouble with Nazi criminals was precisely that they renounced voluntarily all
> personal qualities, as if nobody was left to be either punished or forgiven.
> They protested time and again, that they had no intentions whatsoever, good
> or bad, and that they only obeyed orders. To put it another way: the greatest
> evil is the evil committed by nobodies, by human beings who refuse to be
> persons . . . we could say that wrongdoers who refuse to think by themselves
> what they are doing and who refuse to . . . go back and remember what they
> did (which is teshuvah or repentance), have actually failed to constitute
> themselves into somebodies. (111–12)

Eichmann for Arendt was a 'failed self, one lacking in capacity to think
about others or himself with any insight'.[26]

What she saw, then, as Eichmann's failings, his 'smallness' as a human
being—despite his rank and terrible deeds—was really integral to his evil:
his choice is not to be 'someone', not to claim the agency he had, not to
think or to make proper judgements. It is our judgements that make us
who we are. This is why, in writing to Scholem, to clarify her position
some years after the controversy of *Eichmann in Jerusalem*, Arendt says
that it

> is indeed my opinion now that evil is never 'radical', that it is only extreme,
> and that it possesses neither depth nor any demonic dimension. It can
> overgrow and lay waste the whole world precisely because it spreads like a
> fungus on the surface. It is 'thought-defying', as I said, because thought tries
> to reach some depth, to go to the roots, and the moment it concerns itself
> with evil, it is frustrated because there is nothing. That is its 'banality'. Only
> the good has depth and can be radical.[27]

Evil is powerful not because it is profound but because it is shallow.

This conclusion is echoed in her final, incomplete book, *The Life of the
Mind*, which, like all her work, is tormented by the question of evil, and
by the failure of the philosophical and theological tradition to provide
ways to address the evil of her—and our—age.[28] ('No Platonic dialogue

---

[26] King, *Arendt and America*, p. 197.

[27] Hannah Arendt, *The Jewish Writings*, ed. Jerome Kohn and Ron H. Feldman (New
York: Schocken Books, 2007), p. 471.

[28] Arendt, *The Life of the Mind* (London: Harcourt, 1978). Page references to this
volume are given in parentheses in the text.

deals with the question of evil' (150); '. . . the question of evil which is hardly touched upon by Cicero' (161) and so on). In her discussion of thinking, she explores the 'possible interconnectedness of non-thought and evil' and expands her ideas on the 'two-in-one' from her earlier essays (179). Part of her conclusion is, perhaps appropriately, in parenthesis: '(The sad truth of the matter is that most evil is done by people who never made up their mind to be or to do evil or good)' (180).

To sum up: this new form of evil that Arendt analysed has several linked characteristics. It is not the work of devils, 'satanic' or 'radical', or the action of psychopaths, nor is it related to the forms of evil we know best from fiction. Rather it is day-to-day, systematic work by ordinary human beings working within huge systems (this is not one whit to reduce their guilt). Yet the evil—in which these people are complicit and into which they have been initiated—has rendered them, or they in being evil in this manner have rendered themselves, 'inanimate' and no longer comprehensible to others. In a profound sense, they cannot think, and can no longer talk to themselves or others in authentic speech. Their thinking is 'empty'; they can no longer empathize; they have no memory or, rather, no 'depth' or rootedness as human beings: this new evil is shallow. They are no longer—they have actively stopped themselves being—somebody even if they are 'somebody important', a large 'cog' in the system. Before looking in detail at a range of texts by or about real and fictional Nazi perpetrators, I want to suggest that literature or testimony about perpetrators should, if Arendt is right, have several linked characteristics. First, if these 'inanimate men' are incomprehensible to themselves and to others, the literature about them will also be in some way incomprehensible. Literature is, of course, excellent at expressing or 'thinking through' the large and petty selfishnesses that are part of what it is to be human: this is central to, for example, the work of George Eliot, where the lesser and greater faults of everyone are on display and explained (if not forgiven). And there is no shortage in great or genre literature of monsters, from Richard III to Milton's Satan to Sauron and Voldemort. But if Arendt is right, literature should be very bad—terrible, actually—at the representation and so the understanding of this 'banal' evil: counter-intuitively, we should be able to learn nothing *directly* from perpetrator literature about evil.

Second, this literature should be very boring. Part of the point of naming the 'banality' of this form of evil was to try to downplay a public fascination with 'monsters' and focus, instead, on the wider systems and processes. But literature—with exceptions—is not so good at processes and prefers characters and monsters: Satan, Richard III. Compared to these, the real perpetrators of banal evil are dull and shallow: literature is not good at presenting what is boring. (The testimony of survivors, by contrast, is usually very gripping.) Literature is (usually) about 'somebody' (even Dostoyevsky's 'Underground man' is a somebody, a subjectivity; Coetzee's Michael K is somebody even in his wish to escape even himself). These texts about perpetrators should be about *nobodies* in this sense, failed selves (like Eichmann) rejecting an active, thoughtful subjectivity for thoughtlessness and forgetfulness. (In contrast, testimony by survivors is often about trying to remain or to recover the 'somebody'.) More, the large, complex systems which make up the 'banal' evil are precisely aimed at negating subjectivity, personal agency, and choice, the representation of which are core to much literature.

Third, as a corollary of these two, the characters in these texts will evade memory, empathy, roots, and responsibility. Fourth, there is the sense that we too might be implicated in the evil (as in *Never Let Me Go*) in a way which makes readers and audiences uneasy. Finally, the banality of evil is irredeemable: there no way out for the 'cogs' of the machine, no repentance. In fiction, and especially in genre fiction, there remains the idea that the narrative might end in happy redemption: in the representation of this evil, that should not be possible.

This means that books by or about perpetrators should be dull and not offer the glamour of fictional evil. They should contain incomprehensible, boring, evasive, and rootless characters, and implicate us in some way and offer no redemption. If they are so, they will have succeeded in representing the banal evil Arendt names. And it's with this understanding of a new form of evil in mind that I turn to two different sorts of texts. The first are texts by perpetrators, and could even be called 'perpetrator testimony': they are often very popular, widely read and successful in the public sphere. The second make up a more recent wave of 'perpetrator fiction'.

PERPETRATOR TESTIMONY

Alan Rosen remarks that 'at first glance one is surprised to find' works by perpetrators at all because—he cites Christopher Browning—'unlike the survivors . . . the perpetrators did not rush to write their memoirs after the war. They felt no mission to "never forget". On the contrary they hoped to forget and be forgotten as quickly as possible.'[29] However, he points out that there are texts by 'government officials such as Franz von Papen, Ernst von Weiszacker and Albert Speer, military figures such as Wilhelm Keitel and Karl Donitz; ideologues such as Alfred Rosenberg; police officials such as Walter Schellenberg and concentration camp administrators such as

---

[29] Alan Rosen, 'Autobiography from the Other Side: The Reading of Nazi Memoirs and Confessional Ambiguity', *Biography* 24:3 (2001), 555–69, p. 555.

Perry Broad and Rudolf Hoess'. As I have suggested, these texts have a number of strange generic characteristics, of which the strangest is that they do not do what is expected of them. Sereny, cited at the start of this chapter, describes the (quite widespread) sense of a need to find out about why the perpetrators committed their crimes: indeed, it is this urge to understand, to 'penetrate' into the 'why' of the Holocaust that makes these texts (and their fictional counterparts) so popular. But, as I argue, they fail to offer any 'penetration', fail to offer anything like this 'understanding' in a traditional sense.

The first reason for this is that they are by 'nobodies'. By this, following Arendt, I do not at all mean that the authors were unimportant figures in the regime: quite the opposite, many were very significant, large 'cogs' in the Nazi machine. Nor do I only mean that in terms of the historical record, texts by perpetrators are at best unreliable and at worst are characterized by 'forgetfulness, repression, distortion, evasion and mendacity' in their use of camouflaging language, omission of key moments, and secret manipulation of sources.[30] It has been suggested that Speer, for example, was weeding out incriminating documents from his archives in 1944. These undoubted characteristics have a deeper philosophical, existential significance in relation to evil: they are a rejection of subjectivity. These accounts fail to constitute their own selves as persons, as 'somebody', and in general rather portray themselves as unrooted and at the whim of the currents of history.

The most obvious manifestation of this is that most 'perpetrator texts' are not really by the perpetrators in any sense we more usually recognize. In his famous essay 'What is an Author?', Michel Foucault analyses what he calls the 'author function': he shows that the role of the author has altered over time because it is constructed by a series of changing regulatory controls on authorship and, more importantly, on interpretation. For example, 'the author' as a locus for revelatory authenticity, he suggests, is a construction that stems from Romanticism. Foucault concludes his essay by suggesting that the older characteristics of the 'author function' have passed, and new questions might be usefully asked:

> What are the modes of existence of this discourse?
> Where does it come from; how is it circulated; who controls it?
> What placements are determined for possible subjects?
> Who can fulfil these diverse functions of the subject?[31]

---

[30] Christopher Browning, *Ordinary Men: Reserve Police Battalion 101 and the Final Solution* (London: HarperCollins, 2nd edn., 1998), p. 210.

[31] Michel Foucault, *Language, Counter-Memory, Practice*, ed. Donald Bouchard (New York: Cornell University Press, 1977), p. 138.

In the light of these questions—often foregrounded in postmodern fiction, interestingly, and hidden in the activity of ghostwriting—it is possible to see that several key perpetrator testimonies have a strange relationship to their authorship. Indeed, one might say that 'nobodies' can't be authors or, if they are, as in the case of Speer, it is a pretence and evasion.

Some survivors have ghostwriters, or have their testimony published in conjunction with historians (for example, Mark Roseman's *The Past in Hiding* is also Marianne Ellenbogen's testimony) or through other means (see, for example, the problematic creative work in the medical humanities of Frances Rapport).[32] In a contrasting parallel, work on perpetrators is done by or with other writers, or with very unusual pressures—a sort of 'second person' testimony. In most cases testimony is explicitly dragged out of the 'author' and many—the most celebrated—are written not by the perpetrator but about and with the perpetrator, willingly (Sereny on Speer), unknowingly (Moczarski on Stroop), or unwillingly (most legal testimony). These are different from a more traditional biography precisely because both author-figures (Speer *and* Sereny, Moczarski *and* Stroop) are foregrounded in the testimony. There are complex gradations, too, within these texts: Hoess's extremely dull, tendentious, and self-serving manuscript, which became *Commandant of Auschwitz*, was forced from him by the Polish Court as a confession; other trial confessions are more willing, or the result of direct interrogation. Similarly, Sereny portrays herself as a willing collaborator with Speer, rather than an interrogator. An even more attenuated example is Carmen Callil's *Bad Faith*, where the author is linked to the subject, the French anti-Semite and fascist Louis Darquier, only through a friendship with his deceased daughter.

Even when the author is less unproblematically the perpetrator, there is a 'splitting' between the narrative voice (in the present) and the perpetrator (in the past). Generally, texts by Holocaust survivors strongly stress the sense that the past victim is the present narrator, as a form of recovering the 'somebody': by contrast, in these perpetrator accounts the 'present narrator' is at pains to distance himself from the past perpetrator. In the forced confessions, the split is enacted by—as Browning says—mendacity and pleading: 'I was never cruel, and I have never maltreated anyone, even in a fit of temper' wrote Rudolf Hoess in a Polish prison.[33] In the case of Speer, the most significant of all these texts, the split is enacted by a sense of his pre- and post-Spandau life: a life of action turned to a life of

[32] See Frances Rapport with Anka Bergman, Terry Farago, and Edith Salter, *Fragments: Transcribing the Holocaust* (Swansea: Hafan Books, 2013).

[33] Rudolf Hoess, *Commandant of Auschwitz*, trans. Constantine Fitzgibbon (London: Pan Books, 1959), p. 203.

reflection. Speer's own account—as opposed to Sereny's double of it—contains a moment in early 1945 where he records his Arendtian-sounding realization that he had 'become part of this perverted world... I had lived *thoughtlessly* among murderers' (my italics).[34] This splitting of the perpetrator has an analogous corollary in the splitting of the reader, who is constantly drawn into the text, with moments of almost unwitting sympathy (when, say, Stangl's wife is threatened in *Into that Darkness*) and simultaneous repulsion (by the fact that he was the commandant of Treblinka). These texts, then, have estranging relations to their own 'taking up' of authorship. Where, usually, victim testimony tries to offer a unified narrated subject, a 'somebody' (given the damage done by trauma), perpetrator testimony leaves a 'nobody' unless interpellated by the other writer: Stroop's testimony (like Marlow's in *Heart of Darkness*) is told through Moczarski. This is symptomatic, I suggest, of the sense of their being 'nobodies'—that is, of a rejection of responsibility and so subjectivity.

Arendt suggests that these inanimate men are 'incomprehensible'. These texts do not, in fact, offer anything like 'understanding' in a traditional sense. Stroop is unrepentant, and for him the genocide was deserved. He will not debate the matter much further: he is still just a monster and the representation of his character seems to serve propaganda rather than research. (Moczarski, for example, describes Stroop's disgust with the mess that a dead man's blood has made on his boot during the Warsaw Ghetto clearance.) Hoess and others, in forced confessions, offer pleading and excuses. Most interestingly, in Speer's own book and in Sereny's recapitulation of it, no 'comprehension' is achieved. Sereny fails to uncover Speer's 'secret' and instead records the issues of guilt, his 'battle with truth', rather than his motivation. This is not only because Speer is attempting to evade responsibility but because the secret that she is trying to uncover is not really a secret but a shallow, banal evil. It is the failure of Sereny's *magnum opus* to reveal anything in a traditional manner that is the matter of interest: its failure tells us about the nature of that evil.

Perhaps in response to the impossibility of understanding this new, shallow form of evil, these accounts are often not revelatory or explanatory, but—following the model of *Eichmann in Jerusalem*, which began the genre—accusatory. *Tout comprendre c'est tout pardoner*: if one cannot understand anything, no forgiveness is possible, and the opposite, accusation, remains. Arendt's imagined judicial summing up speech at the end of the book is the most obvious symptom of the 'book as trial and these

[34] Albert Speer, *Inside the Third Reich*, trans. Richard and Clara Winston (London: Pheonix, 1995), p. 575.

texts are about, or are in themselves, acts of punishment. Forced confessions, like the formal recantation of views by heretics, are not simply stating facts: they are themselves part of the form of punishment and so impose related genre requirements, a type of extra-judicial punishment for the person and their name following a set pattern. Events witnessed and testimonies written, then, act not simply as a chronicle of events but as a wider, *literary* calling to judgement. For example, *Into that Darkness* ends with Gitta Sereny making Stangl confess. He moves past his courtroom words '[M]y conscience is clear about what I did, myself' through to 'I never intentionally hurt anyone' through to 'in reality I share the guilt . . . my guilt . . . only now in these talks . . . my guilt is that I am still here'.[35] Nineteen hours after this, he is dead. 'I think he died', Sereny writes,

> because he had finally, however briefly, faced himself and told the truth; it was a monumental effort to reach that fleeting moment when he became the man he should have been.[36]

That is, he became 'somebody', taking on his own guilt through dialogue ('only now in these talks'). There is more than a hint here—not least from the form itself, the location of this comment in the narrative flow of the text—that Sereny, or Sereny's actions have in fact killed him: and that final sentence—when he 'became the man he should have been'—is very ambiguous. Is the man he should have been truthful, and so honest and decent? Or one who admitted his guilt, and so evil and wicked? Or one who was not cheery and positive—as he was in his discussions generally—but bent and grey with guilt? But perhaps it means something more Arenditan: that he moved from being a 'failed self', a nobody, to a somebody, the person he should be, and only then was able to take up the burden of —and be crushed by—his guilt. Perhaps we could read this book as a sort of Arendtian moral therapy, returning Stangl, through dialogue, memory and thought, to selfhood, and so to facing what he had done. (The unanswerable question would then be: how much of this was real and how much shaped by the genre demands of 'accusatory biography'?) Sereny revisits this type of crux in the final pages of her book on Speer: here she finds his refusal to die, though 'he needed and longed to die', of great significance.[37]

This 'accusatory' form—itself a symptom of the lack of response from the perpetrators—is central to Sereny's book on Speer (ironically, she is often taken by her critics as too sympathetic to him). Much of Sereny's judgement on Speer hangs on his presence or absence at Himmler's speech

---

[35] Sereny, *Into that Darkness*, p. 364.   [36] Ibid., p. 366.
[37] Gitta Sereny, *Albert Speer: His Battle with Truth* (London: Picador, 1995), p. 704.

at Posen on 6 October 1943 and so about whether he actually (officially, as it were) knew about the 'Final Solution': it was 'absolutely central to an understanding of him', a 'landmark date'.[38] Joachim Fest's major account of Speer, too, argues this is a 'crucial' date.[39] This concentration on a factual matter stands out because Sereny's book draws so much on the 'total texture' of his life and his battle with truth. But the reason for this is clear: the question of his presence or absence becomes a narrative touchstone where the non-empirical tapestry of a life can be pinned down to a specific, provable truth or falsehood, and so held to account. As I suggested in Chapter 1, the point of this speech, and some others, by Himmler was to bind unequivocally the higher ranking Nazis into collusion with the 'war crimes'—putting their guilt 'on the record' in this way served to warn them what would happen should Germany lose the war, and so perhaps encourage them through fear. However, Himmler was only making explicit what was implicit and widely known. Nevertheless, like a good detective story approaching a denouement, Sereny builds up the suspense. First, she stresses how important it is for him not to have heard the speech. In 1971, Speer hears about an article by Erich Goldhagen which alleged he had been present: it sends Speer into cold sweats and makes him sleepless. Sereny shows this article to be faulty (the allegation is the result of an unedited proof). Then Speer lists all reasons he could not have been there: he claimed that no night landings were possible back in Germany and Hitler's appointment book showed his return and so on. Then, piece by piece Sereny takes these away:

> the fact is that the more Speer tries to explain away awkward facts, the clearer it is that he is desperately trying to avoid facing the truth. There is simply no way that Speer can have failed to know about Himmler's speech, whether or not he sat through it.[40]

This date becomes an epiphanic moment, a concrete historical fact that can be proved or disproved. It is a moment where meaning illuminates truth, and truth illuminates meaning. Moreover, research undertaken since Sereny's book reveals that Speer cannot have failed to have known about the 'final solution'. In fact, the text itself, in the final pages (the chapter called 'The Great Lie') allows that Speer himself 'sensed dreadful things were happening with the Jews': in a cited letter to the South African Board of Deputies he writes of his guilt for 'my tacit acceptance of the

---

[38] Ibid., pp. 397, 399.
[39] Joachim Fest, *Speer: The Final Verdict* (London: Weidenfeld and Nicolson, 2001), p. 185.
[40] Sereny, *Speer*, p. 401.

persecution and murder of millions of Jews'.[41] Sereny pauses over the translation of 'tacit acceptance': *Billigung*. Speer himself glosses it as also 'looking away, not by knowledge of an order or its executioner'.[42] Thus, Speer (and so Sereny) admits a general sense of knowledge, to which one incident (official though it may be) is not crucial, nor landmark. Yet Sereny's text focuses on the moment of Himmler's speech precisely because it can be pinned down and discussed. It is not the secret, but the encryption of the secret, its hiding and denial, that is the issue: we learn about Speer, and other perpetrators, *indirectly*. The accounts of Speer and by Speer are still controversial. Was his Spandau-self still mendacious and deceitful, a 'nobody' denying the depth and commitment of his engagement and, as it were, hiding in plain sight? Or did he properly go back and remember and so try to constitute himself as a person? (Perhaps it is only in fiction and in law that the answer to such questions can be so clear cut.)

If, then, accounts of real perpetrators fail to 'penetrate the personality' because there *is* no real personality, because the perpetrators of this evil cannot really 'think' in Arendt's terms and remain 'incomprehensible', how does fiction respond to the same problem?

PERPETRATOR FICTION

In her now celebrated article 'Beginnings of the Day: Fascism and Representation', Gillian Rose proposed a thought experiment in order to investigate the relationship between the representation of perpetrators and of fascism and what she calls (with, to be fair, a hint of melodrama) the 'fascism of representation' in literature and film: by this, she meant the ways in which representation ineluctably interpellates us in an identity. 'Let us make a film', she imagined,

> which follows the life story of a member of the SS in all its pathos, so that we empathise with him, identify with his hopes and fears, disappointment and rage, so that when it comes to killing, we put our hands on the trigger with him, wanting him to get what he wants.[43]

She suggested that such a film involving such a full identification with a perpetrator is impossible since we would know the identity of the SS

[41] Ibid., pp. 706, 707.   [42] Ibid., p. 708; See also Fest, *Speer*, p. 333.
[43] Gillian Rose, *Mourning Becomes the Law* (Cambridge: Cambridge University Press, 1996), p. 50. Further page references to this volume are given in parentheses in the text.

protagonist from the start and would prevent ourselves from wanting what this evil man wants. Subtly, Rose implied that Kazuo Isiguro's novel, *The Remains of the Day*, achieves just this without us noticing. We find ourselves, through the play of empathy, identifying with the butler Stevens, who turns out to be, in many ways, very unpleasant. Interestingly, she notes that the butler, in espousing dignity in his role, is at the same time abnegating exactly the sort of ability to make judgements that lies in the 'liberal, representative notion of citizenship' (52) in order to serve his master: that is, he chooses to become a 'nobody'. The moments in which the audience feels for him most are in his attempts—through attempting to realize a romance—to take up his agency, to become a 'somebody'. These distressing themes (an almost unrecognized but profound complicity with evil; a failure of any form of redemption) are Isiguro's own, of course.

But this form of disguised, quasi-allegory is not new: Rose might easily have looked at another 'perpetrator fiction', Muriel Spark's 1961 novel *The Prime of Miss Jean Brodie*. This remarkable parable, written during the Eichmann trial (which Spark attended) is clearly about the Nazis and perpetration but the reader only just notices this because it is set in an Edinburgh school for girls.[44] Not only is Jean Brodie an admirer of Hitler ('a prophet-like figure like Thomas Carlyle, and more reliable than Mussolini') and fascism in general, but she also turns her 'set' of girls into 'fascisti', as the most observant girl, and eventually 'betrayer' of Brodie herself, points out.[45] Miss Brodie even has a scapegoat, Mary Macgregor (who was 'famous for being stupid, and always to blame' (14)), who dies in a hotel fire, in a horrible scene, clearly—in the context—evocative of the Holocaust:

> She ran one way: then turning, the other way; and at either end the blast furnace of the fire met her. She heard no screams, for the roar of the fire drowned the screams; she gave no scream, for the smoke was choking her. (15)

In the less-subtle film version, much of the parable is lost and Brodie—in the novel a pander, a hypocrite, and a bully—is seen as someone simply with misplaced charisma.

---

[44] See, *inter alia*, James Bailey, 'Repetition, Boredom, Despair: Muriel Spark and the Eichmann Trial', in Jenni Adams and Sue Vice (eds.), *Representing Perpetrators in Holocaust Literature and Film* (London: Valentine Mitchell, 2013), 165–84. A fictionalized version of the trial is part of Spark's novel *The Mandelbaum Gate* (1966): for a clear discussion, see Stonebridge, *The Judicial Imagination*.
[45] Muriel Spark, *The Prime of Miss Jean Brodie* (London: Penguin, 2000), pp. 31, 97. Further page references to this volume are given in parentheses in the text.

It is not altogether sure that Rose's original conjecture—that we cannot knowingly identify with the wicked in fiction—is correct. Despite knowing he is set out to prove a villain, does the audience not enjoy, perhaps guiltily, Richard III's cleverness and sly wit, as, for example, he seduces the woman whose husband and whose father he has killed? ('Was ever woman in this humour woo'd? / Was ever woman in this humour won?' *Richard III* Act 1 sc. ii). Similarly, at least in Stanley Fish's reading, our identification with Milton's Satan and our knowledge that he is the ultimate evil sets up the complexity of *Paradise Lost* and its view of rhetoric's untrustworthiness. This bears out Arendt's point: that within this fictional evil there is still some nobility, some 'despair-born envy' absent from Holocaust perpetrators, some moment of real or failed courage, of the sort felt for Macbeth in his final scene, for example, or for Stevens' forlorn love. Perhaps these representations do not touch 'real evil'. Yet the questions Rose raises about identification may still remain. The second part of Rose's conjecture, that such fictions and films explicitly based on perpetrators are impossible, was not the case then (to name two more novels explicitly about perpetrators: Amis' *Time's Arrow* (1981); Michel Tournier's *Le Roi des Aulnes/The Ogre* (1970 French, 1972 English)) and in any case been disproved by time: many 'perpetrator fictions' now exist, including one very significant novel specifically about an SS officer, Jonathan Littell's *The Kindly Ones*. Rose was right that *The Remains of the Day* is a sort of post-Holocaust perpetrator fiction, in which the protagonist's abandonment of his own judgement, his choice, makes him a 'nobody'. However, her assertion that it is the play of identification which makes them problematic does not go far enough. The problem lies, as I have argued, in the nature of the evil these texts are trying to represent.

Despite or perhaps because of this difficulty over evil, there has been a boom in the last twenty years or so across Europe and America of work that deals with or focuses on the perpetrators and which makes the questions Rose asked about identification and aesthetic enjoyment even more acute. This boom includes novels like Bernhard Schlink's *The Reader* (1995 German, 1997 English) and Martin Amis' *The Zone of Interest* (2014). The reasons for this wave of novels are complex and various. The growth of *Täterforschung* (historical research into perpetrators) over the last twenty-five years or so is clearly an influence and source: many novels, good and bad, draw on recent historiography (often Christopher Browning's best-seller *Ordinary Men*). The continual popularity of the historical novel, set fifty (or, after Walter Scott, sixty) years in the past is another, as is the dominance and importance of the memory of the Second World War and its changes as the global political situation shifts: that is, the memory of the Holocaust during the Cold War is not the same as it is during, say, the régime of Vladimir Putin.[46] Further, the Holocaust has been used as a 'vector' or 'screen memory': the growth in these fictions seems tied in with the developing role of the Holocaust, rightly or wrongly, as a cultural metaphor for other events and as a 'proxy' for different, and perhaps more recent, atrocities. However, underlying all these is, I think, the fascination evoked by the question of evil, voiced by Sereny (and many, many others): why did this happen? Yet I am going to suggest that, like perpetrator testimony, most perpetrator fiction, even the most perceptive, 'swerves' from engaging or explaining this evil. The mechanics of the 'swerve' varies from book to book.

Maureen Myant's *The Search* (2009), while not internationally successful, can be seen as typical of the subgenre. The protagonists at the start are two fictional children, Jan and Lena, who survive the massacres at Lidice. In revenge for the killing of Reinhard Heydrich by partisans, the Nazis murdered all the male villagers of this Czech village and sent the women and children to concentration camps. Jan hides, then is reunited with his mother and sister. The *donné* here is that a few children, according to the historical record, were chosen for 'germanification', for integration into German families. Jan and Lena are split up and then Jan vows to find her again: the 'search' of the title echoes, of course, the John Ford/John Wayne movie in which the protagonists search for a stolen child: 'once upon a time in Nazi-Occupied Europe' as Quentin Tarantino might have it. Jan then undergoes the (rather predictable) literary Holocaust tourist itinerary: a sort of Nazi Dotheboys Hall in Germany where he is told that here 'you have no sisters, no brothers', an echo of Primo Levi's epiphanic moment of understanding at Auschwitz; he befriends a Jewish boy; they escape to Poland; he's picked up by partisans, straight out of the movie *Defiance*, and is initiated into violence and vodka; he sees boxcars of Jews being sent to their death. Finally, Jan discovers the German farm where his sister is living, where the dénouement, signalled by the title and the intertextual *Searchers* reference occurs.

However, while the novel begins focalized through Jan, at the beginning of Chapter 9 the story suddenly diffuses. It starts to be seen through the eyes of the 'good German' family who now have Lena, and the novel becomes much more clearly about 'perpetration'. Their son is in a killing squad in Poland and later deserts. On his return to the farm, he tells his father that in

[46] See, for different discussions of the war's more complex legacy, Paul Gilroy, *After Empire: Melancholia or Convivial Culture?* (London: Routledge, 2004); Marianna Torgovnick, *The War Complex* (Chicago: University of Chicago Press, 2005); Dan Stone, *Goodbye to All That?* (Oxford: Oxford University Press, 2014).

one village not far from here, they gathered us together one morning and told us that what we had to do might not be all that pleasant . . . They said some of the older men might want to avoid it, and if they did then they could back out. And some of them did. Us younger ones laughed and made fun of them.[47]

The following comes from the widely anthologized first two-page chapter of Christopher Browning's *Ordinary Men*, reporting a speech from Major Trapp:

> The battalion . . . had to perform a frightfully unpleasant task . . . There were Jews in the village of Józefów . . . [and they] were to be shot on the spot by the battalion . . . if any of the older men amongst them did not feel up to the task that lay before him, he could step out.[48]

Here, Myant's prose is simply not very good: this is not simply of aesthetic importance. It is not a question of plagiarism here (authors are allowed—indeed, in Holocaust fiction should have—sources), or lack of accuracy (Józefów is in central Poland, not close to any German farms, on the pre-war borders at any rate), or of lack of originality (though, to be sure, this historical scene is now widely known), but of the *blurring* here. Mynat's 'they gathered us' contrasts sloppily to Browning's precise discussion and translation of Major Trapp; her long circumlocution 'what we had to do might not be all that pleasant' blurs Browning's military euphemistic 'frightfully unpleasant task'; the older men can 'avoid it' as opposed to the more military 'step out'. But this blurring is not just at the level of lexical choice: the deserter son, hidden by the 'good Germans', is wracked with guilt and eventually commits suicide, but not before, Christ-like, telling his father to look after Jan as an act of redemption. This is not to say that soldiers were not wracked with guilt—some were—but that these issues, especially issues of guilt and redemption, are much more complicated than the novel suggests. There are two sorts of swerve going on here. The first happens just because the writing is poor and clichéd. This prevents the novel saying and, as it were, thinking more. This cliché in style leads to the second swerve: a cliché in thought, the suicide of the son, which just avoids the issue all together in an easy redemption. Here, cliché avoids an engagement with evil.

Another form of swerve occurs in Steve Sem-Sandberg's award-winning novel, *The Emperor of Lies* (2009 Swedish, 2011 English). At nearly 700 pages, complete with maps, historical documents, photographs, a glossary, an afterword, and a dramatis personae, this is a huge historical

---

[47] Maureen Myant, *The Search* (London: Alma Books, 2009), p. 6.
[48] Browning, *Ordinary Men*, p. 2.

novel, of the sort that journalists easily call epic, set in the Łódź Ghetto—
the Germans renamed the city Litzmannstadt—from 1942 to 1945.
While the Swedish title is *De fattiga i Łódź* (*The Poor of Łódź*), and this
reflects the multiple narratives, the English title focuses the attention on
the central character and main strand, Chaim Rumkowski. Rumkowski is,
to say the very least, a controversial figure, and the historical bibliography
on him is extensive. Dan Stone, summing up the views of historians,
comments that most would agree that 'although Rumkowksi was an
unpleasant character, he was no traitor' and that his collaboration was
undertaken in the hope that it was serving the interests of those in the
ghetto.[49] This aspect, at least, echoes Levi's discussion of him in 'The
Grey Zone', perhaps the most acute piece written on the subject of forced
collaboration. Levi argues that Rumkowski was addicted to power, was a
morally weak man, and probably a Nazi dupe. But despite this, he is still
an ambiguous figure, and his life ruling the ghetto is shot through with
this ambiguity: 'if he had survived his own tragedy, and the tragedy of the
ghetto which he contaminated... no tribunal would have absolved him,
nor certainly can we absolve him on the moral plane. But there are
extenuating circumstances', writes Levi.[50]

However, in *The Emperor of Lies* there is no sense of this 'grey zone' at
all, and it is this that makes the novel, although it concerns the lives of
many, into a perpetrator fiction and, at the same time, creates its particular
swerve. Rumkowski in this novel is not only petty and vainglorious, weak
as well as utterly corrupt, but an abuser of women and a paedophile rapist:
indeed, the translated English title carries a satanic tang. In an echo of
death camp selection, he picks a child from a group of children awaiting
deportation: his 'eyes pass swiftly over the skinny, the lame and the
deformed. He is looking for that single, *perfect* child, the one who can
act as redress for the thousands he has been forced to sacrifice.'[51] This boy,
his chosen, becomes his adopted son and catamite. I single this out
because, while to some degree substantiated by the historical record, it is
made a central emblematic incident: as if ordering the deportation of tens
of thousands was not enough to convince the reader that Rumkowski was
more than morally compromised, he is a child-abuser too. He is already a
monster and thus there is nothing much more to say about him. Later,

[49] Stone, *Histories of the Holocaust*, p. 86. Stone follows a study by Michael Unger,
Reassessment of the Image of Mordechai Chaim Rumkowski (Jerusalem: Yad Vashem, 2004).
However, other historians find more to censure.
[50] Levi, *The Drowned and the Saved*, p. 49.
[51] Steve Sem-Sandberg, *The Emperor of Lies*, trans. Sarah Death (London: Faber and
Faber, 2009), p. 278.

predictably duped by the Nazis, he displays 'almost schoolboyish innocence' in his surprise.[52]

The novel achieves no depth in its study of evil, offers no explanatory power: in part this is the fault of the narrative voice, which is full of chronological slippages, as well as changing uneasily from a judgemental historical omniscience to more located free indirect discourse. A rabbi, for example, tells the story of Sabbatai Zevi, a false messiah, who when given the choice between death and conversion, chooses the latter, and so was clearly no redeemer: a heavy-handed narrative voice says that the Rabbi 'did not need to say it out loud; but it was still apparent that he viewed Chaim Rumkowski as a self-appointed redeemer of the same kind' and then—even more heavy-handedly—adds that he was a 'man who had learnt to put his fear above his faith'.[53] The narrator here—as elsewhere— tells, explains, and judges, ruling out any sense of complexity or difficulty in the desire to condemn. But if the moral judgement is explicit and heavy-handed in this novel, so is the use of historical material. The novel, as the afterword makes clear, is very reliant on the ghetto chronicle and other surviving documents. Speeches—such as Rumkowski's famous one about the deportation of the children from the ghetto—are inserted whole, and the novel begins with the Nazi memorandum that set up the ghetto. There is, of course, a tradition of the 'non-fiction novel' and this, in some sense, fits that model. But this material, unexplained, lacking in a wider context, does not allow the question of Rumkowski's evil to be asked: indeed, it avoids it.

Another form of swerve, more interesting and more demanding, occurs in the Serbian novelist David Albahari's *Götz and Meyer*. The protagonist and narrator, a writer in the present, knows only (from a telegram sent in mid-March 1942) that the drivers of the truck that killed almost all the women in both his parent's families were called Götz and Meyer. They were entirely 'aware of the nature of their assignment, being simultaneously the herald of death and death itself' and the protagonist begins not to research them but to, as it were, imagine them.[54] He begins by picturing the more mundane things they do: one 'probably smoked. Everyone smoked back then' (11) and then, slowly, fills out their lives with the almost Beckettian twist that he never tells the difference between them:

> Once, for instance, they talked for a long time about the importance of prunes for regular digestion, and another time Götz, or was it Meyer, the one

---

[52] Ibid., p. 584.   [53] Ibid., p. 292.
[54] David Albahari, *Götz and Meyer*, trans. Ellen Elias-Bursać (London: Vintage, 2005), p. 16. Further page references to this volume are given in parentheses in the text.

who was not, perhaps, married, pointed out to Meyer, or was it Götz, the one who probably was, that fresh fruit, if you had enough of it, was just the sort of thing to ease his daughters sore throats. (32)

This trope of the inability to identify each one manages to maintain the tension between the two as perpetrators individually responsible and nobodies, shallow, grown over with evil. At the same time, the protagonist fills out in more concrete detail his dead family and imagines them: 'I would become, by turns, one of my vanished cousins, sometimes a woman, sometimes a little girl or boy, or perhaps an old man resting his hand on a prayer book' (45). But as the novel continues, the imaginative investment begins to overwhelm the narrator: while his relatives become fuller and fuller in his mind (he need only look at his own face to be reminded), Götz and Meyer become more and more a 'void' (65). Comparing himself to the Rabbi of Prague, he becomes afraid that the two men he has constructed are like the Golem, bought blasphemously to life but empty: it—and they—exist only to deal death or, he worries, to die, to be killed in revenge. Götz and Meyer enter the narrative and talk with the narrator-protagonist. But there is no sense of being able to explain

why was it that the war was fought? Götz and Meyer had no way of answering, and they looked at me as if I might answer their questions. I don't know anything, I told them. Götz and Meyer raised their index fingers simultaneously, and admonished me. You know how to turn us into lighthouses, they shouted, but you don't know how to tell us over which shore our sea light shines, how can that be? I replied that sea is too strong a word, that their light, a feeble light at best, was shining on a puddle, nothing more. I savoured, no point in pretending I didn't, the wince of disgust flitting across the void of their faces. (99–100)

Here, some of the crux issues with perpetrator fiction are made clear. The characters are bought into fiction, set up as 'lighthouses' which should illuminate the issues, the sea: but they cannot, because first, in this postmodern, reflective novel, they are created characters, only able to repeat what they are created to say; second because, as lowly truck-drivers, they only have access to a tiny piece of the whole pan-European atrocity, only a puddle (and the puddle itself in contrast to the sea is also an image of shallowness and meaninglessness); and third because, as Arendt's nobodies, they have nothing to offer. The two characters—despite their thoughts on prunes—are so faceless, so much 'nobody', as to be indistinguishable from each other. The swerve here, in this thoughtful novel, is about the limits of the present in understanding the evil of the Holocaust. The historical events are discussed in detail, the impact in the present is made clear, but an attempt to understand, to come up with a secret or an answer is simply blocked: the lighthouse illuminates only a shallow puddle. Eventually, as it were working through the memory of the murder of his family, he imagines meeting the two Germans as old men, talking with them not about the war but about nothings.

Laurent Binet's award-winning novel *HHhH* (2009 French, 2012 English) gives the impression of being a perpetrator fiction, as it appears to take Reinhard Heydrich as its subject. Inspired in its form by the historiographical metafiction of the 1980s, it is divided into 257 separate sections and it tells the story of Heydrich's assassination, setting it in the context of the war, the annexation of Czechoslovakia, the German's own war aims, the lives of the very heroic assassins and, most importantly, in the life of the implied author. As in *Götz and Meyer*, the implied author appears frequently in the text, and it is this that makes the novel different from a more traditional realist historical fiction. The narrator is constantly worrying about the historical status of the work:

> [h]ow impudent of me to turn a man into a puppet—a man who's been dead for a long time, who cannot defend himself. To make him drink tea, when it might turn out he liked only coffee.[55]

More, in the recognizable shift of 'mimesis of product to mimesis of process' (as identified by Linda Hutcheon), the implied author praises or condemns characters (who were real people) as he goes along, spots his errors, and corrects his mistakes as he does more research.[56] Indeed, as I discuss below, even works published during the process of writing change the shape of the novel: he discusses *The Kindly Ones*, for example. Yet with this postmodern apparatus comes a more traditional historical novel: prime ministers say things for which there is no record; heroic commandos prepare themselves; Nazis preen; Czechs suffer. Indeed, these more realist patches—the account of the chase, battle, and capture of Heydrich's killers for example—make up the longest and most compelling part of the novel. The swerve here is that the text is not really interested in Heydrich—he plays only a minor role—save as a figure on which to hang a historiographically metafictional disassembled novel.

However, the most significant work of Holocaust fiction in recent years is Jonathan Littell's *The Kindly Ones* (*Les Bienveillantes*) which is not only a dense, highly researched masterpiece, but engages with many of the

---

[55] Laurent Binet, *HHhH*, trans. Sam Taylor (London: Harvill Secker, 2012), n.p., section 91.

[56] See, *inter alia*, Linda Hutcheon, *A Poetics of Postmodernism: History, Theory, Fiction* (London: Routledge, 1988).

problems with Holocaust perpetrator fiction. On its publication in France it caused a scandal and a sensation, winning the Prix Goncourt in 2006, and it continued to cause controversy and polarize critics in waves in Germany, the UK, and the USA.[57] The book has been more than a *succès de scandale* and has gone on to generate an academic mini-industry since its publication. I want here, below, to offer a reading of this challenging novel which develops as a process.

The book, as is well known, is the story of an SS officer, Maximilian Aue, who, in the literary traditions of the historical novel, experiences a very wide series of events—indeed, too many events to be plausible— during the Second World War. He is involved in the genocidal activities of the *Einsatzgruppen*; then with his friend and ally in the SS, Thomas, also sees action and is badly wounded at Stalingrad (a symbolic bullet to the head that seems to open his 'third eye'). He recovers and sees service in western Russia and the Ukraine, and visits Auschwitz. As this story goes on, the reader learns more of Aue's own personal life: about his father, a war veteran who joined the *Freikorps*, and was presumably killed; about his mother who is remarried to a Frenchman, Moreau (a nod to Jules Verne), who Aue hates; and about his sister, with whom Aue has had an incestuous affair, seemingly resulting in twins, Tristram and Orlando (both names of characters traditionally driven mad by love), unknown to or unacknowledged by Aue; about his own—illegal in the Reich—homosexuality and other sexual predilections. We also learn about his connection to shadowy figures called Herr Leland and Dr Mandelbrod, who seem to be pulling strings behind the scenes in the Reich. About halfway through the novel, Aue murders his mother and step-father and apparently has no memory of this (he falls asleep and, on waking, comes downstairs to find them horribly killed with an axe. But, as with all the complexities of this novel, this lack of memory is not certain and may be a trick. When confronted about the murder by Herr Leland, the blood drains from his face, and the last line of the novel, the 'kindly ones were onto me' is suggestive: Aue, well-educated, knows surely that the Furies pursue those who have killed their parents). Two *Kriminalkommissars*, Clemens and Weser, take up his trail and pursue him throughout the novel. As an SS officer, he is involved with Eichmann and the work of the 'desk killers' and, as the novel becomes more phantasmagorical and includes an oneiric masturbatory section, Aue makes a fraught return to besieged Berlin aided by a band of feral Nazi children, where he meets Hitler and bites his nose.

[57] A good range of these responses are well covered in Margaret-Anne Hutton, 'Jonathan Littell's *Les Bienveillantes*: Ethics, Aesthetics and the Subject of Judgement', *Modern and Contemporary France* 18:1 (2010), 1–15.

Then, as Berlin falls, he escapes both the Nazis and the Allies, but not Clemens and Weser. As they close in, both are killed (Weser by enemy fire; Clemens by Thomas): Aue then murders Thomas, steals his documents and money, and flees to France. The novel begins with his description of his life after the war as the general manager of a lace factory in France, and his decision to write an account of his time at war.

The book draws not only on a huge range of Holocaust historical scholarship (it is almost possible to trace the origins in the historiography of some of the more detailed sections) but, as Debarati Sanyal argues, it also reflects the new wave of Holocaust and genocide scholarship, contextualizing the Holocaust in a wider colonial and postcolonial world.[58] The first chapter, in the English edition, clearly bears this out through a long discussion of the Vietnam War (whereas the French edition discusses Algeria) as do discussions of the Belgian Congo, the American Frontier, and British India.[59] The book also uses other major writers on the Holocaust (such as Antelme and Grossman) and other, less celebrated ones (Ka-Tzetnik's book *Pipel* is referenced (613); the two *Kriminalkommissars* take their names, Weser and Clemens, from Klemperer (they are the two 'principal torturers of the Jews in Dresden, and they were generally differentiated as the hitter and the spitter')).[60] Even more noticeable, however, is the array of philosophers and theorists, sometimes explicitly named (Blanchot, Heidegger) but more often implicitly, anachronistically and rather brilliantly deployed: these include Arendt, Sartre, Bataille, Theweliet, and Levinas. (Indeed the novel offers one of the best glosses on one of Levinas' most obscure passages.)[61] The protagonist also

---

[58] Debarati Sanyal, 'Reading Nazi Memory in Jonathan Littell's *Les Bienveillantes*', *L'Esprit Créateur* 50:4 (2010), 47–66.

[59] Jonathan Littell, *The Kindly Ones*, trans. Charlotte Mandell (London: Chatto and Windus, 2009), p. 590 *inter alia*. Further page references to this volume are given in parentheses in the text.

[60] Klemperer, *The Language of the Third Reich*, p. 12.

[61] An SS doctor—Eduard Wirths, who is a major figure in Lifton's *The Nazi Doctors*, pp. 384–414—tells Aue that 'I came to the conclusion that the SS guard doesn't become violent or sadistic because he thinks the inmate is not a human being; on the contrary, his rage increases and turns into sadism when he sees that the inmate, far from being a subhuman as he was taught, is actually at bottom a man, like him, after all, and it's the resistance, you see, that the guard finds unbearable, the silent persistence of the other, and so the guard beats him to make their shared humanity disappear. Of course, that doesn't work: the more the guard strikes, the more he's forced to see that the inmate refuses to recognise himself as a non-human. In the end, no other solution remains for him than to kill him, which is an acknowledgment of complete failure' (p. 624). Emmanuel Levinas writes, in a dense and allusive two pages in *Totality and Infinity* (trans. Alphonso Lingis, London: Athlone Press, 1999), of how the 'Other is the sole being I can wish to kill' (198). Someone who struggles against murder is a 'quasi-nothing' easily 'obliterated because the sword or bullet has touched the ventricles or auricles of his heart' (199): the victim will

has a fondness for Edgar Rice Burroughs' Martian novels and bases a memo to Himmler on an aspect of them (822–3) about childrearing, which in turn reflects Plato's *Republic*. Indeed, the novel, in its inverted picturesque travels around the world of the Second World War does occasionally resemble John Carter's combative adventures on Barsoom: the war and the Holocaust make our world almost a science-fiction *novum*, a perpetrator's version of claims by victims that Auschwitz was like an alien planet.[62] Similarly, the amoral gods of H. P. Lovecraft appear: Aue dreams 'I was a great Squid God and I was ruling over a beautiful walled city of water and white stone' (152): Cthulhu in R'lyeh. The novel also takes in canonical French literature (Stendhal, Flaubert); Russian literature (Lermontov); and, of course, *The Eumenides* (*The Kindly Ones*), the third play of the *Oresteia*.[63]

The book is about the question of evil and perpetration. In a 2006 interview, Littell commented that the

> perpetrator is the main issue the historians of the Shoah have been exploring for the last 15 years. The only remaining question is the motivation of the killers. Having read the works of the great researchers, it seems to me that they have hit a brick wall. This is very clear with Christopher Browning. He has created a list of potential motivations and has no way of arbitrating between them. Some prioritize anti-Semitism, others ideology. But in the end, they don't know. The reason is simple. The historian works from documents, and so from the words of the perpetrators, which are themselves an aporia. And where can one go from there?[64]

Well, indeed, where does one go? Does this novel also 'swerve' away from coming to terms with evil?

The Kindly Ones does seem to fulfil some of the criteria developed from Arendt: hardly surprising as Arendt's work is an intertext throughout, from the first line 'Oh my human brothers...' (1). First, Aue is an 'inanimate man'. Even in the most reflective section, the first chapter,

---

clearly lose. But there is a resistance here in the 'very transcendence of his being' (199), an 'infinity, stronger than murder, already resists us in his face, is his face, is the primordial expression, is the first word: "you shall not commit murder"... the resistance of what has no resistance—the ethical resistance' (199).

[62] Raul Hilberg, *Perpetrators Victims Bystanders: The Jewish Catastrophe 1933–1945* (London: Harper Perennial, 1992), p. 187.

[63] This has been explored by many critics: Jonas Grethlein, 'Myth, Morals and Metafiction in Jonathan Littell's *Les Bienveillantes*', *PMLA* 127:1 (2012), 77–93 is an especially good take. It also offers another source for the police officer Clemens' name: 'for *clemens* can serve as a Latin translation of the Greek *eumenēs*'.

[64] Interview by Samuel Blumenfeld: http://thekindlyones.wordpress.com/littell-interview-with-samuel-blumenfeld/. Article published in the 17 November 2006 edition of *Le Monde des Livres*.

'Toccata', Aue does not explain or think much of himself: 'I suddenly had a lot of free time, and I began thinking... I was slowly overcome with dread. I realised thinking is not a good idea' (6). While the novel is set up as an exercise in seeing the past, for Aue, it is not, oddly, an act of memory or reflection, nor an act of thought or dialogue: 'even though I'm addressing you, it's not for you that I am writing' he writes to the implied reader and perhaps also to himself. He is unable to talk to anyone (if his secretaries found his manuscript 'they'd have a shock, the poor things, and my wife too' (8)). It's true, of course, that an SS-*Obersturmbannführer* can 'have an inner life, desire, passions, just like any other man' (23), but his profounder motivations are often a blank to him. During the war years he says of himself that 'I observe and do nothing, that's my favourite position' (252). This is not entirely true, although it is the case that he is primarily an observer: at an early murderous 'action' (80–7) for example. Even at Babi Yar, it is his body that seems to take off ('then my left arm detached itself from me and went off all by itself down the ravine, shooting left and right' (130)) and he is left observing it. When he does have some power (in Hungary with Eichmann, for example), he is suddenly (and uncharacteristically) evasive ('ah, but what's the point of relating all these details day by day?' (778)). After the war, of course, he has to hide his identity and deny his own experiences. Aue's memory of the war is less like a memory, in fact—not re-called, re-membered—and more like a newsreel or traumatic memory, simply played over and over again. And, of course, of his murder of his mother he has no memory at all, apparently. In this sense, he is a nobody, refusing to engage with his memory or himself. As I have said, Laurence Binet mentions *The Kindly Ones* several times in *HHhH*. His publisher urged him to remove many of the citations (an example of one remaining is section 189). However, the edited sections are available online.[65] One passage states that

> there is a real problem with *The Kindly Ones*: the tone of the imaginary SS veteran's supposed confession is unbelievably neutral, almost like a history book.... But what is the point of writing in the first person if you are going to erase practically all trace of subjectivity?

But this is precisely the point (and where Littell's insight is greater than Binet's): the subjectivity of the perpetrators had to be self-erased. Aue sees but does not experience.

More, much of the very long book is—or could be seen as—dull. For example, there is an interminable (forty or so pages) pre-meeting, meeting,

---

[65] At   http://www.themillions.com/2012/04/exclusive-the-missing-pages-of-laurent-binets-HHhH.html.

and post-meeting wrangle about whether the 'Mountain Jews' of the Caucasus are really Jewish or not (if so, they would be murdered; if not, the Reich is keen to develop 'good relations with the anti-Bolshevist minorities' (291)). This in itself is banal, everyday stuff, but the outcome of the meeting will lead to an act of mass murder. There is a great deal of detail about everything: there are no real sudden epiphanies for example. But again, the excessive dullness (leavened by the acuteness of historical observation) is part of the point about how this form of evil works: evil-as-fungus is not exciting or glamorous. This means that when searching for the evil in *The Kindly Ones*, we should not be looking for some core moment or essence—a point that even the older Aue gestures towards, in his existential despair and evasion in the preface—but in precisely the huge mass detail about the production of the day-to-day of the genocide: the routinization of evil.

The novel, too, is full of speeches but little 'real speech'. Aue's constant justifications to himself and others are open to question not only because they are wrong (he is a Nazi, after all) and self-serving but also because he is simply very good at playing the 'counters' of rhetoric and logical argument. Aue often asks the characters (real and fictional) he meets what they think—sometimes about prescribed matters, such as the 'Final Solution'—and even when this is not clichéd there is little dialogue: minds are not changed, real conversation fails to happen. Where speeches are effective, the words are used purely as sophistic tools: Aue's seduction of a fellow officer, for example, deploys the Nazi rhetoric of the warrior and masculinity for a highly illegal homosexual seduction. Aue, too, is rootless and shallow. His family has moved frequently, he lacks a father, he rejects his mother and various mentors, and is easily led by his desires; he is (more or less) blackmailed into becoming an informer; towards the end of the novel he ruthlessly and efficiently murders the lover he has had for longest, the Hungarian attaché, Mihaï. (Earlier, Aue seems stung by Herr Leland's comments that, while it was 'all the same to us' if he had 'murdered his mother', he didn't do it properly and was left compromised (832): Mihaï's murder is certainly done properly in that respect.) Aue is led by the nose through the ranks by his friend Thomas, and this friendship means nothing to him—he murders Thomas with barely the flicker of a thought. While he recalls much of his wartime experience (there would be no book otherwise), he does not realize that the twins are (obviously) his children from his sister, and he blanks utterly from his mind the matricide. Aue is unable to find roots, unable to be more than shallow.

The novel is also very clear that acts of atrocity and even genocide are not limited to the Nazis. While this is, of course, part of Aue's attempt to confuse the implied reader of the manuscript he's writing (sometime in the 1970s), his comparison (in the English edition) of the war in the East and the Holocaust to the war in Vietnam—and later in the novel, other comparisons to colonial atrocities—is telling. The reader is implicated in this way and also, perhaps, through the relentless focalization through Aue who insists he is a human 'brother'. And finally, there is no redemption for Aue: his work is 'free from contrition' (5) and the final line of the novel— '[T]he Kindly Ones were on to me' (975)—clearly implies a weight of guilt, 'the entire weight of the past, of the pain of life and of inalterable memory' (975) which will go with him. In all these ways, *The Kindly Ones* seems an ideal Arendtian Holocaust perpetrator fiction, one that is able to show us something precisely about the 'banality of evil'. It does not offer a 'why' but rather tries to explain, and in its form affectively demonstrate, why there is no why, no depth, to this new sort of evil.

However, there is a fundamental problem with this reading of the novel. Susan Rubin Suleiman's illuminating article locates two stories within the novel—'the public history and the family tragedy'.[66] There are, in fact, three strands, although the third is minor and disappointing.

The first is the 'genocidal' strand. This is the dominant part of the story which covers the history of the war and Aue's experiences. As I've suggested above, Aue offers a range of justifications for his actions and the novel is full of speeches—often tense if shallow ones—between Nazi officers on these matters. He cites one example from many, Frank's *Führerprinzip*, a perversion of Kant's Categorical Imperative, 'Act in such a way that the Führer, if he knew of your action, would approve' (366). Yet Aue—highly educated, refined—is also beyond such 'rational' sounding justifications, a committed Nazi. For example, he is assigned by Himmler to the task of working out how to feed the camps. Himmler makes it clear, while discussing provisions, that the aim is to starve the camps, of course, and, as Aue says, 'increased production remains the main objective' (one sign of Littell's mastery of the material is the confidence with which he represents the 'upside down' language of the perpetrators in these matters). As a result of this increased responsibility, Aue declares that he 'felt as if I was floating in my boots. Finally I was being given a responsibility, and authentic responsibility. So they had recognised my true worth' (637). In this strand of the story, the novel portrays and tries to engage with the evil of perpetrators as 'ordinary men': Arendt's (and Littell's) starting point. If the novel had only this strand, the

[66] Susan Rubin Suleiman, 'When the Perpetrator becomes a Reliable Witness of the Holocaust: On Jonathan Littell's *Les bienveillants*', *New German Critique* 36:1 (2009), 1–19, p. 18.

Arendt-inflected interpretation would be unproblematic. Bernhard Schlink wrote that Jonathan Littell presents

> an SS officer's career and inner life because, as he explains in an interview that I read, he wanted to find out what evil is like from the inside. But there are as many insides of evil as there are evil people and there isn't that much to find out about them.[67]

The trick of the glamour of evil is to direct our attention to individuals, when perhaps it is people's interactions, wider cultures, and histories that also need investigation.

Yet, in relation to this absolutely central question of perpetration and evil, this novel undergoes a swerve because of the second strand, the 'family tragedy'. Aue's family life is complex: his father missing, his mother remarried, Aue's intense incestuous sexual obsession with his sister. This obsession, it is strongly implied, is at the root of Aue's convoluted sexuality: he desires men precisely because he desires—*desires to be*, in fact—his sister ('I wanted to be her' (25)). And in the long masturbatory sequence towards the end of the novel, he fantasizes about her, has sex with a dog (probably) and with a tree (definitely (901)) (trees both actual and metaphorical—family trees, German forests, roots—are a recurring symbol in the novel). Aue's sexuality is a complex matter. He is not simply a 'gay Nazi' like Donna Barr's intelligent and charming graphic novel character the 'Desert Peach', Rommel's fictional younger brother. For Aue sexuality is a driving and destructive force. These complexities lie at the fulcrum of the 'family tragedy' of the novel. While apparently in a deep sleep, Aue strangles his mother and kills his stepfather with an axe. It is here that the primary reference to the 'Kindly Ones' of the title comes into focus: the Eumenides from Greek myth are the Furies, those who avenge the killing of family members by family members. Centrally, in Aeschylus' *Oresteia*, they seek to avenge the murder of Clytemnestra by her son Orestes.

The third strand, and by far the least convincing, concerns Dr Mandelbrod and Herr Leland. These two are villains from a more 'pulp' tradition. Dr Mandelbrod even has a 'sleek tabbycat with white paws' (450) in a nod towards Blofeld, James Bond's arch-enemy. Herr Leland, as his name suggests, is clearly a devil figure (Herr Woland from Bulgakov's *The Master and Margarita*; Leland Palmer, the demonically possessed murderer from *Twin Peaks*). These two figures, who reappear from time to time in the novel and take Aue to Posen to hear Himmler's speech and escape from Berlin (to Moscow) before its fall, are a sort of 'conspiracy theory' evil: people who pull the strings behind the scenes. They are

---

[67] Bernhard Schlink, *Guilt about the Past* (London: Beautiful Books, 2010), p. 126.

almost comic in their role in the text and represent a sort of 'satanic' form of evil, more common in fiction (and frequent in pulp fiction).

Centrally, however, the act of matricide has consequences for the meaning of the novel in relation to the question of evil. If we assume that Aue has been, as it were, driven mad by complex incestuous and Oedipal rage, we can assume he is a psychopath, and his evil as a genocidal perpetrator is not that of an 'ordinary man' (or even a 'willing executioner') but an expression of this pathology. Most perpetrators did not murder their parents and step-parents in addition to their terrible crimes, and were not—or did not begin as—psychopaths (there are not, as Aue claims, 'psychopaths everywhere' (21)). This means that Aue is not a 'typical Nazi perpetrator'—not a zealot, vulgarian, or the bearer of a burden, as Raul Hilberg classifies them—and so his justifications, if we take the novel only as an exploration of the evil of the genocide, a thought experiment about perpetration, does not work. Indeed, it is about only this specific man or ogre and his monstrous actions. Conversely, if we assume that Aue was only able to commit the murders in his unconscious sleep, precisely because he had already been unbalanced by his actions at Babi Yar and on and behind the Eastern front, we are still left with the conclusion that the impact of these genocidal events on his particular mind drew out his implicit criminality (something Aue suggests, in fact). This murder and matricide is not an ordinary killing and this difference is expressed in the novel's use of mythopoesis in the echoes of the *Oresteia*.

It is this 'family' story that represents the swerve of the novel, as if the dark sun of the evil of the 'ordinary Nazi' is actually too much to bear, despite the research and the depth of the novel and despite much of what Aue claims. The novel has to look away from the evil in the 'genocidal' strand and, as it were, excuse it or 'redeem' it, in the sense of 'paying it off', with the evil of the 'family tragedy'. Aue, despite his assertions on the first page that he is a man like us, is not: he is already a psychopath and/or a mythic figure, before becoming a genocidal perpetrator. Psychopaths and mythic figures, while they tell us about psychopathology and myth, tell us very little about the day-to-day evil of the perpetrators of Third Reich atrocities. In this sense, the 'family' story and the 'genocidal' story work against each other: the former (the 'Satanic evil' murderer) 'discredits' the latter (the ordinary man) and represents the swerve of the *The Kindly Ones*.

But this may not be the end of the process of interpreting this novel. The two strands, the genocidal and the family, come together only once in any significant way. (Even pursuing police are not allowed to interfere between the strands of the story.) There is a crucial passage which occurs at Aue's mother's house in France just before the murder. Aue has been (significantly, given the role of trees in the novel) chopping wood:

> As I worked, I thought: in the end, the collective problem for the Germans was the same as my own; they too were struggling to extract themselves from a painful past, to wipe the slate clean so they'd be able to begin new things. That was how they had arrived at the most radical solution of them all: murder, the painful horror of murder. But was murder a solution? I thought of the many conversations I had had about this: in Germany, I wasn't the only one to have my doubts. What if murder wasn't a definitive solution, what if, on the contrary, this new fact, even less reparable than the ones before it, opened in turn onto new abysses? Then, what way out was left? (526)

There is much to note about this passage which occurs just before his (unconscious) act of matricide: it is one of the very few times in which Aue recollects his own thought processes, including his doubts, rather than just presenting events; it contains an actual moment of reflection, of proper thought development. It is almost as if, despite Babi Yar and the other atrocities he has seen, there is a moment of escape offered to Aue. Yet importantly it also separates Aue from the Germans ('they' not 'we Germans') while simultaneously linking him to 'them' (the problem is 'the same'): this is because, surely, while he has been chopping wood he has arrived, unconsciously, at 'the most radical solution of them all', the Nazi solution, and has blocked it from himself. More significantly, however, is the linking of Aue in his family life (as Orestes) to Aue the SS officer, an echo of Joyce's 'mythic method': here, at this one moment, the two strands are linked in the idea that in both cases, the extraction from a 'painful past' involves 'wiping the slate clean', beginning again. Alon Confino writes that

> the extermination of the Jews was imagined by the Nazis...as an act of creation, in the sense of genesis, in which the Jewish world would be destroyed to make room for the Nazi one. As an act of creation, it was perceived as producing a cosmic result, as either salvation or eternal damnation; as being a human experience that lacked historical precedence, which every creation is by definition; and, as such, a transgression, in the sense that it was a violation of all past known practice. The notion of creation...was the organising metaphor used by its victims, perpetrators, other Germans and Europeans to make sense of what was happening to the Jews after 1941.[68]

This idea of genesis relies on a view of time itself which both faces down the past and plans a new Nazi epoch: this view of time is, if we accept

---

[68] Confino, *Foundational Pasts*, p. 61.

Confino's view, for the Nazis, the starting premise of totalitarian thought that Arendt suggests. It relies on the 'total eradication of the Jews' as 'the basis for a new page of history' because, Confino argues, the Nazis imagine the 'Jew as a symbol of historical time that had to be removed for Nazi Germany to arise'.[69] More, by 'excising the Jews, Nazis and other Germans excised part of their own religious and historical origins'.[70] This is akin to Aue's unconscious realization about his own family and personal life: the past must be destroyed for his own self to arise. The murder of his mother and step-father and the murder of the Jews are the same step, one in a kitchen in France, the other as a pan-European atrocity. But this Nazi messianic time has in it a trap: for the self to arise in messianic time, that same self, with its roots, attachments, thought, must also be destroyed. To make the self rootless, shallow, is to leave it only at the whim of its bodily desires, fantasies, and outside of the social. This is precisely what happens to Aue. This is the origin of his strange sexually transgressive stay in Una's house. It is also the reason—the lack of reason, perhaps—that leads him to bite Hitler's nose: 'Even today I would be unable to tell you why I did this: I just couldn't restrain myself'.[71] This gesture—'I hadn't premeditated it ... I'd just gone blank'[72]—is precisely the act of the blank, the rootless, and the ungrounded self, whose whims are based only in bodily desires. These and other similar incidents, the novel implies, for both Aue and for the Germans are the result precisely of the Nazi destruction of the past and of the Jews.

Aue, in this crucial moment from *The Kindly Ones*, goes on to wonder if murder is 'a definitive solution': does it, instead, leave time irreparable with 'new abysses'? For the Nazis, and for Aue, it does. This then, is the great theme of *The Kindly Ones*: time and inalterable memory. Aue can never restart his life, as he claims to have done. (In parallel, Gyuri in Kertész's *Fateless* says to his family, on his return: 'I made it clear to them that we can never start a new life, only ever carry on the old one.')[73] This is not time in the sense that *HHhH* can alternate between the historical record, the invented past, and the writer in the present. Nor is the novel proffering a redemptive time by which evil can be expunged. Rather, in its detail and density, it offers a sense of time in which nothing is forgotten and nothing can be forgiven: the time Littell's novel offers is a past lacking in redemption or escape, in which the weight of past events, into which one has been thrown and with which one is complicit, cannot be evaded. It brings together historical time and juridical time: there is no

---

[69] Ibid., pp. 151, 150.   [70] Ibid., p. 150.
[71] Littell, *The Kindly Ones*, p. 960.   [72] Ibid., p. 961.
[73] Imre Kertész, *Fateless*, trans. Tim Wilkinson (London: Vintage Books, 2006), p. 259.

new life. The police officers pursuing him are not the kindly ones, but a sort of pre-emptive vision of pursuit and its evasion. Primo Levi writes that a victim's injury cannot be healed and that 'the Furies, in whose existence we are forced to believe...wrack the tormentor (if they do wrack him, assisted or not by human punishment)'.[74] Aue, obsessed by violent suicidal fantasies, chooses not to try to live with himself, deadening himself with drink and petty (to him) life, because the kindly ones are within him.

A novel, even one full of philosophy and historical detail, is not a treatise and does not need to offer definitive answers or views. *The Kindly Ones*, in its length and depth, raises issues and offers ways of thinking about complicity and guilt, subjectivity and agency, Nazism and the individual, and about the relationship between evil and time which gives it profound power. Perhaps it does 'swerve' from coming to terms with evil, but the swerve, it seems to me, is consistent both with the picture of evil offered by both this novel and the thought of Hannah Arendt. *The Kindly Ones* is a contemporary meditation 'on the fundamental question of post-war Europe', a reflection on why the question of 'why' does not have an answer. It leaves instead 'the entire weight of the past, of the pain of life and of inalterable memory'.[75]

CONCLUSION

This chapter has argued that the many perpetrator testimonies and per-petrator fictions seem to set out to answer the fundamental question of 'why', that is, the question of evil, but they swerve and fail to answer the question they set themselves. On a superficial level, the recognition of this swerve stems from the genre conventions of many books of this sort: in addition to many factual details, both fiction and perpetrator testimonies seem to promise relatively straightforward answers. Richard Bernstein notes that in the discourse about evil there 'is something deep in us that desires a reassuring closure'.[76] This is generally truer in fiction than in philosophy. In fiction we want the solution to a mystery, in history or testimony a convincing account; yet these books, even the accusatory biographies, do not deliver this. Following Arendt, I have suggested that there is a more profound reason for this: that the evil of the Holocaust (indeed of the totalitarian epoch, for Arendt) simply could not be inter-rogated, in testimony or fiction, in this manner. This evil was not

---

[74] Levi, *The Drowned and the Saved*, p. 12. [75] Littell, *The Kindly Ones*, p. 975.
[76] Bernstein, *Radical Evil*, pp. 226–7.

profound, offering a deep secret to be uncovered, but shallow, fungus-like, routine. This is not to downplay or diminish this form of modern evil: rather it is to begin to explore precisely why it was so powerful, so dominant and catastrophic. The perpetrators of this form of evil avoided authentic thought through the destruction of language by cliché; they destroyed their roots and memory (in opening the chimeric possibility of a new Nazi epoch); and they destroyed their own subjectivity and judgement, choosing to become evasive 'nobodies'. (None of these characteristics, incidentally, call for a lack of emotion, as Confino suggests: indeed, the removal of roots and refusing the capability of judgement might liberate many forms of repressed emotions and drives.)[77] The accounts of the perpetrators—and their pathetic self-justifications—bear the traces of these phenomena just as the accusatory accounts bear frustrations with them. These phenomena left the perpetrators 'incomprehensible': not in a mystical or sublime sense, but in the sense that, bereft of common compass points, dialogue, and depth, they could not be understood.

Although the question of perpetration underlies much post-war fiction, recent literature has turned to these issues with a new interest for reasons I suggested above. Yet, even given the greater freedom of fiction, these texts, too, swerve from evil. As I have argued, some because of simplistic cliché; some because they fall into the trap of making the perpetrators monsters; some because, in their fictional engagement with the perpetrator, it appears that there is not much to say. Jonathan Littell's *The Kindly Ones* perhaps gets closest to Arendt's sense of evil—Arendt's work is present in the novel in many ways, so perhaps this is to be expected. Yet even this important novel swerves from evil, because of the interplay between the genocidal and family plot strands, even if the relationship between these can be read in a way which offers some further insight into Arendtian evil and its Nazi instantiation. But this novel too, offers a truism: that humans are not rootless, that lives cannot really be restarted, that we are, as Arendt suggests, trapped within ourselves.

Arendt's notion of evil has a precedent, which both illumines her work and the texts about perpetrators. In *Being and Time*, Heidegger outlines the various existential characteristics of Dasein. One of these, indeed, one of the most contentious, is what he named 'the "falling" of Dasein'.[78] Heidegger stresses that he does not intend any 'negative evaluation' by this (clearly negative) term, but that it 'is used to signify that Dasein

---

[77] Confino, *A World without Jews*, p. 18.
[78] Martin Heidegger, *Being and Time*, trans. John Macquarrie and Edward Robinson (Oxford: Blackwell, 1962), H. 175. Further page references to this volume are given in parentheses in the text.

is . . . alongside the "world" of its concern' (H. 175)). This is as may be, but 'falling' turns out to be a kind of Being that is 'completely fascinated by the world and by the Dasein-with of Others in the "they"' (H. 176). 'Falling' is a fall from authentic Being and the 'they' for Heidegger is an important concept that runs throughout *Being and Time*. The 'they-self' constantly pulls at Dasein to make it inauthentic: it is described as 'dictatorship of the "they"' (H. 127): we 'take pleasure and enjoy ourselves as *they* take pleasure; we read, see and judge about literature as *they* see and judge . . . we find "shocking" what *they* find shocking' (H. 127). But this is not just a matter of taste but of all aspects of life. Because the 'they' presents every judgement and decision as its own, 'it deprives the particular Dasein of its answerability . . . [I]t was always the "they" who did it, and yet it can be said that it has been "no one"' (H. 127). The 'they-self' is not a person or people but an attitude that can be accepted, a take on the world:

> Everyone is the other, and no one is himself. The 'they', which supplies the answer to the 'who' of everyday Dasein, is the 'nobody' to whom every Dasein has already surrendered itself in Being-among-one-another. (H. 129)

The 'they-self' is that of 'inauthenticity and failure to stand by one self' (H. 128). Authenticity and inauthenticity is one of the core themes of *Being and Time*.

But this way of describing the 'fall' to the 'they-self' has an echo in Arendt, for whom the idea of authenticity remains of often unspoken importance. The 'they-self' has a historical and political instantiation in the concept of the 'mob' in *The Origins of Totalitarianism*. More, the analysis of the 'they-self', even in a truncated form, clearly echoes Arendt's account of those perpetrators like Eichmann, unable to speak or think except in cliché and who, in the name of the Reich, denigrate their own subjectivity, renounce their personalities, and rather than rooting themselves in themselves or their own past, chose instead to attach themselves to the others that surrounded them. That is to suggest that the banality of evil is held in parallel with an understanding of authenticity and inauthenticity. It is as if Arendt is accusing the Nazi perpetrators, despite (or, in fact, because of) all their talk of authenticity, of being subsumed utterly in inauthentic life. The texts by perpetrators, with their mendacity, evasion, and pleading, seem to bear this out. The novels about perpetrators, too, have this ring of inauthenticity. The point of this is not simply to begin to trace an idea through in the history of philosophy, but to suggest that, if we accept this idea of evil from Arendt, then it also opens up questions of what we mean by authenticity and inauthenticity, questions that (from Heidegger to Adorno to postmodernism), we thought that we had long passed beyond. Do we judge Aue's evasions as inauthentic? At the end of

The Remains of the Day, Rose's model of the representation of fascism, Stevens learns to 'banter' with his new American boss: is this a welcome authenticity, or just a new jargon of inauthenticity and banality?

The representation and understanding of evil is important not only for literary or aesthetic reasons. This chapter began by citing Tony Judt on how the memory of the dead of the Holocaust has become a 'definition and guarantee' of Europe's humanity. For Arendt, all these experiences can provide a 'politically most important yardstick for judging events in our time, namely: whether they serve totalitarian domination or not'.[79] Arendt warns (again, prophetically) that 'with populations and homelessness everywhere on the increase, masses of people are continuously rendered superfluous if we continue to think of our world in utilitarian terms' and so 'totalitarian solutions may well survive the fall of totalitarian regimes in the form of strong temptations which will come up whenever it seems impossible to alleviate political, social or economic misery in a manner worthy of man'.[80] That is to say, the 'thoughtless', banal evil of making humans superfluous, the core of totalitarian domination, is not limited to totalitarian states and might easily surface at any time. Its symptom is the vilification of others: its result is mass murder.

---

[79] Arendt, *The Origins of Totalitarianism*, p. 442.   [80] Ibid., p. 459.

3

Stasis

INTRODUCTION

The idea of 'working though' the past has played a central role in many of the important literary, historical, philosophical, and wider cultural debates about the Holocaust. The phrase is originally Freudian, from the 1914 essay 'Remembering, Repeating and Working Through', which suggests that the patient has to 'work through' the resistance that leads them to repetition rather than just have that resistance named and identified by the analyst. Actively and affectively doing so will lead to the patient discovering the 'repressed instinctual impulses' which are creating the resistance, so that the patient can properly remember and come to terms with their symptoms.[1] However, the term—and especially the idea that it is 'working through' a resistance—has become so detached from these roots that it is now almost free-floating. Adorno used it in his influential 1959 essay and broadcast, 'The Meaning of Working through the Past', in which he thunders against the idea: 'its intention is to close the books on the past and, if possible, remove it from memory'.[2] Yet he sees, in his dialectical manner, that there is a desire to 'break free of the past',

> rightly, because nothing at all can live in its shadow, and because there will be no end to the terror as long as guilt and violence are repaid with guilt and violence; wrongly, because the past that one would like to evade is still very much alive.[3]

---

[1] Sigmund Freud, 'Remembering, Repeating and Working-through', *Standard Edition*, 1914, vol. 12, p. 155.

[2] Theodor Adorno, 'The Meaning of Working through the Past', in *Critical Models; Interventions and Catchwords*, trans. Henry W. Pickford (New York: Colombia University Press, 1998), 89–103, p. 90. Pickford translates 'Aufabreitung' as 'working through' and notes that it 'does not wholly coincide with the psychoanalytic term "working through" (Durcharbeitung), though it is related' (337). Some politicians and historians with less sensitivity to language than Adorno began using the term in reference to the need to reappraise, or '"master" the past . . . Vergangenheitsbewältigung' (337–8): Adorno, *Critical Models*.

[3] Adorno, 'The Meaning', p. 103.

However, he concludes by arguing that

> [the] past will have been worked through only when the causes of what happened then have been eliminated. Only because the causes continue to exist does the captivating spell of the past remain to this day unbroken.[4]

The causes to which he refers are both detailed and fine brush—the complex politics of 1950s post-war Germany—and, as it were, broad stroke—post-Enlightenment modernity: for Adorno it is unlikely that the latter would be eliminated quickly. The term is central, too, for Saul Friedländer, in essays like 'Trauma, Transference and "Working through"', where it begins to form the underlying intellectual methodology of his *magnum opus*, *Nazi Germany and the Jews*. For him, it doesn't necessarily mean an ending or a completion or a 'hasty ideological closure'.[5] Rather, it signifies a form of engagement that allows process and change, and so understanding and a clearer sense of the past. It is a term used in trauma theory too: again, it signifies not a closure—events are rarely finally 'worked out'—but an active engagement. Indeed, it is hard not to 'work through' in this less technical sense: narrative, for example, either testimonial or fictional, almost inexorably 'works through' events.

However, this chapter argues that two major writers, the Nobel laureate and survivor, Imre Kertész and the hugely celebrated German writer W. G. Sebald, for divergent reasons, refuse 'working through' and aim instead at what I will call 'stasis' or perhaps, better, 'stasis-as-resistance'. This stasis-as-resistance emerges in different ways: in the form, in the narrative, and in characters in their work. The refusal of 'working through' in their oeuvre is not simply the denial of closure that is common to most survivor testimony and to many writers on the Holocaust. Nor is it the sort that Lawrence Langer praises, admiring writers who do not use the evil of the Holocaust to support some 'moral reality, community responsibility, or religious belief' because to do so does, certainly, seem to 'close the books' by what he calls 'pre-emption'.[6] Nor is this refusal an admirable, poignant, or traumatic holding close of a memory.

Rather, the refusal which I characterize by the term stasis-as-resistance is in fact a turn, in the name of memory, against the flexibility and fluidity of memory itself. Memory, especially the sort of complex, politicized and aesthetic memories that are involved in writing about the Holocaust, is

---

[4] Ibid.

[5] Saul Friedländer, 'Trauma, Transference and "Working through" in Writing the History of the "Shoah"', *History and Memory* 4 (1992), 39–59, p. 51.

[6] Lawrence Langer, *Pre-empting the Holocaust* (New Haven: Yale University Press, 1998), p. 1.

never immobile or fixed but rather moving, shifting, intentionally or unintentionally reworked. However, I argue that these writers attempt to resist precisely this movement. More, stasis-as-resistance is a refusal of the basic principles or drive of narrative (at its most basic: to go from here to there—or, because narrative is temporal, from *then* to *then*, and involve change in the process). But so strong are the two linked forces of the movement of memory and the narrative drive, so all-pervasive across collective and personal biographies, literary, testimonial, and historical works, and so engrained in expectations that the refusal to become engaged in the process of 'working through' turns out to be a complex and demanding endeavour at the level of form, plot, and character. Stasis-as-resistance—an aesthetic, literary, memorial, biographical, and historical term—is achieved only with great effort, swimming upstream against a strong current, and perhaps is doomed to fail.

Both Kertész and Sebald have been described as 'Holocaust writers', and in both cases this attribution is both right and too simplistic. Sebald deeply disliked the term 'Holocaust literature' ('it's a dreadful idea that you can have a sub-genre and make a specialty out of it; it's grotesque': I discuss this further, below).[7] Yet he has become understood as 'a post-war German author addressing the Holocaust (and other historico-political and ecological disasters) in a manner the reading public had never before witnessed' combining, for Jacobs, 'an ethics of melancholy outrage' with a moral position laid out 'with an astonishing sense of self certitude'.[8] In his Nobel acceptance speech, Kertész said that it

> is often said of me ... that I write about a single subject: the Holocaust. I have no quarrel with that. Why shouldn't I accept, with certain qualifications, the place assigned to me on the shelves of libraries?[9]

In this way, at least, Kertész and Sebald are clearly both 'writers of the Holocaust'. But for both writers, there is more. Kertész in the same speech discussed how it was precisely the experience of the suppression of the 1956 Hungarian Revolt by the USSR that 'for me was the petite madeleine cake that ... evoked ... the flavour of bygone years'.[10] His experience of Eastern Europe's communist domination, of how 'an entire nation could be made to deny its ideals', and his understanding that 'ethics in general ... is but the pliable handmaiden of self-preservation', shape his

---

[7] http://www.theguardian.com/books/2001/sep/22/artsandhumanities.highereducation: *The Guardian*, Saturday, 22 September 2001.
[8] Carol Jacobs, *Sebald's Vision* (New York: Columbia University Press, 2015), p. x.
[9] Kertész, 'Heureka!', p. 607.
[10] Kertész, *The Holocaust as Culture*, p. 42.

understanding of the Holocaust and of the world afterwards.[11] 'Even today' he said, in 2010, 'once can see significant differences in the way the Holocaust has been treated as a historical memory in the East and in the West': he mentions, for example, how in communist Hungary, the Jewish specificity of the Holocaust was erased (they 'used "persecuted" instead of "Jew" . . . so in a way we became invisible').[12] Despite his Nobel Prize, the 2005 film of his first book, *Fateless*, and his relative celebrity in Germany, Kertész is not well known in the Anglophone world.[13] In part this is due to his uncompromising opinions about the Holocaust and the West's complicity in the post-war settlement, in part because of the difficulty of his fiction, and in part because of the usual Anglophone prejudices against writers from minority languages. In the case of Sebald, too, the experiences growing up in post-war Germany explicitly shape his views, as the occasional autobiographical statement—about the bombing damage, for example—confirms. Both writers also tend towards the experimental in their prose. And the majority of their work cannot be easily classified as either exactly fiction or exactly non-fiction. Kertész's Nobel citation, 'for writing that upholds the fragile experience of the individual against the barbaric arbitrariness of history' reflects this (the term 'writing' is neutral on the fictiveness or not of the prose); much of the criticism on Sebald discusses the relationship between the historical record, the photographs he uses, and the texts he writes. However, their strongest resemblance lies in the admittedly different ways in which they refuse the idea of 'working through'.

TWENTY MINUTES OF *FATELESS*

Central to Kertész's *Fateless* is the question of agency and it is in relation to agency that stasis-as-resistance emerges most explicitly.[14] The book is the story of Gyuri, from just before his deportation, through the experience of the camps, principally Auschwitz and Buchenwald, and his return to Hungary. However, the novel seems as if the first-person narrator, Gyuri, is describing not his own experiences, but almost those of another, a third person. Things happen to the narrator, even when he does them

---

[11] Kertész, 'Heureka!', p. 606.

[12] Kertész, *The Holocaust as Culture*, pp. 43, 44.

[13] On Kertész's fame in Germany, see Peter Bergmann, 'Kertész among the Germans', *Hungarian Studies* 18:2 (2004), 235–42.

[14] The book is better translated as 'Fatelessness' for reasons that will appear: however, the excellent translation by Tim Wilkinson leaves it as *Fateless*: I will use that title.

himself: his agency—even his internal agency—is curtailed. For example, at the start of the novel his father is about to be deported: yet Gyuri's experience of his farewell is almost something that happens to another. The narrator does not describe his feelings, but when he starts to cry he notes his tears as an observer might: 'I don't know if my tears stemmed from that or from exhaustion or maybe even...I had somehow been preparing all along to shed them unfailingly'.[15] Indeed, this is at the core of all of Kertész's work. Even in his Nobel speech, he says that 'I have been feeling the steady, searching gaze of a dispassionate observer on my back'; the short story 'The Union Jack' stresses this by using an innovative pronoun form 'he (I)' a number of times.[16] Miller describes this as the 'narrating I and the experiencing I'.[17] But it is more than that: this trope—the external/internal observer, fused as 'he (I)'—is the key to his work, as I will show, because it marks both a destruction of agency and a declaration of agency in that very destruction.

Another widely recognized feature of *Fateless* is its irony. The narrator does not find the SS troops frightening, but instead rather well turned out. Or, on arrival, sick, at Buchenwald, he wishes to 'live a little longer in the beautiful concentration camp!' (189). Finally, while the narrator expects everyone to ask him about the horrors and the depravations, he declares that he will talk about 'the happiness of the concentration camps' (262). Andrea Reiter argues that this technique is employed because the protagonist is a child and that the narrator 'never departs from the perspective of the child, nor does he explain with hindsight he knows better'.[18] This is right but there is a profounder reason for this: it too is a symptom of the more fundamental revelation of the novel, the idea of fate/fatelessness, the impossibility of agency.

Gyuri comes to understand this in a moment of revelation which occurs in the final pages, as he is talking in a rush, on his return, to some members of his family:

> if there is such a thing as fate, then freedom is not possible...If, on the other hand...there is such a thing as freedom, there is no fate. That is to say...we ourselves are fate, I realised all at once, but with a flash of clarity I had never experienced before. (259–60)

[15] Kertész, *Fateless*, p. 26. Further page references to this volume are given in parentheses in the text.

[16] Kertész, 'Heureka!', p. 604.

[17] J. Hillis Miller, *The Conflagration of Community: Fiction before and after Auschwitz* (Chicago: University of Chicago Press, 2011), p. 219.

[18] Andrea Reiter, *Narrating the Holocaust*, trans. Patrick Camiler (London: Continuum, 2000), p. 262.

At first glance, this complex revelation might look like an existentialist declaration of authenticity ('we ourselves are fate') or something akin to Heraclitus' famous saying 'a man's character is his fate'. However, it is not. It does not rule out 'fate', some force (God, history) over which the individual has no control, nor does it rule out the freedom of the individual to make the world. It leaves these two undecided, aporetic. We can think of ourselves as victims of Eliot's 'vast impersonal forces' or we can also think of ourselves as our own freedom. But either way, it happens to us in a way that we cannot escape: 'we' happen 'to ourselves'. Levinas—also a returnee from a Nazi camp—writes in his early book *Existence and Existents* about a similar idea. He draws apart the 'I' and the 'there is': this latter is the being of the I that the I experiences, making itself both subject and object of its thought. He uses insomnia as an example, in which the 'I' experiences the intentionless 'there is' of anonymous wakefulness. Certainly Gyuri's family find this hard to understand:

> It was impossible, they must try and understand, impossible to take every-thing away from me, impossible for me neither to be winner or loser, for me not to be right and for me not to be mistaken that I was neither the cause nor the effect of anything; they should try to see, I almost pleaded, that I could not swallow that idiotic bitterness, that I should merely be innocent. (260–1)

This is what Kertész on the first page of *The Union Jack* calls 'either the consequentiality of fate or the absurdity of fate' which are 'in any event our fate'.[19] They still happen, they cannot be avoided, however much one digs and hides. What happens, happens, and if one wills it, one is also an impersonal force acting on oneself ('he (I)'). *Fateless* is precisely about the life that leads to this insight and *Kaddish for an Unborn Child*—in which the act of resistance is not to act, to maintain a stasis—is its clear sequel. Yet, as Gyuri's speech suggests, this realization is affective: it cannot be logically argued, only lived through or only shown.

And it is in the literary form of *Fateless* that Kertész tries to show this. Many testimony texts play with the flow of time, employ narrative devices, analepsis, prolepsis, and complex narrative frames. As novels like *Fiasco* and *Liquidated* show, Kertész is willing to use these devices, but in *Fateless* he maintains a consistent, linear narrative. In his Nobel Lecture he discusses the reasons for this. One is his political and social context: 'I have to conclude that in the West, in a free society, I probably would not have been able to write . . . *Fateless*', he said. In the 'free marketplace of books and ideas' in the West, he might have wanted 'to produce a showier

[19] Imre Kertész, *The Union Jack*, trans. Tim Wilkinson (New York: Melville House, 2010).

fiction' by, for example, breaking up time and narrating 'only the most powerful scenes'.[20] But, and this is the crucial revelation,

> the hero of my novel does not live his own time in the concentration camps, for neither his time nor his language, not even his own person, is really his. He doesn't remember; he exists. So he has to languish, poor boy, in the dreary trap of linearity, and cannot shake off the painful details. Instead of a spectacular series of great and tragic moments, he has to live through everything, which is oppressive and offers little variety, like life itself.[21]

This very linearity is crucial for Kertész:

> It did not allow me, say, to skip cavalierly over twenty minutes of time, if only because those twenty minutes were there before me, like a gaping, terrifying black hole, like a mass grave. I am speaking of the twenty minutes spent on the arrival platform of the Birkenau extermination camp—the time it took people clambering down from the train to reach the officer doing the selecting.[22]

His memory, his reading of the work of writers like Borowski and of the famous photographs in what is called the 'Auschwitz Album' (a photographic series of Hungarian Jews arriving at Auschwitz-Birkenau) all suggest that these twenty minutes are recalled and passed over too quickly:

> I saw lovely, smiling women and bright-eyed young men, all of them well-intentioned, eager to cooperate. Now I understood how and why those humiliating twenty minutes of idleness and helplessness faded from their memories. And when I thought how all this was repeated the same way for days, weeks, months and years on end, I gained an insight into the mechanism of horror; I learned how it became possible to turn human nature against one's own life.[23]

The very moments of agency are turned against life: as in his Nobel speech, 'I understood that hope is an instrument of evil'. For Kertész, these twenty minutes ('quite a lot of time') (258) are the utter point of being stripped of agency: 'will it be gas immediately or will it be a reprieve for the time being?' (257) and it is these minutes that give him the interlinked insights I suggested above. The first is about the relationship between fate and choice, between individual agency and the impersonal forces over which the individual has no control. The second is insight is that what happens, happens anyway. Agency, wresting one's subjectivity from the impersonal, however authentically, is no guard against atrocity (worse, as I suggest below, for Kertész, it in fact reinscribes the same

---

[20] Kertész, 'Heureka!', p. 606.   [21] Ibid.   [22] Ibid.
[23] Ibid., p. 607.

gesture). Paralleling Kertész, Emmanuel Levinas argues that if 'I am reduced to my role in history I remain unrecognised'. History, he writes, 'recounts enslavement, forgetting the life that struggles against slavery' and historians 'interpret, that is, utilise the works of the dead'.[24] Kertész in *Fateless* uses the form of the novel to stand for history itself and Gyuri is trapped within the linear narrative. *Fateless* is a novel not a testimony; not, facilely, because the narrator and author have different names, but because the insights about the nature of fate are enacted though the style, narrative, and linear form of the novel. The novel finishes (it does not end) when Gyuri, in a sense, recognizes this trap. This trap of linearity is sprung (and resprung) in the sequel, *Fiasco* (1988 Hungarian, 2011 English). In this, the same character, now an 'old boy', recalls and rewrites the story of himself as a returned young writer.[25] More, it is this trap, this 'fate' that underlies the internal or external Moloch in *Kaddish for an Unborn Child*.

SUBMERGING/STOICISM

Kaddish for an Unborn Child is a demanding prose poem act of mourning for a child that the narrator has decided not to have, an explanation of that choice, and a painful exploration of agency, fate, and paralysis. Following Marianne Hirsch's work, there has been a scholarly exploration of 'postmemory', the ways in which the children of survivors relate to the memory of the Holocaust.[26] Kertész's work might count as a sort of 'negative prememory', about the refusal to hand down or pass on a legacy of any sort. Indeed, the book brings to the fore a strand of ideas that other survivors have rarely expressed and enacts a complex act of resistance to the processes of memory. It is about refusal and resistance in the light of fate. That is, *Kaddish for an Unborn Child* takes from *Fateless* the insight that 'we ourselves are fate', that our agency is always 'he (I)', and that we can easily become our own dictators (and betray ourselves with hope), and excavates from these a form of stasis-as-resistance, resistance to the processes of memory, to 'working through' and even to the self. In it, three strands are interwoven.

The first is the narrator's relationship to Judaism. The recurring image of Jewishness comes, for the narrator, from accidentally seeing his aunt

[24] Levinas, *Totality and Infinity*, pp. 228, 252.
[25] Imre Kertész, *Fiasco*, trans. Tim Wilkinson (New York: Melville House, 2011), p. 1.
[26] See, *inter alia*, Marianne Hirsch, *The Generation of Postmemory: Visual Culture After the Holocaust* (New York: Columbia University Press, 2012); Marianne Hirsch, 'The Generation of Postmemory', *Poetics Today* 29:1 (2008), 103–27.

without her wig: 'a bald-headed woman was seated in front of the mirror in a red negligee'.[27] Judaism is not, as it is for many survivors, something to be cherished or inhabited, but rather something that has to be endured. His rejection of Judaism, of community, is summed up in his refusal to have a child. This has some parallels with others, principally Jean Améry, who Kertész admires, and who wrote of 'the Necessity and Impossibility of Being a Jew'.[28] From an assimilated family, like Kertész's narrator ('urban Jews, Budapest Jews, which is no kind of Jews, though not Christian either of course' (20)), Améry writes that if 'being a Jew implies having a cultural heritage or religious ties, then I was not one and can never become one', but that if 'to myself and to the world... I say: I am a Jew, then I mean by that those realities and possibilities that are summed up in the Auschwitz number.'[29] In the final pages, as his marriage breaks up, Kertész's narrator echoes Améry:

> from this perspective alone am I willing to be Jewish, exclusively from this unique perspective do I regard it as a fortunate, indeed a blessing... to have had the opportunity of being in Auschwitz as a branded Jew and yet, through my Jewishness, to have lived through something and confronted something. (118–19)

This 'something' leaves a bleak comprehension of the world.

This bleakness is the second strand of the novel. For Kertész, Auschwitz reveals that the world has always been beyond the possibility of salvage. It is, for the narrator, not Auschwitz but precisely the absence of Auschwitz in previous history that needs to be explained:

> Auschwitz has been hanging around in the air since long ago, who knows, perhaps for centuries, like dark fruit ripening in the sparkling rays of innumerable disgraces, waiting for the moment when it may at last drop on mankind's head. (36)

The fruit here is clearly an echo of the apple in Eden, a symbol both of knowledge and fall. It is this mixed insight, that what underlies Auschwitz underlies everything, which leads the narrator to reject fatherhood, indeed 'all Führers, Chancellors and other titled usurpers' (27) together. The narrator's recall of his schooling reflects this: the headmaster who pulled open the door like the 'Gestapo' (106); *rapports* on Saturday afternoons

---

[27] Imre Kertész, *Kaddish for an Unborn Child*, trans. Tim Wilkinson (New York: Vintage International, 2004), p. 21. Further page references to this volume are given in parentheses in the text.

[28] See, for his numerous comments, Kertész, *The Holocaust as Culture*.

[29] Jean Améry, *At the Mind's Limits*, trans. Sidney Rosenfeld and Stella P. Rosenfeld (London: Granta Books, 1999), p. 94.

like the 'Appel at Auschwitz' (108). His (English-style) boarding school was a preparation for Auschwitz. More, too, the 'warmhearted paternal rule of terror' (108) of his father existed in the same vein: 'the words father and Auschwitz elicit the same echo within me' (112) and he continues, 'if the assertion that God is a glorified father figure holds any truth, then God manifested himself to me in the image of Auschwitz' (112). It is this that the narrator has seen in Auschwitz: that the whole world is, and has been, a death camp, that the structures of power are the same throughout. Levi's description, at the end of *The Truce*, is of the post-*Lager* world dissolving as a dream, leaving him back in the camp, awaiting the dawn command of Auschwitz: Kertész refuses even this oneiric illusion. There is no outside or after Auschwitz, and in 'my writings, the Holocaust could never be present in a past tense'.[30]

For Kertész the Holocaust is not a conflict between Germans and Jews, nor the 'longest hatred'. Instead, he writes, that what

> I discovered in Auschwitz is the human condition, the end point of a great adventure, where the European traveller arrived after his two-thousand-year-old moral and cultural history.[31]

This is the reason that the narrator refuses to have a child. It is not only that he fears bringing a Jewish child into the world ('I would have to walk with head hung low before it (you) because there is nothing I could give it (you), no explanation, no belief, no ammunition' (88)). It is because he will not take on the role of the father, the culture of which Auschwitz is part: 'I could never be another person's father, destiny, god' (90). The narrator refuses any complicity with Auschwitz and so refuses fatherhood: the consequence is the 'death' of his unborn child for whom he is metaphorically saying Kaddish. And, as I have suggested, he is also refusing a certain sense of 'self-fatherhood', a more conventional sense of agency. Kertész strongly suggests that the sense that the whole culture is like a death camp stems from his experience of the totalitarian oppression in Hungary: 'a spider's web seemed to cover everything', forcing people into complicity.[32] ('In the West, at least, one is allowed to say so', Adorno wrote, during the Cold War.[33]) However, it is clear that it is the barbarism of all of Europe that the narrator is addressing.

---

[30] Kertész, 'Heureka!', p. 607.   [31] Ibid.
[32] Sandor Marai, *Memoir of Hungary, 1944–1948*, trans. Albert Tezla (New York: Corvina, 1996), p. 305.
[33] Adorno, *Negative Dialectics*, p. 367.

The narrator's refusal of fatherhood, actually and metaphorically, is his ethical resistance to Auschwitz. This is the third strand of the book, the narrator's taking up of his fate in resisting it. His 'No', repeated throughout the text is a taking up of a burden (in an English tradition, it might be described as Blake's version of Milton's Satan's denial of God). His denial of a community is the making of a point. This is why the text is called a Kaddish: it is mourning, and, as such, an affirmation of the community. Yet his Jewishness exists in a paradoxical negative sense: his affirmation of the community is in its denial. He is taking on his own fate himself and so declaring himself not fateless. The only agency available to him, the only way to avoid complicity with Auschwitz, is this negative choice which leads, purposefully, nowhere. Yet, once again, he is trapped: the logical conclusion of his refusal of being 'father, destiny, god' (90) is his refusal of being his own father, fate, god. The narrator refuses any complicity, even his own self-authorship. His refusal of agency and community includes even his own agency: an aporietic form of agency, an agency without agency. Thus: 'let me submerge' (120), the command to make commanding impossible, the choice for the impossibility of choice. He has made peace with 'the absurd order of chance, which reigns over our lives with the whim of a death squad' by surrendering himself even to himself.[34]

Kertész's understanding of 'fate' and agency was forged in the Holocaust and then shaped by the experiences of 1956 and the Kádár regime. This not only makes 'working through' impossible but is the theme of his work: stasis-as-resistance. This is a form of post-Holocaust stoicism. As Arendt writes, in a passage that seems to fit Kertész perfectly, there is a tradition of thought which accuses

> freedom of luring man into necessity . . . because its results fall into a predetermined net of relationships, invariable dragging the agent with them, who seems to forget his freedom the very moment he makes use of it. The only salvation from this kind of freedom seems to lie in non-acting, in abstention from the whole realm of human affairs as the only means to safeguard ones sovereignty and integrity as a person . . . [This] materialised into a consistent system of human behaviour only in stoicism.[35]

While Sebald's work also embodies stasis-as-resistance, it does so for different reasons and in different ways.

---

[34] Kertész, 'Heureka!', p. 609.
[35] Hannah Arendt, *The Human Condition*, 2nd edn. (Chicago: Chicago University Press, 1998), p. 234.

THE PARALYZING HORROR OF THE TRALFAMADORIAN QUINCUNX

One of the few German writers to be widely acknowledged in the Anglophone world, largely perhaps because of the English settings of his works and his life as an academic at the University of East Anglia, W. G. Sebald has been discussed as a writer gripped by European, and especially German, memory and with the Holocaust.[36] A critical consensus has grown up that his work is about how 'the writing of memory makes sense of the past'.[37] More than this, in the words of Ernestine Schlant, his work is 'steeped in images of the Holocaust and a language of mourning and melancholy so pervasive that it applies even when the text speaks of other events and times'.[38] However, many critics—and Sebald himself—find the category of 'Holocaust writing' unsatisfactory for his strange, elegiac writing (only the last book published before his death in an accident is a novel, *Austerlitz* (2001)). This is for three reasons: first, unlike Kertész, this German writer, born in 1944, had no direct experience of the Holocaust although, as his lectures *On the Natural History of Destruction* make clear, his life was shaped in the literal and metaphorical ruins of postwar Germany.[39] Second, many writers (for example, Iain Sinclair, Robert MacFarlane, and Teju Cole) have found in the *form* of his writing—reflective, neither clearly fact nor fiction, intertextual, archival—a fertile way of developing their own writing, and there is nothing, perhaps, de facto to do with the Holocaust in his formal innovation. (Although this is

---

[36] There is by now a huge bibliography on Sebald's work, including J. J. Long and Anne Whitehead (eds.), *W. G. Sebald: A Critical Companion* (Edinburgh: Edinburgh University Press, 2004), as well as many book-length studies and articles in English and German. More, his work is a significant feature of many books that address the Holocaust or the Second World War: see, *inter alia*, Richard Crownshaw, *The Afterlife of Holocaust Memory in Contemporary Literature and Culture* (London: Palgrave Macmillan, 2010), chs. 2 and 3; Torgovnick, *The War Complex*, ch. 5; Christopher Bigsby, *Remembering and Imagining the Holocaust: The Chain of Memory* (Cambridge: Cambridge University Press, 2006).

[37] George Kouvaros, 'Images that Remember Us: Photography and Memory on Austerlitz', *Textual Practice* 19:1 (2005), 173–93.

[38] Ernestine Schlant, *The Language of Silence* (London: Routledge, 1999), p. 234.

[39] J. J. Long in *W. G. Sebald: Image, Archive, Modernity* (New York: Columbia University Press, 2008) argues that while his work does deal with the Holocaust, its focus is the experience of modernity as a whole. Paul Sheehan argues that, toward the end of his life, 'the center of gravity of his work' shifted to the bombings of German cities: while this was always an interest of Sebald's, it's not clear that this was the central thrust of his later work, even in his lectures on the subject, which ends, meditatively, on the invention of urban bombing by Germany and on the killing of 40,000 civilians at Stalingrad. Paul Sheehan, 'A History of Smoke: W. G. Sebald and the Memory of Fire', *Textual Practice* 26:4 (2012), 729–45, p. 740.

not to say that in Sebald's case the formal decisions were not linked to reflections on the Holocaust.) Third, it is suggested that Sebald's work has a wider range than 'just' the Holocaust, covering a huge number of historical events: herring fishing, massacres in China, translations from Arabic, and so on—an encyclopaedic list, in fact. But, as Schlant suggests, this range has an illuminating and complex relationship with the Holocaust in his work. In a 2001 interview with Maya Jaggi, Sebald said that it

> was also clear you could not write directly about the horror of persecution in its ultimate forms, because no one could bear to look at these things without losing their sanity. So you would have to approach it from an angle, and by intimating to the reader that these subjects are constant company; their presence shades every inflection of every sentence one writes. If one can make that credible, then one can begin to defend writing about these subjects.[40]

Michael Rothberg's concept of 'multidirectional memory'—designed to help understand the relationship between the Holocaust and postcolonial movements and thought—fits Sebald's work well.[41] Rothberg develops the term from Freud's idea of a 'screen memory', in which a reassuring memory from childhood covers up a more distressing, repressed one. Yet (in part through a felicitous translation), the comforting memory acts as a screen not only because it 'screens off' the traumatic memory ('because no one could bear to look at these things') but because it is also a screen for the projection of these memories ('their presence shades every inflection of every sentence one writes'). Aware that the 'screen' then is the site for many different movements of memory, and moving the idea from a psychoanalytical to a wider register, 'collective and historical, although . . . never divorced from individuals and their biographies either', Rothberg suggests that this idea can be better seen as 'multidirectional': a 'remapping of memory in which links between memories are formed and redistributed'.[42] These 'multidirectional memories' can offer 'insights about individual and collective processes of meaning making' and frequently 'juxtapose two or more disturbing memories and disrupt every day settings'.[43] This is what Sebald's work does: however, I will argue that

[40] https://www.theguardian.com/education/2001/dec/21/artsandhumanities.highereducation.

[41] Michael Rothberg discusses Sebald in 'Multidirectional Memory and the Implicated Subject: On Sebald and Kentridge', in Liedeke Plate and Anneke Smelik (eds.), *Performing Memory in Art and Popular Culture* (London: Routledge, 2013), pp. 39–58.

[42] Rothberg, *Multidirectional Memory: Remembering the Holocaust*, p. 14.

[43] Ibid.

Sebald's work itself demonstrates, in a sort of double movement, some of the problematic implications of this spatial (rather than temporal) metaphor—the risks of stasis-as-resistance.

Memory is not like an unmade jigsaw puzzle to be put together, nor a possession like a mental photograph album, recalled to the mind's eye and opened at the right page (Gyuri in *Fateless* writes that he cannot 'give orders to my memory' (256)). Memory is inextricable from its effects upon the self, although not reducible to them, even when its effects are enervating or paralyzing. Indeed, in the case of Kertész's work, the protagonists and texts work hard to maintain a stasis, swimming upstream, even drowning, against currents both existential (temporality itself, narrative) and contingent (the pressure to reproduce, the desire to 'trump' others' experiences or say something uplifting about the Holocaust). Across Sebald's oeuvre there is a similar tension between stasis and the sense that memory shifts and changes. Specifically, and contra much critical consensus, I argue that his work does not offer a process towards 'a recuperated self' or even to 'seek out the dead and make them welcome' in an act of redemption.[44] Instead, I want to suggest that there is a more disturbing aspect to stasis-as-resistance in Sebald's writing which stems from the trope that dominates his work.

Sebald's work is dominated by the Tralfamadorian trope that turns time into space: thus, the 'places of memory'.[45] It is the case, as John Zilcosky shows, that Sebald's individual works draw on different genres (the novel, travel writing, history, and criticism among others) but within these this spatial trope, however worked and reworked, remains central.[46] In *The Emigrants*, for example, the five characters, one in each section and the narrator who holds them together, are exiles in space because they are exiles in time: the central metaphor of the Holocaust, the reason for migration, is the Alpine guide Johannes Naegeli who falls into a glacier crevasse in 1914 and whose hobnailed boots and polished bones emerge in 1986, seventy-two years later. He is the pre-war life that is both frozen and forced forward by inexorable movement of temporality. The first emigrant, Henry Welwyn (Hersch Seweryn) is tormented by homesickness as

---

[44] John Zilcosky, 'Lost and Found: Disorientation, Nostalgia, and Holocaust Melodrama in Sebald's *Austerlitz*', *MLN* 121:3 (2006), 679–98, p. 969; Torgovnick, *The War Complex*, p. 126.

[45] The aliens from Tralfamadore in Kurt Vonnegut's *Slaughterhouse-Five* (1969) move about time as we move about space. In his account of 'creaturely life' Eric Santner argues persuasively that 'everywhere present' in Sebald is dust and ash: 'the single most poignant embodiment of death, decay and transience': this is true, but dust and ash are not tropes but, perhaps rather, symbolic or associative. Eric Santner, *On Creaturely Life* (Chicago: University of Chicago Press, 2006), p. 99.

[46] Zilcosky, 'Lost and Found', pp. 684ff.

he gets older. The second is a teacher in exile who 'had been prevented from practising his chosen profession' during the Third Reich, served in the Motorized Infantry 'and doubtless saw more than any heart or eye can bear': his fascination with trains—the means of his suicide—casts a darker shadow.[47] Each one, each case, transmutes time into space. Similarly, the vertigo of *Vertigo* is not simply due to height: it is due to the height of time, the vast temporal and the protagonist's dizzying sensation of looking back down through time at his old home town.[48] (The same image occurs in *On the Natural History of Destruction*: '[s]uch is the backward and abysm of time. Everything lies all jumbled up in it, and when you look down you feel dizzy and afraid.'[49]) Indeed, this version of his basic trope may well be the *ur*-image in Sebald's work: turning time into the specific space of a depth or abyss into which one looks. But it is precisely this wider trope which prevents and delimits a 'working through' with the Holocaust. A careful examination of the form of *The Rings of Saturn* and the narrative structure of *Austerlitz* reveals both an awareness of the strength and weakness of this idea.

Introduced by a discussion of Thomas Browne, *The Rings of Saturn* (1995 German, 1998 English) is governed by the shape of the Quincunx, a pattern that recurs 'in the seemingly infinite diversity of forms'.[50] Composed 'by using the corners of a regular quadrilateral and the point at which its diagonals intersect . . . Browne identifies this structure everywhere, in animate and inanimate matter', in animals of all sorts, in the 'root of the water fern, in the seed husks of the sunflower . . . in the pyramids of Egypt and the Mausoleum of Augustus' (19–20). This shape stands for the relation of all of things to each other. More, it is the instantiation of the 'time as space' metaphor in this work, and so to the multidirectional (in Rothberg's terms) interweaving of events, time, and memory. Thus, the non-linear narrative of the book goes from a TV programme on Casement to Conrad's life; the narrow gauge bridge over the Blyth leads to a discourse on British complicity with the suppression of the Taiping rebellion; the destroyed village of Dunwich leads to the life and death of Swinburne, moving from point to point, as it were, on the

[47] W. G. Sebald, *The Emigrants*, trans. Michael Hulse (London: Harvill Press, 1996), pp. 55–6.

[48] W. G. Sebald, *Vertigo*, trans. Michael Hulse (New York: New Directions, 1999).

[49] W. G. Sebald, *On the Natural History of Destruction*, trans. Anthea Bell (London: Hamish Hamilton, 2003), p. 74.

[50] W. G. Sebald, *The Rings of Saturn*, trans. Michael Hulse (London: Harvill Press, 1999), p. 19. The quincunx is illustrated on p. 20. Further page references to this volume are given in parentheses in the text.

quincunx. But this spatial metaphor which interweaves the world is conjoined to Browne's realization that on

> every new thing there lies already the shadow of annihilation. For the history of every individual, of every social order, indeed of the whole world, does not describe an ever-widening more and more wonderful arc, but rather follows a course which, once the meridian is reached leads without fail into the dark! (23–4)

Even though this admits a sort of movement to decay, it is still a spatial metaphor: history as the movement of the sun arcing from dawn to dusk. The silkworm, omnipresent in *The Rings of Saturn*, changes time (the time of its life) into space (the fabric of silk itself) and marks the relationship between the insights of the interweaving of all things and the descent into darkness of all things. And this darkness lies behind the book. It describes, in the first person, a walking tour around Suffolk that gave the narrator not only an 'unaccustomed sense of freedom' (3) but also a sense of 'paralysing horror' when 'confronted with the traces of destruction, reaching far back into the past, that were evident even in that remote place' (3). This horror led to his hospitalization which starts the book: the first photograph is of a quincunx-like wire mesh security window which frames the 'colourless' sky and proleptically echoes the quincunx (2).

It is in this context of the woven fabric of memory, spatially understood and connected always to destruction, that the Holocaust appears in the text. A darkening evening calls to mind an odd story about a former Major who had been present at the liberation of Belsen and, in the years afterward had become increasingly eccentric—engaging a housekeeper to eat with him, on the condition that she was silent. The text has a two-page picture of Belsen—corpses among the trees (60–1) (it is like a *coup de theatre*; the reader turns the page and suddenly the image is there, free of text). The Holocaust appears as a text or subtext in other places, too: in a discussion of how much fuel one needs to burn a body, of the Allied carpet-bombing in the Second World War, in the context of ethnic cleansing in Bosnia, in relation to Kurt Waldheim. It is one of the major intersections of the quincunx and everything is irreducibly linked with it. (In David Grossman's *See Under: Love*, a character says 'suddenly I'm talking about the Holocaust again. I don't even know how I got back to it. I can get there from anywhere. I'm a regular Holocaust homing pigeon': there is this sense, too, in Sebald's text).[51]

---

[51] David Grossman, *See Under: Love*, trans. Betsy Rosenberg (New York: Farrar, Strauss and Giroux, 1989), p. 151.

Yet this constant return to the Holocaust—as if the quincunx and its interconnections were a railway system and the Holocaust a central station from which trains of thought travel out, around the network and then return—means that the events are removed from chronological time. Like the rather shocking picture of the dead of Belsen, the events are held static by the dominating trope, in the image of the Tralfamadorian quincunx, time-as-space, unchanging, simply to be visited. The material traces that link to the destructive events are found in the 'archive' of the Suffolk walking tour, held up for investigation and then simply left. The stories do not engage with or change each other, they simply accumulate: there is no movement in time. It is as if the narrator could simply return (on the lines of the quincunx) and have exactly the same thoughts (indeed, the narrator of *Austerlitz* does do exactly this, as I will show). This is not, as Marianne Torgovnik argues, 'a process' but rather its opposite: a resistance to process and to 'working through'.[52]

INTERLOCKING SPACES

The sense of stasis—as well as a concern for trains and terminals—is both heightened and perhaps critiqued in Sebald's *Austerlitz*, a novel in which the Holocaust exerts not an implicit force on the works but appears in a specific and detailed way. More driven by narrative than his previous works—indeed, it is through the narrative movement that the self-critique, such as it is, occurs—*Austerlitz* is still founded upon the same trope of time as space. Jacques Austerlitz, as if an alien from Tralfamadore himself, says that 'I feel more and more as if time did not exist at all, only various spaces interlocking according to the rules of a higher form of stereometry, between which the living and the dead can move back and forth as they like.'[53] These interlocking spaces recur again and again in the text of the novel: Terezin, Liverpool Street station (literally and meta-phorically the entry to the underworld), the iron frame that holds the railway station roof together, Lucerne station, the Saarlouis fortress, the interlocking forts around Kaunas, the Bibliothèque nationale in Paris. It is an obsession with architecture that marks out Austerlitz's 'substitute or compensatory memory' (198): indeed, this obsession with architecture is the novel's image of the space-as-time trope (as the quincunx was in *The Rings of Saturn*). However, is it precisely this trope which is and empowers

---

[52] Torgovnick, *The War Complex*, p. 117.
[53] W. G. Sebald, *Austerlitz*, trans. Anthea Bell (London: Penguin, 2011), p. 261. Further page references to this volume are given in parentheses in the text.

(in Freud's terms) the resistance which prevents Austerlitz remembering. In order to recover his childhood memories (and so himself), Austerlitz must, and will, redemptively, escape back into time from his 'substitute or compensatory' time-as-space memory.

The novel, like all Sebald's work, is full of intertexts. Stuart Tabener points out a long section drawn from writer and Holocaust survivor H. G. Adler's 1955 study *Theresienstadt*;[54] some of the section set in Wales echoes a memoir, *Bad Blood* (2000), by his colleague at the University of East Anglia, Lorna Sage; and Susi Bechhofer's *Kindertransport* story is an acknowledged inspiration.[55] However, two other revealing intertexts demonstrate how *Austerlitz* works in relation to the Holocaust. The first concerns Jacques Austerlitz himself; the second, the narrative strategy and the relationship between the narrator and Austerlitz.

Austerlitz draws on *When Memory Comes*, the memoir of Holocaust historian Saul Friedländer. Friedländer, like Jacques Austerlitz, is a Czech-born Holocaust survivor: he was hidden by his parents and baptized in a French school during the war. Like Vera in *Austerlitz*, he remembers Hitler's speeches, 'the incantatory repetition of the word *tausand*, like the panting of some monstrous locomotive': in *Austerlitz*, a 'thousand, then ten thousand, twenty thousand, thirty-seven thousand, two hundred and forty thousand, a thousand times a thousand, thousands upon thousands: such was the refrain he barked out in his hoarse voice' (236).[56] Friedländer's book is in part a search—or a memory-search—for his murdered parents and stolen youth—the sort of search that, after a revelatory crisis and breakdown, Jacques Austerlitz begins. For Friedländer, baptized as Paul-Henri Ferland, the 'first ten years of my life, the memories of my childhood' had to disappear, 'for there was no possible synthesis between the person I had been and the person I was to become', just as, too, Austerlitz's life is split and divided.[57] And indeed, the title and leitmotif of Friedländer's memoir describes Austerlitz's character well.

The Prague-based Czech occult writer Gustav Meyrink claimed that '[W]hen knowledge comes, memory comes too, little by little. Knowledge

---

[54] Stuart Tabner, 'German Literature and the Holocaust', in Alan Rosen (ed.), *Literature of the Holocaust* (Cambridge: Cambridge University Press, 2013), p. 81. This is examined in detail in Helen Finch and Lynn L. Wolff (eds.), *Witnessing, Memory, Poetics: H. G. Adler and W. G. Sebald* (New York: Camden House, 2014).

[55] Susi Bechhofer, *Rosa's Child: One Woman's Search for Her Past* (London: I.B. Tauris, 1996).

[56] Saul Friedländer, *When Memory Comes*, trans. Helen R. Lane (New York: Discus Books, 1980), p. 25. For other accounts of historians' memoirs, see Jeremy Popkin, 'Holocaust Memories, Historians' Memoirs: First-Person Narrative and the Memory of the Holocaust', *History and Memory* 15 (2003), 49–84.

[57] Friedländer, *When Memory Comes*, p. 80.

and memory are the same thing.' Significantly, for Friedländer, the sequence is inverted: 'when memory comes, knowledge comes too'.[58] This is the case for Austerlitz. At first his recall of events is not even, to use Henri Raczymow's phrase, 'memory shot through with holes', but just blank, leaving only an impulse to investigate the idea of networks as a substitute memory; then he is plagued by fragments of his own memory; then, finally, inspired by a vision of himself as a boy in Liverpool Street station, he begins a search for knowledge (Austerlitz says that he 'knew nothing about the conquest of Europe by the Germans and the slave state they set up, and nothing about the persecution I had escaped, or at least what I did know was not much more than a salesgirl in a shop' (197)). He discovers himself, his identity, and he aims to uncover the fate of his parents. For Friedländer and for Austerlitz, the process of discovery is not static but a process of change. Indeed, it is precisely when he says that 'I am going to continue looking for my father and for Mme de Verneuil as well' (408), when he has discovered who he is, that the narrator no longer has any time for him. And the crucial significance of this moment is illustrated by the second intertext.

The narrative strategy and the relationship between the narrator and Jacques Austerlitz is a parallel to Conrad's *Heart of Darkness,* a novella which looms large for Sebald (in *The Rings of Saturn* certainly). Most of that novella is a tale told by Marlow to a second, unnamed, character who, in turn, narrates the story to the reader: an intermediary screen-narrator in fact. The novella, as I will argue in Chapter 4, is about a colonial genocide from the point of view of one of the minor perpetrators: wracked by both fear and guilt, Marlow, the primary narrator, is unable or unwilling to speak or to recall the events clearly, a point that Sebald himself both takes and makes. However, in *Heart of Darkness* it is suggested that the complicity of Marlow and of the narrator are intertwined: in the last lines, the second screen-narrator, for example, sees the 'tranquil' Thames, his river, the centre of the imperial metropolis, flow into the 'heart of an immense darkness' (124).[59] In *Austerlitz,* however, while the narrative structure is similar, the complicities of the narrator and Jacques Austerlitz are different. Critics have been so fascinated by the character of Austerlitz (and his self-redemption) that the role of the narrator has frequently been ignored. Although the German narrator was only a baby during the war, while visiting as a tourist the mess of the SS guards at the fortress of Breendonk, he can

---

[58] Ibid., pp. 20, 182.
[59] Joseph Conrad, *Heart of Darkness with The Congo Diary,* ed. Robert Hampson (London: Penguin, 1995), p. 124.

well imagine the sight of the good fathers and dutiful sons from Vilsbiburg
and Fuhlsbüttel, from the Black Forest and the Bavarian Alps, sitting here
when they came off-duty to play cards or write letters to their loved ones at
home. After all, I had lived among them until my twentieth year. (29)

(It is significant, of course, that Jean Amery offered a full and terrifying
account of his torture at Breendonk: another intertext). In contrast,
Austerlitz is a victim of the Holocaust with no 'at home' to write letters
to: despite living in England and Wales for many years, when speaking
English he clutches his 'worn spectacle case... so tightly that you could
see the white of his knuckles beneath the skin' (42). As Austerlitz tells his
story to the narrator, at intervals of years, he reveals not a sort of mutual
complicity or shared darkness, as Marlow does, but the narrator's unin-
tentional guilt and complicity. Indeed, Austerlitz becomes like a 'native
informant' from the world of the Holocaust, and enacts, for the narrator, a
version of that horror. The narrator, as in other of Sebald's works, is using
Austerlitz to uncover his own feelings of complicity.

For most of the book, Austerlitz mirrors the narrator's stasis, until,
Holmes to the narrator's Watson, Austerlitz uncovers his own mystery.
When this happens, Austerlitz finally manages to move from a static,
frozen relationship to the past to an engaged, changing and developing
one: he is able actively to make decisions and seek out his father's traces in
the archive. But at this point, he can no longer serve the role of whetstone
to sharpen the narrator's sense of guilt and the novel—which has only ever
been about, as it were, the image of Austerlitz in the narrator's mind—has
to finish. Bluntly, once Austerlitz has begun to 'work through' himself,
then he is of no interest to the narrator who refuses any such movement of
memory. At their last meeting, Austerlitz gives the narrator a key to his
house in London (408) and enjoins him to visit the Jewish cemetery that
lies, Austerlitz has discovered, behind it (408). Entering the cemetery, he
says, is like entering a 'fairy tale which, like life itself, had grown older with
the passing of time' (409). Could there be a clearer allegorical sign for
someone to begin a transformative experience than being presented with a
key, an injunction, and an 'older' fairy tale? Instead, the narrator decides to
go back to the Nazi fortress at Breedonk, to where, more or less, he had
begun.[60] From, as it were, the memorialization of the Jewish dead back to

---

[60] Amir Eshel suggests that the narrative is a 'postmodern crypto-Bildungsroman...
[which] follows the story of a young German in search of an idiom that will address what he
finds along the way' (80): while there is something to this, there is no 'Bildung' at all—the
narrator ends back where he started, frozen: he has not learned anything. Amir Eshel,
'Against the Power of Time: The Poetics of Suspension in W. G. Sebald's "Austerlitz"',
New German Critique 88 (2003), 71–96, p. 80.

the memorialization of the perpetrators. For the narrator, Austerlitz is only of interest as an image of the past held in stasis. (One might find in this, perhaps, a distant and convoluted echo of Confino's view that, for the Nazis, the Jews represented the past of historical time.) Once Austerlitz no longer represents this, the narrator has to leave him and find himself another substitute memory. Thus the text turns to the image of Dan Jacobson, looking down into the huge pit of a South African diamond mine:

> [A]nyone who liked could venture to the edge of those vast pits and look down to a depth of several thousand feet. Jacobson writes that it was truly terrifying to see such emptiness open up a foot away from firm ground, to realise that there was no transition, only this dividing line, with ordinary life on one side and its unimaginable opposite on the other. The chasm into which no ray of light could penetrate was Jacobson's central image of the vanished past of his people which, as he knows, can never be brought up from those depths again. (414)

Again, the abyss as time, that is, space as time, Sebald's *ur*-image: Rothberg finds this a moment of 'multidirectional sublime' in which 'cultural memory regenerates itself at the site of historical loss'.[61] But this moment, which is sublime in a sense, is not regenerative. The narrator of *Austerlitz* is static in the face of the Holocaust and the whole panoply of Nazi war crimes, and trapped—as Austerlitz was but is no longer—by the trope of taking space for time. Unable to grasp his own past, to move in process, he is left, as in *Vertigo*, just dizzy. The novel, in this way, contrasts two different ways of facing the Holocaust: Austerlitz's engagement and the narrator's stasis, which, in the light of the final gift and injunction (to visit the Jewish dead) looks increasing problematic.[62]

CONCLUSION

What is at stake in stasis for these two writers? In Kertész's *Fateless*, Gyuri's stasis-as-resistance stems from his revelation that 'we ourselves are fate'. This is the revelation—stemming from that twenty minutes—that we are trapped in linear time, that we happen to ourselves, that we are, for

---

[61] Rothberg, 'Multidirectional Memory and the Implicated Subject', p. 46.

[62] As I suggested, Jacobs' study of Sebald aims to show how he combines 'radical stylistics' with 'moral certitude' (*Sebald's Vision*, p. x). I've suggested that in this novel at least, this combination is not the case: and indeed even Jacobs' closing remarks admit no little puzzlement about the novel because both 'ethical and aesthetic satisfaction elude us' (*Sebald's Vision*, p. 145).

Kertész, 'he (I)'. Importantly, the literary form of *Fateless* enacts the entrapment of the protagonist in that linear time, and strips active agency from him, leaving only his ability to observe, to observe even himself. In *Kaddish for an Unborn Child*, it is within this denuded sense of agency that resistance emerges: a resistance which denies 'working through' precisely because 'working through', if done for one's community, for one's self or for one's unborn child, is opening to a form of 'father, destiny, god' (90) that is the part of the same process that leads to Auschwitz, at least for Kertész in that work. There is nowhere to go from here: only the desire to submerge—which is not the desire to die but the desire, somehow, to maintain an agency-less agency, a sort of stoicism, which leaves the protagonist at peace. As readers, we are not called on to confirm or agree with this powerful and complex chain of ideas, but, at least, to recognize it. In these texts, stasis-as-resistance is a reaction—a complex and difficult one to grasp, to be sure—to what the Holocaust has revealed and to post-war history.

But what are we to make of Sebald's stasis? In *The Rings of Saturn*, it seems to function as a trap: after all, the unaccustomed freedom of the walking tour led to the protagonist's 'almost total immobility' (3) as a response to the horror arising from the contemplation of the traces of destruction. The book, within its own diegetic, is the explanation of that hospitalization, that both real and metaphorical immobility. Is this a warning that to take the past as static, as space, might result in our own paralysis or destruction? Or—like the rings of Saturn themselves—a sort of revelling in the beauty and power of that destruction rather than an active engagement with it? *Austerlitz* can also be read in two similarly divergent ways. One could be called an 'active' interpretation: the narrator (and so text) chooses to abandon Austerlitz because, as a German or even as a non-survivor, he knows he can never enter into Austerlitz's world, nor properly respond to his request to honour the dead, nor 'work through' the Holocaust.[63] Instead, he actively resists kitsch and facile attempts to 'work though' and returns to where he began, to the fortress, the site of his Nazi history. This might be seen as an admirable refusal to 'close the books on the past', a rejection of easy redemption as a 'fairy story' and a resistance to the processes of memory. However, this seems to involve taking Austerlitz's redemption as an easy fairy story, too (Austerlitz's sudden and unconvincing recovery of all his Czech language is slightly like a 'fairy story'). That is, if it is admirable to resist 'working through', what are we to make of Austerlitz doing it? Is the idea that this resistance is

[63] On this, see Brad Prager, 'The Good German as Narrator: On W. G. Sebald and the Risks of Holocaust Writing', *New German Critique* 96 (2005), 75–102.

admirable for Germans and not for Jews? (Should Jews be able to 'close the book'? Is there some form of restitution for Jews and not Germans?) Or is the implication that what Austerlitz is doing is somehow facile, like a fairy tale?

A 'passive' interpretation suggests that the narrator abandons Austerlitz because his own resistance to remembering is too powerful. Perhaps the trope of time-as-space, which Austerlitz displays, so narcissistically fascinates the narrator because it is the structuring mechanism of his own resistance: for the narrator time is space and so cannot be changed. It is simply too strongly fastened and, while he may desire to, he simply cannot 'work through' it. Yet, as a German and as a European, refusing to work though the past, refusing to respond to it, finding it simply a paralyzing abyss is also problematic as it marks a form of refusal. In this reading, the way in which Austerlitz's character 'works through' the trauma is both a critique of the narrator's stasis, and possibly a complex model for overcoming it. But—precisely because a novel is not a treatise—both active and passive readings are aporetically undecidable. Perhaps the stasis-as-resistance in Sebald reflects the complexities of life better than a simpler conclusion.

More widely, the work of these writers might indicate that an engagement with Holocaust memory is also an engagement with Holocaust time. That is, they explore how a reflection on the events of the Holocaust changes or destabilizes the processes of temporality and memory, and in so doing, processes of agency and representation. Both refuse, in different ways, to let the memory of the Holocaust sit within 'normal' time: stasis-as-resistance may not open a new form of time, but it does question the taken for granted temporality.

The issue of stasis and its (almost) overcoming is central to Otto Dov Kulka's book (not quite a memoir, not quite a mediation) *Landscapes of the Metropolis of Death*. Kulka, a very eminent Holocaust historian, a survivor and son of a survivor from Auschwitz, writes in fractured, modernist prose mixed with photographs, and is clearly influenced by the work of W. G. Sebald.[64] He tells of his thoughts, dreams, visits, moments of epiphany and memory, and of his 'mythology' of the 'Metropolis of Death', of Auschwitz. He names the 'Great Death' (the gas chambers) but also the 'Small Death' (the electrified fence) and the 'Life beyond Death', recalling the occasion where he was electrified on the fence, hanging a moment 'after death' ('I am dead, and the world as I see it has not

---

[64] Anna Hájková makes some criticisms of various omissions, too: 'Otto Dov Kulka Tells Auschwitz Story of a Czech Family That Never Existed', 30 October 2014, *Tablet*: http://www.tabletmag.com/jewish-arts-and-culture/books/186462/otto-dov-kulka.

changed! Is this what the world looks like after death?'): he was saved by being pushed off the fence by a Soviet prisoner of war.[65] Most of all, perhaps, it is about his attempts to face his own history by linking his 'Holocaust' time to his present.

Between his memory and his historical work is a diremption within himself, even though his historical work concerned the 'family camp' in Auschwitz in which he himself was held (as if Austerlitz had spent his career investigating the *Kindertransport* without formally recognizing that he had escaped in that manner). Kulka was aware of the 'tremendous "meta-dimensional" baggage and tensions' (82), philosophical and personal, which underlay his historical work but lived these out as a 'paradoxical duality' (82) in which he was both historian of that period and avoided 'integrating any detail of biographical involvement' (82) in his history. This division was so successful that, in 1978, on hearing he planned to visit Auschwitz, a well-meaning colleague suggested that he ignore the main camp and 'go to Birkenau—that is the real Auschwitz' (3).

Kulka writes that he hoped that his highly regarded historical research would be 'infused' with a consciousness of the intensity of events he witnessed, or that the 'scientific historical research' (82) would somehow help him break into the 'metropolis of death'. However, he finds that

> the truth, as it seems to me now, is that I only tried to bypass here the barrier of that gate, to enter it with the whole force of my being, in the guise of, or in the metamorphosis of, perhaps, a Trojan horse, intended, finally, to smash the gate and shatter the invisible wall of the city forbidden to me, outside whose domain I had decreed that I would remain. (82)

Disguised or hidden as a historian he sought to come to terms with, to work *at*, not 'work through', the childhood experiences from which he had exiled himself. But quite the opposite happened: the 'safe and well-paved way of scientific discipline' (82) led him to skirt precisely the violence, murder, and torture he had seen ('as perhaps I skirted the piles of skeletons in Auschwitz on my way to the youth hut' (83)). The 'safe passage' (83) of the discipline of history prevented him from being able to convey 'the message' (83) that was 'burned into' (83) his being but at the same time helped him to cope with precisely that inability to tell it. The contrast Arendt draws between the quest for truth and the quest for meaning seems apt here. Yet, he writes that the message that he could not tell, that made him 'cower at the vague awareness that I had no way, and would never attempt, to embark on the path of an attempt to disclose' (83–4) is that

---

[65] Otto Dov Kulka, *Landscapes of the Metropolis of Death* (London: Penguin, 2013), pp. 34, 35. Further page references to this volume are given in parentheses in the text.

'the world, with the Metropolis and the immutable law of the Great Death having been, can no longer, and will never again be able to free itself of their being part of its existence' (84). It is in the textual exploration of the stasis-as-resistance itself that this message emerges.

In his memoir, Kulka writes that he avoids artistic and memorial representations of the Holocaust because 'I cannot find in them what they seek to convey' (80). However, he turns to Kafka's 'Before the Law' as a way of coming to understand how he can arrive at the 'gate' of comprehension but not pass through it. Kulka suggests that his mythology exists, perhaps, only for himself, and no other 'gate' will open for him. However, he recalls that, in Kafka's story, the man sees, faintly, a light glowing from behind the gate of the law.

Kulka's stasis, held in place oddly precisely by history, is different again from both Sebald's and Kertész's. But that stasis occurs so often in these more complex accounts of memory should, perhaps, give critics and others pause about the ubiquity of 'working through' in literary, historical, critical, and theoretical discourses. Of course, it is easy to question the relatively straightforward closures of some forms of 'working through'. However, even what Dominick LaCapra (amusingly) calls the 'non-Pollyanna understanding of working through the past' still finds ways to dominate discourse, not least because of the links between the drive of narrative itself and movements of memory, and, as Adorno writes, of the desire to escape guilt and violence.[66] More, the desire not to 'work through', not to engage with past might be seen as lachrymose or, worse, to be tied to chthonic forms of nationalism or communal identity, although these two alternatives are, in fact, quite as much a form of 'working through' as any other. But this chapter has explored what is at stake in stasis and suggested that the many uncomfortable ways in which 'working through' is refused illuminates the past, memory, and its living complexities. And while these refusals might lead to unsettling conclusions about the selves and communities scarred by the events of the past, they cannot be seen as evasive.

---

[66] Dominick LaCapra, *Writing History, Writing Trauma* (Baltimore: Johns Hopkins University Press, 2001), p. 218.

4

Disorientalism

INTRODUCTION

To lose the East, the Orient, is to become lost, confused: 'disorientated'. Said's *Orientalism*, and the movements of postcolonial theory it helped inaugurate, mark a critique that

> focuses on forces of oppression and coercive domination that operate in the contemporary world; the politics of anti-colonialism and neo-colonialism, race, gender, nationalisms, class and ethnicities define its terrain.[1]

The worlds of the Holocaust and the worlds of colonial and postcolonial genocides are, as Blanchot proposes, the worlds of the disaster. Everything is inverted: doctors torture and do not heal; midwives bring children into the world to let them die or kill them; progress is death. The etymology of 'disaster' is the prefix 'des' (a 'privative sense, implying removal, aversion') plus 'starre', a planet: *désastre*. It means to lose one's guidance, to lose one's star or direction: to become 'disoriented'. This chapter's title is meant to suggest that it is possible to bring together the insights and debates of postcolonial scholarship with those of Holocaust and genocide literature—not to subsume either but to place them together in a dialogue to explore the literary subjectivity of the 'disoriented'. Critics have begun this work: this chapter, and Chapter 5, aims to continue this by exploring, or testing out, these mechanisms of interpretation and their meaning.[2]

[1] Robert Young, *Postcolonialism: An Historical Introduction* (Oxford: Blackwell, 2001), p. 11.

[2] See Rothberg, *Multidirectional Memory: Remembering the Holocaust*; Bryan Cheyette, *Diasporas of the Mind: Jewish and Postcolonial Writing and the Nightmare of History* (New Haven: Yale University Press, 2013); Stef Craps, *Postcolonial Witnessing: Trauma out of Bounds* (Basingstoke: Palgrave Macmillan, 2013); Max Silverman, 'Interconnected Histories: Holocaust and Empire in the Cultural Imaginary', *French Studies* 72:4 (2008), 417–28; Max Silverman, *Palimpsestic Memory: The Holocaust and Colonialism in French and Francophone Fiction and Film* (London: Berghahn, 2013); Paul Gilroy, *Between Camps* (London: Allen Lane, 2000); Debarati Sanyal, *Memory and Complicity: Migrations of Holocaust Remembrance* (New York: Fordham University Press, 2015).

The association has been made already. Victor Klemperer wrote that *Strafexpedition* (punitive expedition)

> is the first term which I recognised as being specifically National Socialist ... For me the word *Strafexpedition* was the embodiment of brutal arrogance and contempt for people who are in any way different, it sounded so colonial, you could see the encircled Negro village, you could hear the cracking of the hippopotamus whip.[3]

Analogously, after the Second World War, Aimé Césaire famously wrote of 'reddened waters', that the 'people of Europe tolerated Nazism before it was inflicted on them' because before 'it had been applied only to non-European peoples'.[4] In *The Origins of Totalitarianism*, a foundational work both in Holocaust and postcolonial studies, Arendt argued that some of the 'fundamental aspects' of imperialism 'appear so close to totalitarian phenomena of the twentieth century that it may be justifiable to consider the whole period a preparatory stage for coming catastrophes': historians and others write of Arendt's 'boomerang' thesis, imperialism returning to Europe.[5] Arendt uses the 'boomerang' metaphor twice in *Origins of Totalitarianism*: once very specifically, in the context of the wider impact of South Africa's racial divisiveness (206) and once precisely to deny such effects on the 'continental imperialism' (238) of the Pan-Germanists and Pan-Slavists, who did not need an 'overseas' for their extra-national claims. Arendt makes clear that 'Imperialism' is not something flung out from the centre, bound to return, but is rather the result of political and cultural processes *internal* to Europe and occur simultaneously there: expansionism, race-thinking, the changing role of the bourgeoisie, the creation of the mob and its relation to capital, the 'Pan-movements', the erosion of rights. Dirk Moses argues that there are

> good reasons today to revise central features of Arendt's account. Her talk of 'the mob' is anachronistic, her views on the Jewish question quixotic, the concept of totalitarianism is suspect, the section on imperialism is based on the superseded views of Hobson and Lenin, and the contention false that empires weakened nation-states.[6]

---

[3] Klemperer, *The Language of the Third Reich*, p. 43.

[4] Aimé Césaire, *Discourse on Colonialism*, trans. Joan Pinkham (New York: Monthly Review Press, 1972, orig. 1955), p. 14.

[5] Hannah Arendt, *The Origins of Totalitarianism*, new edn. (New York: Harcourt, Brace and World, 1966), p. 123. Further page references to this volume are given in parentheses in the text. She does occasionally use the 'boomerang' thesis in her writing elsewhere (e.g. in Hannah Arendt, 'Home to Roost', in *Responsibility and Judgment* (New York: Schocken Books, 2003), p. 271). However, the metaphor has the risk of sounding misleading, not least because of its origins (in this context in cartoons: the point of the boomerang is not just that it comes back but that the return hurts the thrower).

[6] Dirk Moses, 'Conceptual Blockages and Definitional Dilemmas in the "Racial Century": Genocides of Indigenous Peoples and the Holocaust', *Patterns of Prejudice* 36:4 (2002), 7–36, p. 33.

This may be the case: but it does not deny that the processes are internal to imperial centres. A serious disease may have different symptoms in different parts of the body but affects the whole: it does not 'fly back'. Cesaire's 'reddened waters' simultaneously inundated both the imperial centre and the colonial margins: imperialism not only profits but damages the metropolitan centre too.[7]

Other post-war writers, including survivors, brought the experience of the Holocaust and of colonialism together: this link underlies much of Pierre Vidal-Naquet's and other French intellectuals' objections to the war in Algeria. Vidal-Naquet writes that

> I personally entered the fight against the Algerian war and specifically against torture . . . with a constant point of reference: the obsessive memory of our national injustices . . . and of the Nazi crimes of torture and extermination. That reference to Nazism remained in effect throughout out the war. For instance, the day after the Paris pogrom of October 17 (I still regard that term as appropriate), a certain number of intellectuals, at the behest of *Les Temps Modernes*, Jean-Paul Sartre's journal, signed a manifesto . . . . 'We refuse to make any distinction between the Algerian piled up at the Palais de Sports while waiting to be "dispatched" and the Jews stored at Drancy before their deportation'.[8]

Charlotte Delbo, too, makes an explicit comparison:

> Torture in Algeria.
>
> My Language has been appropriated by the executioners.
>
> Villages burned by napalm in Indochina.
>
> Algerians hunted through the streets by the Paris police one day in October of 1961.
>
> Algerians whose bodies were fished out of the Seine.
>
> How often I have thought of you, Hannelore.[9]

Having viewed the film *Come Back Africa*, Jorge Semprun writes that it was 'as though the film were transparent, I kept seeing the quarantine camp, while on the screen were flashing pictures of the Negro suburbs of Johannesburg': a screen memory indeed.[10] Andre and Simone Schwarz-

---

[7] Arendt, *The Origins of Totalitarianism*, new edn. On the boomerang, see Rothberg, *Multidirectional Memory: Remembering the Holocaust*, p. 62ff. For a very full account of Arendt's thought in this area, see Dirk Moses, '*Das römische Gespräch* in a New Key: Hannah Arendt, Genocide, and the Defence of Republican Civilization', *Journal of Modern History* 85:4 (2013), 967–13.

[8] Pierre Vidal-Naquet, *Assassins of Memory*, trans. Jeffrey Mehlman (New York: Columbia University Press, 1993), pp. 127–8. See also Michael Rothberg, 'Between Auschwitz and Algeria: Multidirectional Memory and the Counterpublic Witness', *Critical Inquiry* 33:1 (2006), 158–84.

[9] Charlotte Delbo, *Days and Memory*, trans. Rosemary Lamont (Marlboro, VT: Marlboro Press, 1990), p. 117.

[10] Jorge Semprun, *The Long Voyage*, trans. Richard Seaver (London: Penguin, 1997), p. 161.

Bart's *Un plat de porc aux bananes vertes* (1967) is dedicated to both Elie Wiesel and Aimé Césaire. The Holocaust, and his ambiguous reactions to Jewish identity, haunts Frantz Fanon's work—in his exhortation at the close of *The Wretched of the Earth*, for example.[11] As Bryan Cheyette and Stef Craps have shown, a number of novelists in the Anglophone world—Muriel Spark, Doris Lessing, Caryl Phillips, Anita Desai, Salman Rushdie—have made these associations, too.[12] Colonialism and the Holocaust are closely linked; so are the postcolonial and the post-Holocaust worlds. In Chapters 1–3, I've discussed the way post-Holocaust literary texts have engaged with secrecy and complicity, evil and stasis. In this chapter, and Chapter 5, I want to take these concepts, and others, that have arisen in the study of the Holocaust, and explore 'disorientalism', understanding the literary texts that represent the worlds of genocidal disasters.

Historians have explored similar connections: Sven Lindqvist's extraordinary book of allusive, experimental historiography, *Exterminate all the Brutes* (1992 Swedish, 1997 English), explicitly focuses on the relationship between the Holocaust and the colonial. More formal work by historians from around the turn of the century to the present—Dirk Moses, Dan Stone, Donald Bloxham, Mark Mazower, Timothy Snyder, and Jürgen Zimmerer among others—have analysed these links in more (and more historically respectable) detail.[13] Mazower, for example, notes how Hitler's

imagination was caught by the example of the British in India. Their model of imperial rule, such as he conceived it, struck him as admirable . . . for him the Ukraine was 'that new Indian Empire': the Eastern Front would become Germany's North-West frontier.[14]

---

[11] See Bryan Cheyette, 'Frantz Fanon and Jean-Paul Sartre: Blacks and Jews', *Wasafiri: The Transnational Journal of International Writing* 44 (Spring 2005), 7–12.

[12] See Cheyette, *Diasporas of the Mind* and Craps, *Postcolonial Witnessing*.

[13] Thomas Kühne, 'Colonialism and the Holocaust: Continuities, Causations and Complexities', *Journal of Genocide Research* 15:3 (2013), 339–62 offers a very good survey of this area, but see also Moses, 'Conceptual Blockages and Definitional Dilemmas; Dan Stone and Dirk Moses (eds.), *Colonialism and Genocide* (London: Routledge, 2007); Dan Stone, *History, Memory and Mass Atrocity: Essays on the Holocaust and Genocide* (London: Vallentine Mitchell, 2006); Dirk Moses, *Genocide and Settler Society: Frontier Violence and Stolen Indigenous Children in Australian History* (Oxford: Berghahn, 2004); Jürgen Zimmerer, 'The Birth of the "Ostland" out of the Spirit of Colonialism: A Postcolonial Perspective on Nazi Policy of Conquest and Extermination', *Patterns of Prejudice* 39:2 (2005), 197–219; Donald Bloxham, *The Final Solution: A Genocide* (Oxford: Oxford University Press, 2009); Mark Mazower, *Hitler's Empire* (London: Penguin, 2009); Timothy Snyder, *Bloodlands: Europe Between Hitler and Stalin* (New York: Basic Books, 2010). For a discussion and examples of arguments around this, see Jürgen Matthäus et al., 'Review Forum: Donald Bloxham, *The Final Solution: A Genocide*', *Journal of Genocide Research* 13:1–2 (2011), 107–52.

[14] Mark Mazower, *Dark Continent* (London: Penguin, 1998), p. 150.

And Snyder writes that Hitler 'compresses all of imperial history and a total racism into a very short formulation: "Our Mississippi must be the Volga and not the Niger".'[15]

However, this area of research has proved to be controversial and deeply politicized, full of what Dirk Moses called in 2002 'conceptual blockages'.[16] One of these blockages is the assumption that Holocaust memory is a 'zero-sum' game, and that the memory of one terrible event would drive out or reduce the 'memory-space' of another.[17]

One of the aims of recent work, including Rothberg's, has been to try to work beyond this image of competitive memory and to suggest that 'the result of memory conflict is not less memory, but more'.[18] Indeed, in contrast to these blockages, Moses has suggested that concepts from Holocaust historiography, such as 'cumulative radicalization', 'race branding', and the links between violence, modernity, and state building, have been effective 'heuristic' devices for illuminating other genocides.[19] In parallel, there are analogies for interpreting the literary texts which arise from genocides and other times of atrocity: this chapter makes some of these, while Chapter 5 offers some important qualifications. What critics have learned from reading Holocaust texts can work as a way of seeing, a

---

[15] Snyder, *Black Earth*, p. 20.

[16] These blockages include a desire by the formerly imperial West not to look too closely into its own genocidal colonial past, and a concern for the idea that the Holocaust was unique. Both are (in Moses' terms) liberal theories of colonial genocide that took states to be the principal actors and so ignored cultural factors, and post-liberal theories that focused overmuch on structure and passed over intentionality. Moses argues that a way to further understanding would involve a form of analysis inspired by Arendt's bringing together both structure and culture.

[17] In Tova Reich's satirical novel *My Holocaust*, a caricature activist from the 'United Holocausts rainbow coalition of all Holocausts' gives hyperbolic voice to this assumption by declaiming, over three pages of the novel, solidarity with the

African-American Holocaust... the Women's Holocaust... the Native American Holocaust... the Palestinian Holocaust... the Children's Holocaust, the Muslim Holocaust, the Tibetan Holocaust... The Holocaust past, present and future of nations too numerous to list, from Cambodia to Chechnya, from Russia to Rwanda... plus Ecological and Environmental Holocausts... Nuclear Holocaust, the Herbal Holocaust... the Endangered Species Holocaust of plants and animals from bluegrass to baby seals, to bladderpods to lesser long-nosed seals, plus the personal and private Holocausts of our brothers and sisters everywhere... No one Holocaust is superior to another, no one Holocaust is deserving of special treatment or recognition. (Tova Reich, *My Holocaust* (New York: HarperCollins, 2007), pp. 243–4).

[18] Michael Rothberg, 'From Gaza to Warsaw: Mapping Multidirectional Memory', *Criticism* 53:4 (2011), 523–48, p. 523. See also Dan Stone, 'The Historiography of Genocide: Beyond Uniqueness and Ethnic Competition', *Rethinking History* 8:1 (2004), 127–42.

[19] Dirk Moses, 'The Holocaust and Genocide', in Dan Stone (ed.), *The Historiography of the Holocaust* (Basingstoke: Palgrave Macmillan, 2004), 533–55, pp. 547–9.

'conceptual optics': analysis sensitized to a range of difficulties and questions raised by Holocaust literature, broadly defined, can draw our attention to complex textual matters and to issues of interpretation which in turn may help us understand these atrocities and our relationships to them more clearly. These issues would include, as I have suggested in this book, secrecy and complicity; understandings of evil; and the concept of 'working through', including its failure and resistance to it. They might also include debates over the relationship between representation, fiction, memoir, history, and the events of the past; over genre and form; over writing and how we might understand truth; over ethics and responsibility, and the relation of these to textuality; issues over the 'right to write' and over the relationship between these texts and the public sphere more generally; and over issues often summed up in the term 'trauma' or 'trauma culture'.[20] This is not a full taxonomy but a suggestive list.

This chapter will read the novella *Heart of Darkness* (1899), a foundational text for postcolonial criticism, and suggest that, because it is a text about genocide, by and about a minor perpetrator of that genocide, some of the concepts explored and developed in reading Holocaust literature will illumine some of its celebrated and famously obscure characteristics. Many texts about genocide are overlooked, marginalized, or ignored. However, importantly for work on genocide, this novella is at the heart of the Anglophone canon and this chapter returns it to its context: a colonial genocide. This leads to some very counter-intuitive suggestions about the novella, not least about the role of Kurtz.

OBSTACLES TO READING *HEART OF DARKNESS* AS A TEXT ABOUT COLONIAL GENOCIDE

Because of its canonical importance, *Heart of Darkness* has accumulated a great deal of interpretive 'crust'. In *King Leopold's Ghost*, Adam Hochschild writes of his ignorance of the genocide on the Congo, but then remarks that

> like millions of other people, I had read something about that time and place after all: Joseph Conrad's 'Heart of Darkness'. However, with my college

---

[20] For a sense of the range and depth of these questions, and the body of work on Holocaust literature, see Adams (ed.), *The Bloomsbury Companion to Holocaust Literature*, esp. pp. 237–334. For a discussion of a 'canon' of criticism and theory about Holocaust literature, see Robert Eaglestone, 'Holocaust Theory?', in *Teaching Holocaust Literature and Film*, ed. Robert Eaglestone and Barry Langford (Basingstoke: Palgrave Macmillan, 2008), 28–36.

lecture notes filled with scribbles about Freudian overtones, mythic echoes, and inward visions, I had mentally filed the book under fiction, not fact.[21]

Even though, in the intervening years, postcolonial critics and writers have restored some degree of historical context to how the novel is read, Hochschild's mental filing is perhaps one of the first lessons that a Holocaust-inflected criticism can bring to reading the text. We know from studying Holocaust fiction that texts about genocide are not straightforwardly 'fact' or 'fiction' and, instead, there is a complex aesthetic and ethical interplay between these two categories. Indeed, a number of conceptual obstacles—in addition to the Freudian overtones and so on—prevent *Heart of Darkness* from being seen as a genocidal text.

First, many have been unwilling to recognize that there was genocide on the Congo. The consequence of this is important. Genocide is extreme: doctors torture; midwives kill; freedom means slavery; progress means savagery; work means death. The world of *Heart of Darkness* and of the Congo Free State (CFS) is not simply colonial, it is radically disoriented: the world, after Maurice Blanchot, of the disaster. Without taking this genocidal extremity on board the novel's content, context, and publication history is indecipherable.[22]

The second obstacle concerns Conrad himself and the character Marlow. In *The Rings of Saturn*, Sebald's protagonist writes that during the march from Matadi to Nselemba in June–August 1890, 'Jósef Korzeniowski began to grasp that his own travails did not absolve him from the guilt which he had incurred by his mere presence in the Congo.'[23] While many critics seek to exculpate both Conrad (historically) and Marlow (fictionally), I argue below that, as Sebald evocatively but unambiguously suggests, Conrad (in the historical record) and Marlow (in the novella) are, bluntly and despite their reservations, low-level genocidal perpetrators. As I suggested in Chapter 1, guilt, secrecy, and implication are complex matters, to do with knowing and not-knowing and the interrelations of the public and the private but it is important to engage with them.

---

[21] Adam Hochschild, *King Leopold's Ghost: A Story of Greed, Terror and Heroism in Central Africa* (London: Papermac, 1998), p. 7. Sarah De Mul reads Hochschild's book, too, as imbued with the legacy of the Holocaust: see 'The Holocaust as a Paradigm for the Congo Atrocities: Adam Hochschild's *King Leopold's Ghost*', *Criticism* 53:4 (2011), 587–606, p. 592.

[22] Even where the genocidal context has been mentioned, the full consequences of this have not been explored: see, for example, François Warin, 'Philippe's Lessons of Darkness', trans. Nidesh Lawtoo, in Nidesh Lawtoo (ed.), *Conrad's Heart of Darkness and Contemporary Thought* (London: Bloomsbury, 2012), 123–42.

[23] Sebald, *The Rings of Saturn*, p. 120. Conrad's diary is included in *Heart of Darkness with The Congo Diary*.

This leads to a third issue about the relationship between the past and a literary text. As (at least) three generations of critical and theoretical debate has made clear, the relationship between literary texts and the historical record is not at all simple: indeed, this issue is the source of some of the fiercest theoretical controversy. The autonomy of an artwork from history is important, yet texts about atrocity are bound in some special way to the past. While the historical record cannot offer a full interpretation of a text, it can and does work contrapuntally to reveal important moments of blindness, odd commitments and inconsistencies in texts. I explore a small example below concerning Captain Freiesleben (of the historical record) or Fresleven (as named in *Heart of Darkness*). Similarly, the role of the historical author—a part of the 'author function'—is also different in texts about genocide. It is legitimate to ask about their identity, about their relationship to the events or material and about their responsibilities, in a way that is not, perhaps, so normal or legitimate in relation to other forms of writing. This means that questions can be asked about Conrad, Marlow, and the narrator and about their relationship that might be different for other writers and characters. These are questions of aesthetic ontology and are usefully understood here in relation to Said's concept of 'worldliness', the 'materiality of the text's origin, for in its material being is embedded the very materiality of the matters of which it speaks: dispossession, injustice, marginality, subjection'.[24] Said's first book, *Joseph Conrad and the Fiction of Autobiography*, is, at heart, a comparison between Conrad's letters, personal writings, and his fiction: this stresses his time in the Congo. Said writes that Conrad's 'Congo experience had been so terrible . . . that his disgust with himself had made it very hard for him even to stand himself': he goes on, arguing that although 'a great deal has been written on Conrad's highly developed sense of personal guilt, not enough has been written on his extraordinary sense of shame'.[25] (This shame echoes Arendt's observation that if 'I do wrong I am condemned to live together with a wrongdoer in an unbearable intimacy: I can never get rid of him'.)[26] It is from this study of Conrad that Said's concept of 'worldliness' emerges: and perhaps 'worldliness' emerges as a critical concept less from a consideration of the normal relationship between art and the world and more from precisely their fusing together in the extremes of a

---

[24] Bill Ashcroft and Pal Ahluwalia, *Edward Said: The Paradox of Identity* (London: Routledge, 1999), p. 33.

[25] Edward Said, *Joseph Conrad and the Fiction of Autobiography* (Harvard: Harvard University Press, 1966), pp. 18, 98.

[26] Arendt, *Responsibility and Judgement*, p. 90.

genocidal situation. This core critical and postcolonial idea might better be seen as 'post-genocidal'.

Finally, in these sorts of texts, the relationship between text, its production, and the wider world can be important (for example, the fact that Primo Levi's *If This Is a Man* was turned down by publishers just after the Second World War is, itself, very revealing about the testimony and its context). In this case, I argue, some significant aspects of *Heart of Darkness* were shaped by Conrad's very reasonable desire to avoid legal prosecution by King Leopold's agents.

'AGGRAVATED MURDER ON A GREAT SCALE': GENOCIDE ON THE CONGO

Neal Ascherson writes that the 'moral reflection on the details and implications of the Nazi "Final Solution"... has come to overshadow all assessments of our times. And the discovery that genocide is still with us, in Cambodia or Rwanda, has only made that shadow darker. This change of emphasis has altered perspectives on the history of the Congo Free State.'[27] Indeed, the historian William Samvin writes of the 'slogan' of the Congo Free State, '*Travail et Progès*':

> every officially recognised village 'chief' bore these words, beginning with the year 1892, on a large medallion of nickel nearly two and half inches in diameter hanging from his neck. One is reminded of the agonising irony of these words inscribed in a poster at the concentration camp of Auschwitz: *Arbeit Macht Frei*.[28]

To turn, then, first to the implications of the novella's genocidal context: while *Heart of Darkness* is similar to some other contemporary texts about empire, its genocidal context gives it a radically different timbre. There is no doubt about the fact that there was a genocide in the Congo Free State, even though the term was not coined until 1944. Genocide was 'an inherent part of general practice employed by virtually all colonial powers throughout the colonial period'.[29] As early as 1907, Mark Twain estimated the number of those killed: his Leopold exclaims,

[27] Neal Ascherson, *The King Incorporated: Leopold the Second and the Congo* (London: Granta Books, 1999), p. 8.

[28] William J. Samvin, *The Black Man's Burden: African Colonial Labour on the Congo and Ubangi Rivers 1880–1900* (London: Westview Press, 1989), p. 27.

[29] Christian P. Scherrer, 'Towards a Theory of Modern Genocide. Comparative Genocide Research: Definitions, Criteria, Typologies, Cases, Key Elements, Patterns and Voids', *Journal of Genocide Research* 1:1 (1999), 13–23, pp. 14–15.

[M]y traducers … go shuddering around, brooding over the reduction of the Congo population from 25,000,000 to 15,000,000 in twenty years of my administration; then they burst out and call me 'the King with 10 million murders on his soul'.[30]

Arendt estimates between twenty million and forty million dead; Neal Ascherson, basing his calculations on the 1924 Belgium Census, estimates between three million and ten million; Isidore Ndaywel è Nziem, a contemporary Congolese historian, estimates thirteen million; Adam Hochschild and Georges Nzongola-Ntalaja, ten million.[31] Because the CFS was inherently unstable, 'governed in an absolute fashion by individuals concerned first and foremost with profit maximisation', genocide was the most effective political measure to dominate the area and maximize profits in the short term.[32] Such a policy was, in Ascherson's words, 'too viciously wasteful, too recklessly short term in its conception to deserve even the term of exploitation. It was no more than a prolonged raid for plunder': as Marlow observes, it was 'just robbery with violence, aggravated murder on a great scale, and men going at it blind'.[33] Moreover, if genocide involves the extermination of a whole people and, as Raphael Lemkin insisted, their pattern of life, it is incorrect—and a typical colonial blindness—to judge by total numbers of African dead. It is perhaps more accurate to count the total of distinct peoples eliminated. The Congo had over 200 different ethnic and linguistic groups: Hochschild compares it to 'medieval Europe … a huge collection of duchies, city states and principalities'.[34] The destruction of just one people in the Congo, with their own language and culture, their own pattern of life, counts as a genocide. (In his *A Congo Diary* from 1975, V. S. Naipaul records a symptom of these multiple genocides: 'I tried to find out about old songs, about historical traditions. I drew a blank. History has vanished

---

[30] Mark Twain, *King Leopold's Soliloquy* (London: T. Fisher Unwin, 1907), pp. 38–41.

[31] Arendt, *The Origins of Totalitarianism*, new edn., p. 185; Ascherson, *The King Incorporated*, p. 8, see also pp. 250–3; see Adam Hochschild, 'Dealt an Unlucky Hand', *Times Literary Supplement*, 28 July 2000, 3; Hochschild, *King Leopold's Ghost*, pp. 225–34; Georges Nzongola-Ntalaja, *The Congo: From Leopold to Kabila* (London: Zed Books, 2002), p. 22.

[32] Samuel Nelson, *Colonialism in the Congo Basin, 1880–1940* (Ohio: Ohio State University Centre of International Studies, 1994), p. 112. Nelson also points out that the ivory and 'red rubber' regimes were also an ecocide, damaging the environment permanently. See also Hochschild, *King Leopold's Ghost*, p. 277.

[33] Ascherson, *The King Incorporated*, p. 203; Conrad, *Heart of Darkness with the Congo Diary*, p. 20. Further page references to the novella are given in parentheses in the text.

[34] Hochschild, 'Dealt an Unlucky hand', p. 3. For details, see John K. Thornton, *The Kingdom of Kongo: Civil Wars and Transition* (Madison: University of Wisconsin Press, 1983).

here.... History has disappeared.')[35] While some critics argue that Conrad 'almost certainly had no knowledge and little suspicion that officials of the Congo State were carrying out policies leading to the extermination of the local population', it is clear that, as the campaigner for reform in the Belgian Congo, E. D. Morel wrote, from '1890 onwards the record of the Congo State has been literally bloodsoaked'.[36]

As with the Holocaust, colonial genocide is inextricably intertwined with racism and ideas about the nation: indeed, racism or race-thinking is the 'main ideological weapon of imperialistic politics'.[37] Racism, colonialism, and genocide make up a composite whole. Yet within this, Raul Hilberg distinguishes between different sorts of Holocaust perpetrators ('Zealots, Vulgarians and bearers of burdens').[38] Analogously, Gayatri Spivak analyses three different types of imperialist in India.[39] Indeed, recent historical scholarship has suggested that the monolithic intellectual categories of 'imperialism' and 'colonialism' in fact mask a mosaic of different historically contingent approaches to empire. While each should be condemned, it's possible and important to distinguish between racists in the novella and genocidal perpetrators (Achebe's famous comments both clarified and obscured this).[40] As I will show below, in *Heart of Darkness*, commercialist, paternalistic racists (Marlow, the narrator, and by extension Conrad) become involved and complicit with agents of genocide (the manager of the Central Station and others, but not Kurtz). It is this interaction of different forms of racism and imperialism which generates many of the complexities of the novella.

Marlow embodies, and it is likely that Conrad believed in, a paternalistic racism. Steven Donovan observes that a 'century of scholarship has produced the unlikely consensus that Joseph Conrad entertained

[35] V. S. Naipaul, *A Congo Diary* (Los Angeles: Sylvester and Orpharos, 1980), pp. 9, 13, 42.

[36] Peter Edgerly Firchow, *Envisioning Africa* (Kentucky: University Press of Kentucky, 2000), p. 160; E. D. Morel, *King Leopold's Rule in Africa* (London: W. Heinemann, 1904), p. 103. Morel, a rather amazing figure, is the hero of Hochschild's history. Hochschild compares Morel's role in the shipping company that gave him the information to begin to denounce the CFS to the Holocaust: 'as if, in 1942 or '43, somebody who began to wonder about what was happening to the Jews had taken a job inside the headquarters of the Nazi railway system': Hochschild, *King Leopold's Ghost*, p. 177. However, of course, while Morel worked for a genocidal company, he was not doing so in a genocidal environment. Hochschild also discusses early accounts of the CFS's crimes: George Washington Williams, for example, wrote his condemnation in 1890.

[37] Arendt, *The Origins of Totalitarianism*, p. 160.

[38] Hilberg, *Perpetrators, Victims, Bystanders*, p. 51.

[39] Gayatri Spivak, *A Critique of Postcolonial Reason* (Cambridge, MA: Harvard University Press, 1999), pp. 209–17.

[40] Chinua Achebe, 'An Image of Africa: Racism in Conrad's *Heart of Darkness*', *Massachusetts Review* 18:4 (1977), 782–94, p. 788.

profound doubts about imperialism'.[41] More likely, Donovan decides, is that 'at no time did Conrad *ever* believe that the ideals that had built the British Empire were either "rot let loose in print" or commercial "bad faith"'.[42] Conrad is more likely to have agreed with Morel who asserted that the 'native of Africa is not a brute, but a man, more or less intelligent according to environment, tribal peculiarities and influences from within and without—but still, and always, a man'.[43] In a long descriptive passage from his *King Leopold's Rule in Africa* designed to help his unintuitive reader sympathize with the indigenous peoples, Morel spoke of the way men work or chat in a 'native village' and how the women 'attend to household matters . . . and spend many an hour over the intricacies of their coiffure' (33–4). Morel's message is clear: 'they' are like 'us', down to sharing the same stereotyped gendered habits and concerns. Achebe precisely sums up this ideological position in his assessment of the opinions and actions of the famous philanthropist Albert Schweitzer:

> '[T]he African is indeed my brother but my junior brother.' And so [Schweitzer] proceeded to build a hospital appropriate to the needs of junior brothers with the standards of hygiene reminiscent of medical practice in the days before the germ theory of ideas came into being.[44]

This is Marlow's sort of racism: he recognizes a 'remote kinship' with the indigenous peoples: denying in an oddly reflexive formulation their inhumanity, he declares, 'if you were man enough you would admit to yourself that there was in you just the faintest trace of a response to the terrible frankness of that noise, a dim suspicion of there being a meaning in it which you—you so remote from the night of first ages—could comprehend'.[45] Unlike the district manager, he is able to reason from and even sympathize with the indigenous perspective, as, for example, when he predicts that the steamer will not be attacked again, having intuited the sorrow of his attackers. Passing through abandoned villages on the way to the Central Station, Marlow is even able to imagine what Deal and Gravesend might look like if porterage slavery was brought back to Kent.

[41] Stephen Donovan, 'Figures, Facts, Theories: Conrad and Chartered Company Imperialism', *The Conradian* 24:2 (2000), 31–60, p. 31. See also Benita Parry, *Conrad and Imperialism* (London: Macmillan, 1983).

[42] Donovan, 'Figures, Facts, Theories', p. 52.

[43] E. D. Morel, *The British Case in the French Congo* (London: William Heinemann, 1903), p. 184.

[44] Achebe, 'An Image of Africa', pp. 787–8.

[45] Conrad, *Heart of Darkness with The Congo Diary*, p. 63.

This paternalist racism contrasts vividly with the racist genocidal ideology of the CFS, what Morel called 'the living embodiment of the evil counsels ... given in connection with native policy in West Africa'.[46] The CFS portrayed the African population as inhuman. In the words of one missionary, the 'black race is certainly the race of Ham, the race cursed of God'.[47] In 1891 the Belgian officer Alexandre Delcommune (the uncle of the Station Manager whom Norman Sherry identifies as Camille Delcommune) describes Msiri, king of Garanganja (which the Europeans called Katanga), as scowling more 'like a chimpanzee than a human'.[48] Or, in the words of Léon Rom, a notorious CFS officer and author of *Le Nègre du Congo*, 'it', by which Rom means the African native, was the

> product of a mindless state, its feelings are coarse, its passions rough, its instincts brutish, and in addition it is proud and vain. The black man's principal occupation, and that to which he dedicates the greatest part of his existence, consists in stretching out on a mat in the warm rays of the sun, like a crocodile on the sand.[49]

This racism, espoused by Friedrich Ratzel, whose infamous book Hitler read while composing *Mein Kampf*, readily laid groundwork for genocide. Genocidal atrocities were not simply 'overflows' from the attempt to rescue Emin Pasha or a response to the fate of Hodister's expedition: rather, they were part of a policy enabled by an ideology.[50] The victims 'could by no stretch of the imagination be called enemies' and, although they were 'called criminals' it is clear that Marlow, for one, believes that it is the 'outraged law ... an insoluble mystery from over the sea' (33) that is to blame more than they.

A fascinating and relevant example illustrates the distinction between racism and genocidal ideology, and the role of the historical record. For paternalist racists, commerce was the solution to the problems of Africa: Morel argued that this the only way 'Europe [could] ever hope to rationally develop tropical western Africa in a manner profitable to her peoples and to the peoples of Africa', and that (echoing Marlow) commerce led to 'real work being done in there'; moreover, 'commerce [was] the Negro's one bulwark against ... the new slavery introduced into Equatorial Africa

---

[46] E. D. Morel, *Affairs of West Africa* (London: William Heinemann, 1902), p. 352.

[47] Cited in Nelson, *Colonialism in the Congo Basin*, p. 76.

[48] See Norman Sherry, *Conrad's Western World* (Cambridge: Cambridge University Press, 1971), pp. 45, 86; Thomas Pakenham, *The Scramble for Africa* (London: Abacus, 1991), p. 406.

[49] Cited in Hochschild, *King Leopold's Ghost*, p. 148.

[50] See Tim Young, *Travellers in Africa: British Travelogues, 1850–1900* (Manchester: Manchester University Press, 1994); Sherry, *Conrad's Western World*, p. 111.

by the... Congo state'.[51] Indeed, there had been a flourishing trade on the Congo before the creation of the CFS during the 1880s, with the Africans taking an active role.[52] However, genocidal colonial decrees supported by military force made such trade illegal. When the people of Bolobo-Tchumbiri attempted to defend their trade rights, two 'punitive expeditions' were sent to intervene.[53] In 1891 an employee wrote that the first 'expedition destroyed all the villages between the mouth of the Kasai and the Bolobo. The plantations are ravaged. The inhabitants defended themselves and a great number were killed.'[54] If, as Norman Sherry suggests, this very encounter led to the death of Captain Freiesleben (of the historical record) or Fresleven (as named in *Heart of Darkness*), and thus to the vacancy that Conrad (in the historical record) or Marlow (in *Heart of Darkness*) filled, then this was not what the novella calls a 'misunderstanding' (23) about hens. It was a genocidal attack—a *Strafexpedition* in fact—to assert an illegal trading monopoly. Both Conrad and Marlow's account of this vital detail and wider context illustrates the confusion and complexity of this genocidal situation. This is an example of the way that a historically informed contrapuntal reading challenges the conventions of the fiction.

Heart of Darkness is about the moment in which one form of paternalist racist colonizer becomes complicit with a genocidal ideology. It is not a critique of imperialism in general, nor a specific 'indictment of Belgium colonialism' but an account of genocide.[55]

MARLOW'S AND CONRAD'S COMPLICITY

In *The Rings of Saturn*, Sebald pointedly tells Conrad's, not Marlow's story. Like so many of Sebald's accounts, as I argued in Chapter 3, it is a story of complicity and perpetration. Work on Holocaust perpetrators in the last twenty years or so has created a variegated and complex picture of perpetrators with different motives and different reactions to genocide. These sort of nuanced distinctions usefully illuminate the nature of

[51] Morel, *British Case*, p. 3; Morel, *King Leopold's Rule*, p. 25.

[52] As Robert Harms states, during that time 'the African traders were regularly underselling the Europeans on such items as guns, gun powder, and salt, all the major commodities in river trade'. See Robert Harms, *River of Wealth, River of Sorrow: The Central Zaire Basin in the Era of the Slave and Ivory Trade 1500–1891* (New Haven: Yale University Press, 1981), p. 224.

[53] Sherry, *Conrad's Western World*, p. 20.

[54] Harms, *River of Wealth, River of Sorrow*, p. 225.

[55] Marianna Torgovnick, *Gone Primitive: Savage Intellects, Modern Lives* (Chicago: University of Chicago Press, 1990), p. 143.

complicity in *Heart of Darkness*. Morel, in an unfinished history, while describing the politics of the Congo could be (perhaps even is, in part) summing up Conrad's novella:

> [the] newcomer...with a clean heart or an evil one, was swept into a maelstrom from which there was no escape.... A raw European, with decent instincts might find himself caught in the meshes of a system that compelled him at least to connive at acts of habitual violence and oppression. But in terms of his contract he would be unable to free himself before his three years contract was over, however desirous he might be of relinquishing his employment, or of indicating the character of his employers. And by that time, save under exceptionally favorable circumstances, he would either have sunk to the level of the system or have committed suicide or died.[56]

This sounds, of course, similar to the history of some Holocaust perpetrators. While individuals in the Congo were less subject to propaganda—although as I will show, there were some—and there were perhaps different ideational motivations, there was also group pressure to conform and, more importantly, nowhere for the 'raw European, with decent instincts' to escape to.[57] Soon after Marlow signs on, while passing the knitters at the doorway, he 'began to feel slightly uneasy...as though I had been let into some conspiracy' (25).[58] The doctor he sees remarks that the 'changes take place inside' and Marlow begins to feel like an 'impostor': a sign that there are now two Marlows (27, 29). This experience of duality in perpetrators is common in Holocaust writing: in Gitta Serenys' *Into that Darkness* she comments on the way that Stangl seemed to have two personalities. In speaking of his involvement with the euthanasia programme, for example, 'an alarming change' came over his face: 'it coarsened and became slack and suffused. The veins stood out, he began to sweat and the lines in his cheek and forehead deepened.'[59] This psychic splitting, too, is a central theme in Lifton's *The Nazi Doctors*. Marlow is not historically the equivalent of Stangl but clearly, as he begins to become enmeshed, there is in him also a sense of doubling, a sense that becomes most obvious during his encounter with Kurtz.

Marlow's witness of the atrocities at 'the grove of death' leave him 'appalled, as though by a warning' (34). In effect, they are a warning of his

---

[56] Roger Lewis and Jean Stengers (eds.), *E. D. Morel's History of the Congo Reform Movement* (Oxford: Clarendon Press, 1968), p. 60.

[57] On the specific issue of differences between ideational motivations in colonial genocides and the Holocaust, see Confino, *A World without Jews*, pp. 11–15.

[58] Morel describes his own situation, when he discovered the atrocities while he was a clerk as stumbling across a 'secret society of murderers with a King for a croniman'. He was in the UK, however. Lewis and Stengers (eds.), *E. D. Morel's History*, p. 42.

[59] Sereny, *Into that Darkness*, p. 50.

own subsequent desensitization to the horrors to come. In this vein, Hochschild cites a CFS agent from 1895: 'to think that the first time I saw the *chicotte* administered, I was pale with fright... I could now walk into fire as if to a wedding'.[60] Browning's *Ordinary Men* begins, similarly, with an 'induction': the unit's first act of mass murder at the village of Jósefów and he suggests that such men began as Marlow did, aghast at what they saw yet gradually being drawn into the genocide. As a cog in the colonial genocidal machine, albeit one with reservations, Marlow learns to play his role. On the trip to central station to deal with the slave porters, he gives a 'speech in English with gestures, not one word of which was lost to the sixty pairs of eyes'. A short while later his companion seems 'very anxious' for Marlow to kill somebody, and Marlow reflects ruefully, 'I felt I was becoming scientifically interesting' (40) as he becomes an unwilling genocidal perpetrator.

Accounts from the Holocaust, from both low-level perpetrators and kapos as well as from victims, stress how the genocidal situation put groups into conflict with each other: Hilberg's 'zealots', 'vulgarians', and 'bearers of burdens'. We can use something like these characteristics to map the characters of the novella. Marlow finds himself enmeshed in another sort of struggle, one that reflects the differing colonialist ideologies—genocidal versus paternalistic racism. The Chief Accountant is a model *bearer-of-burdens* type, a paternalistic colonialist with 'backbone' who keeps his books in 'apple pie order' (36, 37). He admires Kurtz, and since he does not trust the post ('with those messengers of ours you never know who may get hold of your letter'), he asks Marlow to convey a message to the effect that 'everything here... is very satisfactory'. It is enough to stay in Kurtz's good graces, so that he may become a somebody in the 'Administration before long' (38). At the Central Station, the genocidal faction is in control, filled with both *zealot* and *vulgarian* types. The fence is ill-maintained: the white men are 'languid' and rude (40). The manager there is a 'common trader... nothing more', lacking initiative, organization, learning, and intelligence, someone who inspires only 'uneasiness' (41, 42).

It is this manager who recruits Marlow to the plot to bring about Kurtz's ruin. Sherry asserts that 'the death of Kurtz is laid at the manager's door', but Conrad's novella allows for a much stronger claim.[61] The manager conceives a plot to kill Kurtz—or, more accurately, to let him die—by wrecking the steamer (an 'affair... too stupid—when I think of it... to be altogether natural' (41) says Marlow, in a slight temporal

60 Hochschild, *King Leopold's Ghost*, p. 123.
61 Sherry, *Conrad's Western World*, p. 47.

interruption of the 'now' into his tale) and so delaying Kurtz's relief. In the manager's conversation with his uncle, which Marlow overhears, the two men have the same thought, hoping that 'climate may do away with this difficulty' (56)—which is to say, with Kurtz. This conversation is a kind of murderous pep talk: 'Anything—anything can be done in this country. That's what I say; nobody here, you understand, here, can endanger your position.' (57). It also reveals the manager's alibi: he states that the 'extraordinary series of delays is not my fault. I did my best' (58), implicitly recalling his own remark about taking 'advantage' of the fire at the station. As Kurtz is dying, the manager 'considered it necessary to sigh, but neglected to be consistently sorrowful' (100). He asks noncommittally, 'We have done all we could for him—haven't we?' (100). After Kurtz's death the 'manager was very placid', and Conrad tells us that 'he had no vital anxieties now' (109) since the '"affair" had come off as well as could be wished' (109). In a genocidal situation, words and meanings, as exchanged by and among perpetrators, are often inverted or euphemistic.

However, for this conspiracy within a conspiracy to work, the ship's captain must also be on side, and thus it is the manager's spy who attempts to recruit Marlow or to warn him at least to be quiet. The spy pumps Marlow for information, trying to ascertain the faction to which Marlow belongs. Marlow is at a loss about all of this: 'I couldn't possibly imagine what I had in me to make it worth his while' (46). At this point there is a strange caesura in the text, as, significantly, the nameless narrator interrupts his account of Marlow's tale: 'I listened on the watch for the sentence, for the word, that would give me the clue to the faint uneasiness inspired by this narrative' (50). This interruption is crucial: for it occurs at the moment in which Marlow tips from *unwitting* to *knowing* complicity. It is true that he has no way of escaping and is being threatened himself (although his position is made a bit safer by his technical expertise). But the nameless narrator is uneasy here because Marlow is about to be recruited into complicity with the murder of another European and this is the sign that, whatever his reservations or personal qualms, he has joined the genocidal faction (unlike Kurtz, as I will show). When the narrative continues, the spy—after talking about 'the necessity for every man to get on' (51) and how 'no sensible man rejects wantonly the confidence of his superiors' (51)— checks the state of Marlow's complicity: 'Did I see it? I saw it. What more did I want?' (51). It is too late for Marlow to claim he has clean hands, so he opts for what will make him seem less guilty: 'What I really wanted was rivets, by heaven!' (51). At which point the spy seems to change the subject: he 'suddenly began to talk about a hippopotamus... "That animal has a charmed life," he said; "but you can say this only of brutes in this country. No man—you apprehend me?—no man here bears a charmed life"' (52). This is both an oblique threat to Marlow and an assertion of what is happening to Kurtz. (It is a sly assertion, too, significant later in the novel. 'Brutes' (84) have a charmed life: those who are not brutes, who still make a claim to be men, do not.)

The hippo, too, comes to stand for everything that is wrong in this genocidal world. Later, hippo meat rots on the journey upriver and is thrown overboard because '[Y]ou can't breathe dead hippo waking, sleeping, and eating, and at the same time keep your precarious grip on existence' (70). If you lose this, you might take 'a high seat amongst the devils of the land' (82) or, if lucky, be 'too much of a fool to go wrong' or you might be such a 'thunderingly exalted creature . . . deaf and blind to anything but heavenly sights and sounds' (82): but 'most of us are neither one nor the other. The earth for us is a place to live in, where we must put up with sights, with sounds, with smells, too, by Jove!—breathe dead hippo, so to speak, and not be contaminated' (82). Dealing with this contamination is where, Marlow says, your 'strength comes in, the faith in your ability for the digging of unostentatious holes to bury the stuff in— your power of devotion, not to yourself, but to an obscure back-breaking business. And that's difficult enough. Mind, I am not trying to excuse or even explain—I am trying to account to myself for—for—Mr. Kurtz—for the shade of Mr. Kurtz' (82). This is not Marlow's attempt to exculpate himself but rather an awareness of how hard it is to dig 'unostentatious holes to bury the stuff in', to hide from oneself, even. Since the whole of this conversation in which Marlow becomes complicit in the plot against Kurtz is given as reported speech, it is at times hard to follow. For Marlow it is a confession trying not to be a confession.

What is the motive for the murder of Kurtz by act of omission by his colonialist compatriots? The answer to this question changes, I think, the widely held view of Kurtz, and I will explore it in some detail. First, there is the competitiveness of the manager: 'look at the influence that man must have', he says. 'Is it not frightful?' (56). Beyond this, there is a much more important reason for Kurtz's murder, which also pertains to the genocidal state of the Congo. Kurtz, while complicit with genocide, is not like the manager, who is actively genocidal. The most important corollary of this is that the genocidal faction is afraid that Kurtz, a person of some influence, will get word out to Europe about the events occurring in the CFS, and therefore they decide he must be silenced: Kurtz is a sort of Casement *avant la lettre*. (In 1904, Roger Casement provided a highly critical report to the British government 'respecting the administration of the independent state of the Congo', which played a large role in the final reform of the Congo 'red rubber' regime.) Indeed, the manager's lack of initiative, clearly stressed by the novella, might be taken to imply that this decision came from higher up. That Kurtz is aware of this threat is shown by his decision not to come down river and by his decision to return the aide he was sent: 'don't bother sending more of that sort. I had rather be alone than have the kind of men you can dispose of with me' (56). Kurtz does not want a genocidally-minded spy as his number two man.

The fact that what the manager says cannot be taken at face value is made clear in the novella. In the conversation with his uncle, he accuses the Russian and declares that they 'will not be free from unfair competition till one of these fellows is hanged' (57). Under the Berlin Act of 1885 and as he well knows, such foreign traders had every right to be there, so that the competition he rejects is fair rather than unfair. So, too, with regard to his accusation that Kurtz's methods are 'unsound'. This again is 'inverted' genocide talk. Kurtz's methods are, in fact, more humane (marginally, because they are not genocidal) than those employed in the rest of the CFS. This is important in understanding Kurtz: like Morel, as cited above, Kurtz believes in trade rather than in genocidal plundering. First, he sends 'ivory . . . lots of it' with an 'invoice' (56) that presumably tells the manager how much to pay the indigenous people who have supplied it. Second, although he is from time to time angry with the Russian, he does allow him to work within the monopoly, following the law as specified by the Berlin Act but in opposition to actual illegal CFS policy. Third, Kurtz does not just steal the ivory. When the Russian says that 'mostly his expeditions had been for ivory', Marlow replies, assuming that 'he had no goods to trade with by that time', and the Russian's subsequent rejoinder is seemingly a bizarre non-sequitur: 'There's a good lot of cartridges left even yet' (92). According to CFS practice at the time, for each cartridge issued, proof—usually a severed hand—was needed that the bullet had been used to kill someone.[62] The fact that Kurtz has cartridges left implies he has not been genocidally plundering in the manner of other colonialists. Each cartridge left signifies an unmurdered life. Fourth, Kurtz, unlike other CFS agents in *Heart of Darkness*, speaks at least one of the native languages. So unusual is this that Marlow remarks on it. Speaking the language was important. The first *Vocabulaire Français-Kisouahili* was published in 1880, and the author of a later version, Charles Lemaire, wrote that

[62] Hochschild, *King Leopold's Ghost*, p. 165. See also: Hunt Hawkins, 'Joseph Conrad, Roger Casement and the Congo Reform Movement', *Journal of Modern Literature* 9:1 (1981–2), 65–80.

[K]nowledge of the native languages is without any question of the utmost importance to those who go to Africa. Every candidate for service in the Congo must study them as early as possible.[63]

They very rarely did, of course, so Kurtz's speaking an indigenous African language shows a surprising degree of dedication on his part and an interest in both his career and the native peoples. It explains also why Kurtz got so much ivory, which the manager describes dismissively as 'mostly fossil' (101). What is fossil ivory? Marlow remarks, confused, that it 'was no more fossil than I am'. Fossil ivory was ivory that was not from freshly killed elephants:

> [prior] to the growth of long-distance trade [i.e. with Europe], ivory had little value . . . Tusks were generally left where an elephant had been killed or they were used incidentally for fences, door posts, and implements such as log wedges, hammer heads and hunting horns. But when village elders learned of the possible rewards that ivory trade could impart, tusks were no longer abandoned.[64]

Kurtz, through his language skills and commercial ingenuity, has persuaded the local people to provide him not only with fresh ivory, but with a great deal of the ivory that was simply lying around. That the tribe 'adored' Kurtz might be seen as reflecting a problematic strategy among certain members of the CFS (for example, Washington had complained that Stanley and others used tricks to convince the indigenous peoples that they were supernatural).[65] A different and less racist reading is also possible: the adoration may be a savvy expression of self-interest by the tribe. As the CFS waged genocidal massacres—over hens, or more accurately over trade—a tribe might quite reasonably seek to keep with them an agent who traded more or less fairly with them—providing invoices!—and prevented them from being massacred. The loss or replacement of such a colonialist agent would open them up to genocidal attack or forced displacement. No wonder that, on Kurtz's advice, the natives choose to attack the steamer coming to remove him, and then bewail his departure.

All this reveals that Kurtz is not so much 'unsound' (101), as his fellow colonialists charge, but is instead a threat to the genocidal situation on the Congo. In the face of such evidence, the manager's view of things continues to be upside down. He reports that the 'district is closed to us

---

[63] Cited in Johannes Fabian, *Language and Colonial Power: The Appropriation of Swahili in the Former Belgian Congo, 1880–1938* (Cambridge: Cambridge University Press, 1986), p. 20.
[64] Cited in Nelson, *Colonialism in the Congo Basin*, p. 66.
[65] Hochschild, *King Leopold's Ghost*, p. 109.

for a time...Upon the whole, the trade will suffer' (101). But this explanation is bizarrely euphemistic: the district is closed only because the natives will expect more raiding parties and are prepared to fight back. Plundering, not trade, will suffer until the people have been subdued by the CFS policy of mass murder. In contrast, to stress that Kurtz is the commercial, paternalistic, non-genocidal form of colonizer, Marlow associates him with England, the stereotypical model for this form of colonization. He is described as having been 'educated partly in England', 'his sympathies...in the right place', 'his mother [having been] half-English' (83); and so too his primary associates the Russian and the clerk are anglicized (the Russian has 'served some time in English ships' and Kurtz's clerk was 'an English half-caste'). Of course, Kurtz has infamously scrawled 'Exterminate all the brutes!' (84)—though he seems forgetful of the fact—on his manuscript. This is often taken as a sign of his genocidal intentions but there are a range of other possibilities. The fact that the 'burning noble words' (83) were written 'in a shakey hand' implies something ambiguous about them. It could be that Kurtz's text, much like Marlow's narrative, is a commentary on the hypocrisy of the Belgian colonial narrative—*Travail et Progès/Arbeit Macht Frie*—and the words refer as Frances Singh argues, to the colonizers rather than to the colonized: 'the only way Africa could develop would be if the real brutes or savages, the colonizers, were removed'.[66] More, the novella has already contrasted 'brutes' (who have a charmed life) and men (who don't), which raises the question of who docs the charming: if a man was an irritant (like Kurtz) he could easily be denied support or aim and so (like Kurtz) die from inaction.

It has become commonplace to suggest that Marlow's view of Kurtz is strange. But Marlow is drawn to Kurtz because he comes to understand that Kurtz is, like him, a person with non-genocidal motivation caught up and made unwillingly complicit in a genocidal world. 'The horror! The horror!' (112) is the horror of the genocidal colonialism with which the trade-minded paternalist Kurtz, despite his best efforts, has also become complicit. He understands that the people with whom he has lived for many years and whose language he has learnt are soon to be massacred in the name of restoring 'trade' to the region. Perhaps, too, the 'horror' is what he wishes for Marlow to take back from the Congo and thereafter to speak of. Thus Marlow perceives in Kurtz 'the expression of some sort of belief', seeing him as a man who speaks with 'candour...conviction...a

---

66 Frances B. Singh, 'The Colonialistic Bias of *Heart of Darkness*', *Conradania* 10:1 (1978), 41–54, p. 50.

vibrating note of revolt in its whisper' (113). In his words Marlow hears 'an affirmation, a moral victory paid for by innumerable defeats, by abominable terrors, by abominable satisfactions. But it was a victory!' (114). The victory is to have seen the horror *as* horror, and not to pretend (as Stangl did in court) that his 'conscience is clear' or that he never hurt anyone. The victory is to have claimed himself as someone, not a genocidal 'nobody' like Eichmann or the manager of the Central Station.

Kurtz, to a greater extent, and Marlow, to a lesser, seem to me fictional analogues to those historical figures under Nazism, such as Kurt Gerstein, who tried to oppose genocidal crimes even while functioning in service to the nation-state and administrative system responsible for perpetrating them. Gerstein, who is the subject of Saul Friedländer's study *The Counterfeit Nazi: The Ambiguity of Good* (1969), a book which is a response to Hannah Arendt's portrait of Eichmann, was an SS officer who tried to smuggle out information about what was going on in the camps. From within his position of agentive complicity with the Holocaust (Gerstein was responsible for the transportation of Zyklon B and managed, at one point, to destroy a shipment of the gas), he also tried to resist it. Gerstein wrote that not 'more than four or five persons have seen the things I have witnessed and the others were Nazis'.[67] An acquaintance of his, Pastor Mochalsky, wrote that, while an opponent of the regime, Gerstein's 'situation was such that he had been obliged to cooperate in carrying out… extermination orders and he himself had become a murderer': very akin to Marlow, and perhaps to Conrad.[68] Gerstein was found dead—either from suicide or by a murder to silence him—in his prison cell in July 1945. Marlow, despite his better intentions, is complicit with the atrocities and brutalities of genocide and with the murderous neglect of Kurtz.

SECRETS AND LIES

Complicity is made manifest as an awareness of secrecy: it seems to Marlow 'as if I also were buried in a vast grave full of unspeakable secrets' (101) and that 'there is a taint of death, a flavor of mortality in lies' (49). Morel wrote that it

---

[67] Saul Friedländer, *The Counterfeit Nazi: The Ambiguity of Good*, trans. Charles Fullman (London: Weidenfeld and Nicholson, 1969), p. 214. There are many similar remarks: see, for example, Pierre Joffroy, *A Spy for God: The Ordeal of Kurt Gerstein* (New York: Harcourt, Brace, Jovanovich, 1971), p. 287.

[68] Friedländer, *The Counterfeit Nazi*, p. 171.

is hard to get news out of the Congo, and when it does come out it is, as a rule, unreliable; moreover, few Belgians would dare to boldly denounce the State, for, as you know, Belgium is not free soil, and fear of the power of the rubber clique is enough to deter any of the returned employees from speaking.[69]

Many have observed that *Heart of Darkness* is a secretive text, full of gaps and silences.[70] Yet when it is read as a perpetrator narrative about a colonial genocide, new reasons for such secrecy begin to come into view.

Most genocidal operations require secrecy. As we know from the Holocaust, the requirement for secrecy emerges in a number of ways: in its day-to-day organization, orders passed up and down through the hierarchy between 'desk killers' and those who literally have the blood on their hands are encoded in secretive or highly euphemistic language; between the face-to-face killers at the time; and perpetrators try to ensure secrecy about the genocide in areas outside their influence (although this often leaks, as I suggested in Chapter 1). As a coda there is often denial, an attempt to make the genocide secret again by denying it happened. The circumstances of *Heart of Darkness*'s publication, as well as some of its textual characteristics and plot, are marked by secrecies like these.

Morel discusses at some length how the CFS maintained and enforced secrecy. In the Congo itself, there was 'judicial machinery which could be invoked against recalcitrant subordinates . . . if and when disclosures filtered through to Europe'. Moreover, half the salary of those in the Congo was retained in Brussels to be paid, or withheld, on return. In addition, Morel says, he 'was bound down strictly in his articles not to communicate any knowledge he might have acquired during his employment. If he made himself a nuisance, his medical and other stores would be unaccountably delayed.' (This is precisely what happens to Kurtz: he is not 'charmed'.) Escape from the CFS was hard too: with the exception of the odd missionary vessels, travel on the rivers relied on government steamers, and the Captain of the steamer 'could, of course, refuse to

[69] E. D. Morel, *The Congo Slave State* (Liverpool: John Richardson and Sons, 1903), p. 68.

[70] See, for example, famous readings by Peter Brooks (a 'detective story gone modernist: a tale of inconclusive solutions to crimes of problematic status'), *Reading for the Plot* (Oxford: Clarendon Press, 1984), p. 238; Nina Pelikan Straus ('the guarding of secret knowledge is thus the undisclosed theme of "Heart of Darkness" which a woman reader can discover'), 'The Exclusion of the Intended from Secret Sharing in Conrad's "Heart of Darkness"', *Novel* 20:2 (1987), 123–37, p. 134; Mark Wollaeger ('the language of mysticism, Marlow's discourse often finds rapture in its inadequacy and consummation in the release into silence'), *Joseph Conrad and the Language of Scepticism* (Stanford: Stanford University Press, 1990), p. 61; and J. Hillis Miller (who sees it as a parable), '"Heart of Darkness" Revisited', in *Heart of Darkness: Case Studies in Contemporary Criticism*, ed. Ross C. Murfin (New York: Bedford Books of St. Martin's Press, 1996), pp. 206–20.

take' someone who was a 'nuisance'. If the potential whistleblower got as far as Leopoldville or Boma, he could easily be arrested for desertion or held for judicial enquiry. Even if he circumvented this obstacle, the fare back to Europe was £24, and the chances of a 'subordinate in the Congo services having this amount of money in his possession was remote'. Finally, even if the complicit colonialist did get out and return home, Leopold's 'reach was a long one, his attention to detail was marvelous and he never forgave'. The whistleblower would find 'a mysterious influence blocking his chances', and if he had spoken out, 'he was literally hunted down and driven to destitution or emigration.' Finally, if the escaped colonialist persisted in his endeavour and got news out of what he had witnessed, he was likely to be discredited. As Morel says, 'who would believe a "dissatisfied ex-service agent against whose character much would be hinted if not positively assessed"'?[71]

Leopold was 'one of the first masters of the modern practice of public relations'. He set up a secret 'Press Bureau' to provide journalists with positive accounts of events in the Congo and to 'emit a stream of public statements of approval from impartial travelers' and others.[72] At times he simply bought people, in the United States and in Europe. An example of this was a 1905 pamphlet, published by 'Congolese Pamphlets', which cites a Lieutenant-Colonel's description of a hunting trip in the Congo and asserts that this 'unquestionable' witness was 'unreservedly in favor' of the CFS administration.[73] That same pamphlet goes on to argue that Morel is treacherous and underhand, providing as evidence for this claim the fact that he refused to engage in debate with supporters of the regime. Morel's position, not unlike Deborah Lipstadt's today when faced with Holocaust deniers, was simply not to debate with the regime's apologists because to 'do so would give them a legitimacy and a stature they in no way deserve'.[74]

One result of all these tactics is that the genocide on the Congo is little known about today, despite the fact that such wide-scale atrocity provided the background to this canonical novel. Even in *Heart of Darkness* there is much secrecy and covering up. The only actual clue that these atrocities

---

[71] All of the quotations in this paragraph are from Lewis and Stengers, *E. D. Morel's History*, pp. 61–2.

[72] Ascherson, *The King Incorporated*, p. 255. See also Hochschild, *King Leopold's Ghost*, esp. 235–52.

[73] Anon., 'A Complete Congo Controversy Illustrating the Controversial Methods of Mr Morel' (Edinburgh: Oliver and Boyd, 1905), pp. 5–6. For another example, see the pamphlet, Anon, 'Dr Guinness Self-Refuted: Inconsistency of the Congo Balido Missionaries' (Edinburgh: Oliver and Boyd, 1905), p. 19.

[74] Deborah Lipstadt, *Denying the Holocaust: The Growing Assault on Truth and Memory* (London: Penguin, 1994), p. 1.

are going on in the CFS is Marlow's remark that he is 'going into the yellow' (25), the region of the map of Africa coloured for Belgium. No proper names of key personnel, besides Kurtz, are given. Conrad's evasive strategy meant that it would be difficult for Leopold or his agents to sue Conrad, as in 1903 they sued Captain Guy Burrows, a British officer who had served in the CFS. After publishing *The Curse of Central Africa*, Burrows was sued for 'criminal libel against certain Free State officers'.[75] Burrows failed to produce any witnesses from the Congo (unsurprisingly) and lost his case: the 'British Judge assessed libel at £500 and ordered the book to be suppressed'.[76]

In his interaction with the 'compassionate secretary', Marlow, as Conrad must also have done, signed a document. 'I believe,' he tells us, 'I undertook amongst other things not to disclose any trade secrets' (25). In the same breath he declares, 'I am not going to' (25) and later repeats the point that, in telling us this story, he has not disclosed any. These professions can be read in two complementary ways. First, as I have suggested, there is a difference for Marlow and Conrad (as for Morel and others) between trade and genocidal colonialism. Marlow is going to reveal secrets, but not secrets about trade. Therefore what he is about to tell us is not covered by this document. Second, this statement, repeated twice, is also a meta-textual statement reaching out from the fiction to the public sphere: a declaration of immunity against Leopold and his lawyers.

One way in which secrecy is foregrounded in Conrad's text is by the concerns surrounding Kurtz's papers. If, as I have suggested here, Kurtz is really opposed to the genocidal methods practised on the Congo, it is possible that the CFS is afraid that his papers might break the seal of secrecy about genocide. With Kurtz's connections in Europe and his reputation, he might have been someone capable of authoritatively uncovering the actions of the CFS. In response, the CFS monitors all Kurtz's correspondence. Marlow surmises that the spy reads the company's confidential correspondence (45, 47). The manager reads Kurtz's post before it is sent on to Kurtz (thus when they bring Kurtz on board, they lay 'him down in one of the little cabins', whereupon he receives 'his belated correspondence, and a lot of torn envelopes and open letters littered his bed' (98)). The manager goes through some of Kurtz's papers on his deathbed, too, although Kurtz had entrusted them, including the report on the 'Suppression of Savage Customs', to Marlow. (One morning, Marlow tells us, Kurtz gave him 'a packet of papers and a photograph—the lot tied together with a shoe-string'. As he does so, he says, 'Keep this for me.... This noxious fool [he refers to the manager] is capable of prying into my boxes when I am not looking.' Marlow admits, 'I was not even sure that he had given me the right bundle. I rather suspect he wanted me to take care of another batch of his papers which, after his death, I saw the manager examining under the lamp' (120).)

After Kurtz's death, the manager twice tries to get the remaining papers from Marlow, and they have 'two rows' on the subject (115). Upon his return to Belgium, and bearing in mind Leopold's 'marvellous attention to detail', Marlow is visited by no less than three people, demanding the papers. The first, a 'clean shaven man, with an official manner', asks for them first circuitously, then in a 'suavely pressing' manner, and then with an affect that is 'darkly menacing... and with much heat' (115). Acknowledging the company's rights, Marlow eventually turns over the report, minus the postscript, which the visitor takes 'eagerly', although eventually he 'sniffs at it' (115). Presumably, his brief perusal of its seventeen pages (minus postscript) informs him that the report reveals nothing. Marlow makes the man leave by threatening court action (a trial would expose the company as trying to keep secrets, which it would only do if it had secrets to keep, of course, and this is precisely what the man, as an agent of Leopold, is trying to avoid). Next, a man 'calling himself Kurtz's cousin' comes and bears off 'family letters and memoranda without importance' (115, 116). Finally a journalist visits and takes the report. This leaves Marlow nothing except a 'slim packet of letters' (116)— carefully pruned, one supposes, by the company and by Kurtz himself through a mixture of complicity and sexism—to give to Kurtz's intended. Except for Marlow's yarn, then, no evidence of the atrocities remains. And thus the yarn itself—not the papers, but the story of the paper's suppression—becomes the witness. In addition, the novel is making the reader aware of the persistence and power of the CFS: stressing how hard it tries to cover up what it is doing.

Like the satirical science fiction novel *The Inheritors* Conrad wrote with Ford Maddox Ford in 1901, the existence of *Heart of Darkness* as a narrative under erasure is testimony to the genocidal policy in the CFS. It is constantly pointing to what it cannot say: but this is not to do with the nature of language per se—after all, Marlow gives quite a full account of the 'grove of death'. Rather, these are limits enforced by meta-textual legal, social, and political pressures not to admit the atrocities in the Congo. Conrad constantly draws our attention to these limits: as when Marlow repeatedly states that he will not reveal trade secrets; or in the pursuit of the papers by Leopold's agents; or in Marlow's final (forced) lie to the intended. Clearly, the 'taint of death', the 'flavor of mortality in lies' (49) that Marlow so hates and detests is the taint of the genocidal CFS.

CONCLUSION

This chapter has tried to read 'disorientally': where Arendt took *Heart of Darkness* as a novel about a colonial atrocity that preceded genocide, this chapter has read it in a genocidal context as a perpetrator narrative. It explores the complexities of the interaction of two colonial racist ideologies, paternalistic and genocidal, to the almost total exclusion of any African voices (this lack echoes some critiques made of Holocaust perpetrator history, and which I address in part in Chapter 5). In this light, Kurtz is not the fiend he is so often taken for but, like Kurt Gerstein, a conflicted figure in a genocidal environment. Guilty and complicit, yet struggling against this: sound and unsound at the same time. I have also argued that there are clear parallels in the induction into genocidal practices between the behaviour of Marlow (in the novella), Conrad (in the historical record), and low-level perpetrators during the Holocaust. All these things emerge because of the complex and perhaps more demanding relationship between history and the work of art in these genocidal circumstances. Finally, the obsession with secrecy, both within the novella and in the context in which it was published can be explained as a consequence of the genocidal situation in the CFS.

F. R. Leavis wrote that the 'details of the journey to and up the Congo are presented to us as if we are making the journey ourselves', and more recently Andrea White has discussed the use of Marlow to 'control our response'.[77] The result is that, vertiginously, readers are placed at the core of a genocide through a voluntary, fictionalized, first person narrative of a perpetrator, with all the complexities and confusion that this implies. Seen aright, the novella is an exploration of our own complicity with forms of genocide as, with the narrator, we see not the Congo river but how our domestic, metropolitan waterways 'lead into the heart of an immense darkness' (124). Reading with 'disorientalism' reveals *Heart of Darkness* to be a perpetrator fiction, about complicity, secrecy, and evil within a genocide in an affective way.

Authors of imperial and colonial adventures (the genre of 'imperial romance') included, in the Anglophone world, Stevenson, Haggard,

---

[77] F. R. Leavis, *The Great Tradition* (London: Penguin, 1962), p. 194; Andrea White, *Joseph Conrad and the Adventure Tradition: Constructing and Deconstructing the Imperial Subject* (Cambridge: Cambridge University Press, 1993), p. 75.

Kipling, Conan Doyle, Henty, and others.[78] *Heart of Darkness*, it has been suggested, both modelled itself on and differentiated itself from these.[79] As postcolonial critics have amply demonstrated, these texts, usually aimed at boys, reflected, shaped, and sometimes—rarely—even critiqued imperialist ideologies of race, nation, power, and gender. There was an analogous wave of stories in Germany. Indeed, the 'bestselling book for German youth up until 1945' was Gustav Frenssen's *Peter Moor's Fahrt nach Sudwest*, which tells the story of one man's adventure in the German colonial war in South West Africa in what is now understood to be the genocide of the Herero.[80] Significantly this colonial genocide has been taken—not uncontroversially—by several historians as a form of early model for the Holocaust.[81] A conversation—akin to some from Marlow's Congo—from this children's book springs out. The protagonist, the young soldier Peter Moor, overhears conversations about the cause of the revolt:

> The matter stood this way: there were missionaries here who said [to the Herero]: 'You are our dear brothers in the Lord, and we want to bring you these benefits—namely Faith, Love and Hope'. And there were soldiers, farmers and traders, and they said: 'We want to take your cattle and your land gradually away from you, and make you slaves without legal rights'. Those two things didn't go side by side . . . Either it is right to colonize—that is deprive others of their rights, to rob and makes slaves—or it is just and right to Christianise, that is to proclaim and live up to brotherly love. One must clearly desire the one and despise the other.[82]

Following the major battle of the war, the narrator discusses matters with his Lieutenant, having shot a straggler (who 'says he has not taken part in

---

[78] See, *inter alia*, Laura Chrisman, *Rereading the Imperial Romance: British Imperialism and South African Resistance in Haggard, Schreiner, and Plaatje* (Oxford: Oxford University Press, 2000). On Conrad in particular, see Linda Dryden, *Joseph Conrad and the Imperial Romance* (Basingstoke: Palgrave Macmillan, 2000).

[79] See, for examples, Linda Dryden, "Heart of Darkness" and "Allan Quartermain": Apocalypse and Utopia', *Conradiana* 31:3 (1999), 173–97; Gareth Cornwell, 'J. P. Fitzpatrick's "The Outspan": A Textual Source of "Heart of Darkness"', *Conradiana* 30:3 (1998), 203–12; Robert Hampson, 'Conrad and the Idea of Empire', in Gail Finham and Myrtle Hooper (eds.), *Under Postcolonial Eyes: Joseph Conrad after Empire* (Cape Town: UCT Press, 1996), 65–71.

[80] Zimmerer, 'The Birth of the "Ostland"', p. 217.

[81] Ibid., *passim*; see also David Olusoga and Casper W. Erichsen, *The Kaiser's Holocaust: Germany's Forgotten Genocide and the Colonial Roots of Nazism* (London: Faber and Faber, 2010); Stone, *Histories of the Holocaust*, ch. 5, esp. pp. 232ff.

[82] Gustav Frenssen, *Peter Moor: A Narrative of the German Campaign in South-West Africa*, trans. Margaret May Ward (London: Constable & Co., 1914), p. 79. Further page references to this volume are given in parentheses in the text. See, for a parallel, Horst Drechsler, '*Let Us Die Fighting': The Struggle of the Herero and Nama against German Imperialism* (London: Zed Press, 1980), pp. 133ff.

the war').[83] The Lieutenant argues that the 'blacks have deserved death before God and man', not for their revolt, but because

> they have built no houses and dug no wells... God has let us conquer here because we are the nobler and more advanced. This is not saying much in comparison with this black nation, but we must see to it that we become better and braver before all the nations of the earth.... To the nobler and more vigorous belongs the world. (236)

This is a simplified version of colonial race-theory. However, later and after reflection, the Lieutenant says 'but the missionary was right when he said all men are brothers' (237). Peter then points out that they have—in fact—killed their brother, and in an attempt to resolve this paradox, the Lieutenant says that for 'a long time we must be hard and kill, but at the same time strive towards high thoughts and noble deeds so that we may contribute our part to mankind, our future brothers' (237). The Lieutenant squares the circle (killing the Herero/all men are brothers) by projecting the fraternal links into the future—a typical totalitarian ideological move—so that the current killing is absolved in the eyes of the material world (not, significantly, a heavenly one) to come. In this imperial romance—again, the bestselling youth book during the period of the Reich—it is not hard to see fertile ground for the messianic race fantasies and genocide of the Nazi age.

Conrad, of course, did not have the term for genocide, but that does not make the 'aggravated murder on a great scale' any the less genocidal or destructive. Conrad later considered the 'physical and moral assault of his African experience the turning point in his life: before then, he told Garnett, he had '"not a thought in [my] head...I was a perfect animal"'.[84] With regard to his time in Africa, Norman Sherry suggests that Conrad's account of his travels involves an omission: the delays he experienced in getting from Boma to Kinchassa 'seem attributable only in part to sickness': 'the lack of reference in his letters to the unusually long time he took over the journey... seems to suggest that there is something he did not wish to admit to.'[85] After his return, Conrad sank into despair. In writing *Heart of Darkness*—in confessing without quite confessing, as it were, to what he had seen—Conrad's memories of his experience were 'evoked and expressed at the end of a year so depressing and unsettling

---

[83] 'In Hereroland itself German death squads made little effort to distinguish between Hereros, Berg-Damaras and Bushmen': David Soggot, *Nambia: The Violent Heritage* (London: Rex Collings, 1986), p. 11.

[84] Ian Watt, *Conrad in the Nineteenth Century* (London: Chatto and Windus, 1979), p. 146.

[85] Sherry, *Conrad's Western World*, p. 46.

that he had written to Garnett; '"I am afraid that there's something wrong with my thinking apparatus. I am utterly out of touch with my work—and I can't get in touch. All is darkness."'[86] He described his famous book to Casement as an 'awful fudge'. 'To fudge' means to blur, with the aim of covering up for oneself or for others. Hinting perhaps at what he would like to have told more straightforwardly, Conrad wrote to Graham that Casement 'could tell you things! Things I've tried to forget; things I never did know.'[87] Reading *Heart of Darkness* informed by what we know about the Holocaust shifts how the novella is understood, makes the issues of complicity, secrecy, and evil stand out more clearly, as well as reminding us that genocide occurs with some frequency and can even hide in plain sight.

[86] Watt, *Conrad in the Nineteenth Century*, p. 146.
[87] Hawkins, 'Joseph Conrad, Roger Casement', pp. 68, 70, 71–2.

5

Disorientalism Today

INTRODUCTION

Chapter 4 defined 'disorientalism' as the bringing together of postcolonial and post-Holocaust concerns and showed how concepts from the study of the Holocaust illuminate texts from other genocides. This chapter follows the same line of thought but, in contrast, suggests limitations to this by looking at correlations—or lack thereof—between the literature of the Holocaust, widely defined, and accounts of the Rwandan genocide and other atrocities in Africa.[1] Because these texts about genocide and atrocity are more recent and because they are aimed at a Western audience, it might seem that the Holocaust would be an immediate point of reference. However, as I will show, this is not straightforwardly the case: even approaching these texts presents a number of theoretical difficulties and problematic concepts which I will examine first.

AFRICAN TRAUMA LITERATURE?

In recent years, there has been a sudden burst of distressing narratives from Africa aimed at Western readers. This in part reflects a guilty Western conscience that has too often passed over the particular and intricate problems and difficulties in Africa, or reduced them to simplistic pieties. Formal political action by Africans and others, media interest, campaigns by non-governmental organizations, as well as the more complex tides of migration and globalization have helped bring these issues to the fore. However, in this context, the term 'African' is itself problematic.

---

[1] Ishmael Beah, *A Long Way Gone* (London: Fourth Estate, 2007); Gil Courtemanche, *A Sunday at the Pool in Kigali* (Edinburgh: Canongate, 2003); David Eggers, *What is the What: The Autobiography of Valentino Achak Deng* (London: Hamish Hamilton, 2007); Uzodinma Iweala, *Beasts of No Nation* (London: John Murray, 2005). *Beasts of No Nation* was made into a film in 2015 (dir. Cary Joji Fukunaga); Paul Rusesabagina, *An Ordinary Man* (London: Bloomsbury, 2006).

It clusters the nations of 'Africa' into a single continent, and passes over the various complications and specific situations, including genocides in Darfur and Rwanda as well as coups and civil wars. Binyavanga Wainaina's much-cited, insightful, and satirical 'How to Write about Africa' makes these points very clearly:

> Some tips: sunsets and starvation are good.
>
> Always use the word 'Africa' or 'Darkness' or 'Safari' in your title...
>
> Note that 'People' means Africans who are not black, while 'The People' means black Africans...
>
> Never have a picture of a well-adjusted African on the cover of your book, or in it, unless that African has won the Nobel Prize. An AK-47, prominent ribs, naked breasts: use these...
>
> In your text, treat Africa as if it were one country.... Don't get bogged down with precise descriptions. Africa is big: fifty-four countries, 900 million people who are too busy starving and dying and warring and emigrating to read your book...
>
> Africa is to be pitied, worshipped or dominated. Whichever angle you take, be sure to leave the strong impression that without your intervention and your important book, Africa is doomed.[2]

The term 'trauma' is also problematic in this context: it could easily be argued that much of African literature in the second half of the twentieth century is 'traumatic' in a broad sense: from Achebe's description of the colonial encounter, to Fanon's Algerian War case studies, to Ngugi's politics in *Matagari* and *A Grain of Wheat*, to Bessie Head's agonized prose in *A Question of Power*, to the trauma of poverty in NoViolet Bulawayo's *We need New Names*. More, trauma does not describe what Rob Nixon names the 'slow violence' enacted on African peoples and the environment.[3] The very act of using the after-effects of the Holocaust to analyse events seems to betray these complexities. However, because the books I will be analysing discuss genocide or genocidal atrocities and because they are Western facing (unlike, for example, Bouobacar Boris Diop's *Murabi, The Book of Bones*, written as part of a pan-African project) it might seem intuitive that they should evoke the Holocaust as a point of reference, implicitly or explicitly.[4]

---

[2] Binyavanga Wainaina, 'How to Write about Africa' (London: Granta 92, 2006).

[3] Rob Nixon, *Slow Violence and the Environmentalism of the Poor* (Cambridge, MA: Harvard University Press, 2011).

[4] Boubacar, Boris Diop, *Murabi, The Book of Bones*, trans. Fiona McLaughlin (Bloomington: Indiana University Press, 2006).

Stef Craps has convincingly explored the problems of a postcolonial context in his analysis of trauma theory.[5] He argues that Caruth's celebrated edited collection, *Trauma: Explorations in Memory* (1995) drew on a wide interdisciplinary range of critics and theorists, film-makers, and medical experts and practitioners and her widely cited introduction to the volume served almost as a 'mission statement' for this branch of trauma theory.[6] But, as Craps makes clear, Caruth's argument goes further in relation to ethics, history, and the relationships between cultures. She expresses the hope that 'trauma itself may provide the very link between cultures', suggesting that trauma could be the site of an encounter between disparate historical experiences and cultures, and could form the bonds of cross-cultural solidarity.[7] However, as Stef Craps argues with great force, this founding text and much that follows has not yet developed this suggestion of cross-cultural ethical engagement. Instead, he argues, it is profoundly Eurocentric, often marginalizing or ignoring traumatic experiences of non-Western or minority cultures. That is, accounts in trauma theory focus on events in the West, centrally the Holocaust, and pass over other traumatic events such as slavery and colonial genocide. More, Craps argues that the 'psychiatric universalism' of trauma theory—the assumption that trauma works in the same way in different cultures—takes for granted the 'universal validity of definitions of trauma and recovery that have developed out of the history of Western modernity'.[8] He cites an emblematic incident from Ethan Watters' 2010 book, *Crazy like Us: The Globalization of the American Psyche*. The Western trauma counsellors who arrived in Sri Lanka following the 2004 tsunami to help the victims simply exported, Watters argues, an American model of trauma, mental illness, and mourning and so 'inadvertently trampled local expressions of

---

[5] Craps, *Postcolonial Witnessing*. Many scholars, such as Jane Kilby, Wulf Kansteiner, and Susannah Radstone, have pointed to flaws, omissions, and areas in which trauma theory needs to be developed and expanded. See Wulf Kansteiner, 'Genealogy of a Category Mistake: A Critical Intellectual History of the Cultural Trauma Metaphor', *Rethinking History* 8 (2004), 193–221; Wulf Kansteiner with Harald Weilnböck, 'Against the Concept of Cultural Trauma or How I Learned to Love the Suffering of Others without the Help of Psychotherapy', in Astrid Erll and Ansgar Nünning (eds.), *Cultural Memory Studies: An International and Interdisciplinary Handbook* (New York: de Gruyter, 2008), pp. 229–40; Jane Kilby, *Violence and the Cultural Politics of Trauma* (Edinburgh: Edinburgh University Press, 2007); Susannah Radstone and B. Schwarz (eds.), *Memory: Histories, Theories, Debates* (New York: Fordham University Press, 2007); Susannah Radstone, *The Sexual Politics of Time: Confession, Nostalgia, Memory* (London: Routledge, 2007).
[6] It is here that the claim is made that trauma consists 'in the structure of its experience or reception: the event is not assimilated fully at the time, but only belatedly, in its repeated possession of the one who experiences it.' Cathy Caruth (ed.), *Trauma: Explorations in Memory* (Baltimore: Johns Hopkins University Press, 1995), pp. 4–5.
[7] Caruth, *Trauma: Explorations in Memory*, p. 11.
[8] Craps, *Postcolonial Witnessing*, p. 22.

grief, suffering, and healing, thereby actually causing the community more distress'.[9] This marginalization and 'psychiatric imperialism' together mean that it is hard for Western scholars even to *see* trauma in some cases. Craps argues that as a result of all of this, rather than promoting cross-cultural solidarity, 'trauma theory risks assisting in the perpetuation of the very beliefs, practices, and structures that maintain existing injustices and inequalities'.[10]

What about the Holocaust? Craps argues that this is taken, in the West, as the pre-eminent model of a historical trauma. Echoing Dirk Moses' analysis of 'conceptual blockages', Craps suggests that the Holocaust can act less as a 'bridge' between the understanding of different historical traumas and more as a block or divide. Worse, it can act more subtly as a lens which shapes the interpretation of other atrocities: the long list of atrocities, satirically and hyperbolically turned into a '-caust' in Tova Reich's novel *My Holocaust* cited in Chapter 4 is an example of this. Zoe Norridge, too, in her powerful and thought-provoking book on African literature raises concerns about the dominance of the Holocaust as a model for understanding both personal and communal trauma: she offers an approach drawing on a comparative and postcolonial understanding of pain and what she names 'social suffering'.[11] In the light of all these issues, any analysis of African trauma literature needs to be both very provisional and perhaps only suggestive: to see where there are bridges and to avoid blocks. More, it needs to be clear about what it aims to do and why.

ATROCITY IN RWANDA AND SUDAN

Indeed, rather than force the shape of a 'Holocaust model' here, it is clear that there is little explicit reference to the Holocaust in any of these texts, even the two which focus on the Rwandan genocide. *A Sunday at the Pool in Kigali*—which is as much about the damage caused by AIDS in Rwanda and about sexual violence as about mass murder—states that the killers' methods were as they were because they were 'too poor to build gas chambers',[12] and the leaders are compared to Nazis (163): there is a 'Rwandan nazism' (210) or 'tropical Nazism' (252). Paul Rusesabagina mentions the Holocaust in a discussion of the term genocide and the need

    [9] Ibid.   [10] Ibid., p. 2.
    [11] Zoe Norridge, *Perceiving Pain in African Literature* (Basingstoke: Palgrave Macmillan, 2012), p. 15.
    [12] Courtemanche, *A Sunday at the Pool in Kigali*, p. 233. Further page references to this volume are given in parentheses in the text.

for a Rwandan Nuremberg,[13] and hints at it with his epigraph from *The Plague*. In Eggers' novel—concerning Sudan—it occurs only once, where a rumour sweeps the Kakuma refugee camp that the new fences erected for census are the prelude to 'a plan like that used to eliminate Jews in Germany and Poland'.[14] It features in Beah's and Iweala's work not at all.

These very slight references contrast interestingly with, for example, Philip Gourevitch's reportage, *We Wish To Inform You That Tomorrow We Will Be Killed With Our Families* (1998), which is haunted by the Holocaust. His epigraph, for example, compares the speed of murder taking place in Rwanda with killings during the Holocaust: between 800,000 and one million in around one hundred days, murdered 'at nearly three times the rate of Jewish dead during the Holocaust'.[15] This claim is striking, and sets the tone for the book: it is not, however, totally accurate. As Christopher Browning suggests, between 50 per cent and 60 per cent of the victims of the Holocaust were murdered in a 'short, intense wave of mass murder' between March 1942 and February 1943, and this itself excludes many others murdered in that time.[16] Indeed, this raises questions of definition, of dating (when did the Holocaust start: 1933? 1939? 1941?) and when exactly it finished (and as Kertész and David Cesarani both suggested, 'finishing' is not a simple issue). To point this out is not to try to 'trump' one genocide with another, but rather to illustrate the complexities that immediately arise when contrasts and comparisons are made. Gourevitch mentions the Holocaust again as a comparison of 'efficiency' (96), in relation to the UN's genocide convention and the USA's lack of action (149ff), in a discussion about reconciliation (240) and at a moment of outrage:

> Rwanda had presented the world with the most unambiguous case of genocide since Hitler's war against the Jews, and the world had sent blankets, beads and bandages to camps controlled by the killers, apparently hoping that everyone would behave nicely in the future. (170)

Indeed, his outrage is rightly focused on both the inaction and the wilful ignorance of the Western powers and media, who confuse Hutus and Tutsis and blame innate 'savagery' rather than analyse the situation.

---

[13] Rusesabagina, *An Ordinary Man*, pp. 174 and 250 respectively. Further page references to this volume are given in parentheses in the text.

[14] Eggers, *What is the What: The Autobiography of Valentino Achak Deng*, p. 345. Further page references to this volume are given in parentheses in the text.

[15] Epigraph in Philip Gourevitch, *We Wish To Inform You That Tomorrow We Will Be Killed With Our Families* (London: Picador, 2000). Page references to this volume are given in parentheses in the text.

[16] Browning, *Ordinary Men*, p. xv.

However, despite this, I want to suggest that the Holocaust and our knowledge of the representation of the traumas and damages of those events shape to some degree the form of these accounts of atrocity and mass death and an interpretation of them, while being wary of 'over-coding' one with the other. Indeed, it may be that the forms of representation—in this case in prose—by which traumatic events of this sort are represented are themselves shaped by Western culture's deep involvement with the after-effects of the Holocaust, and so these explicitly Western-facing texts are shaped by these influences.

AUTHORSHIP

One of the most obvious points of comparison between these traumatic texts about Africa and Holocaust literature concerns the interrelated issues of authorship and genre. I've already cited Foucault's essay 'What is an Author?' in Chapter 2, and suggested that the older characteristics of the 'author function' are no longer so relevant: instead there are new questions which might be usefully asked. Like Holocaust testimony and other Holocaust literature, these texts too pose many of these questions: not in a foregrounded theoretical way, the way post-modern fiction might, for example, but simply in their construction. Paul Rusesabagina's *An Ordinary Man* is co-written with the reporter Tom Zoellner: Ishmael Beah's testimony is his own work, supported by his professors at Oberlin College. While *Beasts of No Nation* is a novel in a straightforward sense, Gil Courtemanche claims that *A Sunday at the Pool in Kigali* from 2003

> is a novel. But it is also a chronicle and eyewitness report. The characters all existed in reality, and in almost every case I have used their real names. The novelist has given them lives, acts and words that summarise or symbolise what the journalist observed in their company. If I have taken the liberty of inventing a little, I have done so the better to convey the human quality of the murdered men and women. (preface)

Indeed, the novelist has done more than this to the work of the journalist: apart from changing the name of the protagonist from Gil Courtemanche to Bernard Valcourt, he describes the inner thoughts of others, scenes at which he was not present, and fictionalizes a diary. He puts monologues into the voices of the characters. In addition, the epigraph to Gentille— the central female character, who more than anyone else symbolizes the violence of the genocide—implies that the author does not know if she is 'dead or alive' (n.p.): yet it is very clear, and centrally important, in the main body of the text, that she, the fictional character at least, dies

('Gentille was dead' (248)). Here, then, the role of the author and the claims to the veracity of the text, in a traditional positivist sense at least, are open to investigation. Is Courtemanche following the codes and conventions that a journalist does, or the more traditional literary creative conventions? This uncertainty seems to confuse some of his claims. In parallel, *What is the What* is subtitled 'The Autobiography of Valentino Achak Deng: A Novel by Dave Eggers'. Eggers is of course famous for his metafictional experimentations: his debut *A Heartbreaking Work of Staggering Genius* also plays off the contrast between a novel and a memoir. Here, the preface by Valentino Achak Deng makes clear the status of the text: the 'real' events are the foundation, but the rest has been novelized, 'concocted' (preface) by Dave Eggers though 'it should be noted that the world I have known is not so different from the one depicted within these pages' (preface). The preface also makes clear the strong didactic and moral purpose of the book.

These sorts of issues and complications over more traditional forms of authorship are well known in Holocaust studies. Some texts resolve this by foregrounding the role of the author, their relation to their own memory and the role that, say, the historian or ghostwriter takes. These texts, especially *What is the What*, follow this in stressing the constructed nature of the text. But the questions concern not only what the author can know and can legitimately tell, but also moral and political issues. For example, Courtemanche put a speech into the mouth of one Cyprien, who has AIDS and suspects the genocide is about to begin: he is not afraid of death, and while the Westerners want him to talk, he states, 'we're dying... I'm going to live and fuck and have a good time' (82). In contrast, Beah describes how afraid he is, captured by rebels: 'I couldn't hear their words, because all I could think about was death. I struggled to avoid fainting'.[17] Indeed, Courtemanche's non-white African characters seem unafraid and almost lacking in agency, while the non-white Africans from the others works—self-authored or ghostwritten—stress their fear and interiority.

While each text makes a concrete claim to its authenticity, the questions suggested by Foucault do illustrate a common theme in these works. Just as Holocaust testimonies are often aimed at those who did not experience the camps and the generations born subsequent to the Second World War, all these trauma texts are aimed at the West, often, specifically, the USA: indeed, like many Holocaust texts, they are all diasporic, by Africans or Americans resident in the West. This is clear not only from the

---

[17] Beah, *A Long Way Gone*, p. 31. Further page references to this volume are given in parentheses in the text.

language but also in the very nature of the authorship itself. Trauma literature not only has forms of authorship and different relations to the historical record from other forms of fictional writing but it is also *read* differently. This means that the affective experience of reading them can be like reading Holocaust testimonies: fascinating and upsetting but not pleasurable. Like Holocaust testimony, they make up a new genre, with new characteristics and, following Foucault, new placements and affectivities.

GENERIC CHARACTERISTICS

At the level of genre, these texts do seem to share many formal characteristics with Holocaust literature and testimony. Traditionally, texts are clustered by national identity, or period, or by genre. Yet, because the Holocaust was a continent-wide event and the borders—both geographic and chronological—are hard to define, texts that concern the Holocaust are often studied beside each other to draw out contrasts and similarities. This form of 'drawing together', the creation of a rhizomatic subject of study, has had a number of beneficial effects. So, too, it might be useful to contrast these texts, which cover Sudan, Sierra Leone, Rwanda, and an unnamed African country (reminiscent of Nigeria, though it could be Sierra Leone again). I have outlined elsewhere a non-totalized selection of characteristics: these include, *inter alia*, the use of discourse usually seen as historical, diverse, and complex narrative-framing devices, moments of epiphany, and consciously confused time schemes.[18] Here I want to suggest how far these texts use these formal characteristics and what this might mean.

Holocaust testimonies and some Holocaust fiction often break from their narrative to discuss or explain wider historical events and movements. They also have a range of meta-textual support including maps and references. These texts offer a parallel. Eggers' novel offers meta-textual historical information: it includes a map of Eastern Africa, and the preface (by Valentino Achak Deng, not Eggers) makes clear its didactic purpose. In contrast to many Holocaust testimonies, however, the historical situation is offered within the diegetic time of the novel rather like the technique described as 'infodumping' in science fiction. For example, a character called Dut offers a lecture, complete with a citation from historical documents, on the colonial history of Sudan (175–9) and

---

[18] See Robert Eaglestone, *The Holocaust and the Postmodern* (Oxford: Oxford University Press, 2004), esp. ch. 2.

Achak often comments on other events. The book is also 'dated' by occasional references to world events such as the death of Princess Diana and 9/11. Holocaust testimonies often list the dead, too: here the book concludes with a long list of people to be thanked, academic books that have proved useful, and a website address for Achak's charity.[19] Similarly, though it avoids historical lectures, *A Long Way Gone* has a considerable amount of meta-textual support: maps, acknowledgements, and a historical chronology of Sierra Leone. *An Ordinary Man* has a map and a bibliography. It is also full of historical background and information which interrupts the flow of the narrative but which makes it more accessible for the less-informed reader. Various passages cover accounts of world events or US reaction: a section begins 'Seven time zones away, in the United States...' and then describes the US reaction, the history of the term genocide, and America's attempts to avoid using the word. Another describes the Conference of Berlin in 1885. These texts explicitly aim to explain and historicize the events they narrate.

In contrast, Iweala's novel does not offer any extraneous detail; indeed, it is not even clear what country the novel takes place in (though 'Beasts of No Nation' is the name of a 1989 record by Nigerian Afrobeat superstar Fela Kuti, suggesting a Nigerian background to the novel, and Iweala is Nigerian). This, with the dialect English and dizzying movement of the narrative, is part of the 'immersion' that the novel wishes to achieve. Oddly, too, *A Sunday at the Pool in Kigali* has no support outside the text: perhaps this is because of its claim to be a novel, rather than a testimony, and a reflection that it is more focused on the experience of the European protagonist. Its aim, as it were, is not to reach outward to the West as an appeal, but to affectively describe, in the way Wainaina analyses, in fact, the state of Rwanda before and during the genocide.

Most Holocaust testimonies—though perhaps not the most celebrated—offer framing devices which structure the narrative: these texts do too. Beah's testimony is framed by a very short chapter set in New York in 1998: his school friends ask him about his life in Sierra Leone, little imagining that he had been press-ganged as a murderous boy soldier. For them, even seeing a war is 'cool' (3). Here the frame subverts what is to come. Conversely, *Beasts of No Nation* simply begins in the confusion of a rebel attack, echoing the start of Amos Tutuola's *My Life in the Bush of Ghosts* (1954). However, perhaps the most demanding use of a narrative frame occurs in *What is the What*. The whole of the first book is told in

[19] http://www.vadfoundation.org/.

flashback while Achak is being robbed and then tied up in his (present-time) Atlanta apartment. The second book takes place during the next day, and includes his visit to hospital and return to one of his jobs. Not only does this (very unsettling) frame destroy, from the beginning, any sense of narrative redemption, but it makes clear that simply being in the USA is far from the answer to the problems faced by Achak and his peers, the 'Lost Boys' of Sudanese refugees and exiles. Indeed, while individuals are praised, the USA as a whole comes out rather badly from this novel.

This unsettlement is emphasized by the use of a trope akin to one quite common in Holocaust testimonies, which I have named 'allegories of failed understanding': figures not involved in the traumatic events are shown misreading, failing to understand, or simply taking over the traumatic events that the victim experienced.

Charlotte Delbo offers a clear example of this in *The Measure of Our Days*. Sometime after the Second World War, the narrator meets Pierre, the husband of her camp-sister friend Marie-Louise. Pierre has an obsessive interest in his wife's experiences and has read her notebooks: indeed, Marie-Louise says that her memories have become his, and he is more aware than she of some of the 'facts' of the events. The narrator is simply horrified by Pierre's claim to memories and experiences he cannot know.[20] Pierre becomes a figure of 'failed understanding', that is, a measure of the impossibility for someone who has not experienced them of understanding the events, of the gap between the survivors and the others, and so, in turn, of the gap between the readers and the survivor/authors. Eggers' *What is the What* often uses something like this trope in a subtly different way, one that does not focus on incomprehensibility but failed empathy: early on Achak (in Eggers) writes that when he

> first came to this country, I would tell silent stories... to people who wronged me... I would glare at them, staring, silently hissing a story to them. *You do not understand*, I would tell them. *You would not add to my suffering if you knew what I have seen.* (32)

Indeed, throughout, he addresses people silently in order to tell them his story: a child belonging to the robbers who tie him up, a receptionist at the hospital, the members of the health club at which he works are all silently told part of his story, and addressed like this. Each is seen as unwilling to grasp the events. In contrast, the widespread community of the Sudanese diaspora—in contact by mobile phone and web—is seen as comprehending and supporting.

---

[20] Delbo, *Days and Memory*.

This issue over empathy touches on a very significant difference between the vast majority of Holocaust testimonies and these texts: in these African texts, there is little sense of 'smothered words'. This is the term used by the philosopher and second-generation survivor Sarah Kofman to describe the aporia which lies between the inability of Holocaust survivors to put into words the evil they survived—its traumatic breakage of the very possibility of narrative—and their duty and often compulsion to do so, which would reform the events into a comprehensible narrative.[21] The accounts are 'smothered words' which both 'say' and 'unsay' the events. These accounts of African trauma, however, offer a different approach to this. There is no sense that the events themselves, while awful, are actually incomprehensible, as is so often claimed for Holocaust testimony. Indeed, the opposite is claimed. In the closing pages of Imre Kertész's novel, *Fatelesss*, Gyuri, the survivor, meets a journalist eager to write about the camps. But after some conversation, the journalist 'covered his face with his hands' and declares that the camp cannot be imagined: 'so, that must be why they prefer to talk about hell instead' thinks Gyuri.[22] In these texts, whether conventionally a novel like *Beasts of No Nation*, or a novelized testimony or a simple testimony, there is a real sense that there can be comprehension, that a story must be told and can and should be grasped by others in the West. Indeed, the end of Iweala's novel consists of his learning to enunciate his story. More movingly, the second half of Beah's testimony concerns his care at Benin Home, where he learns to 'work through' his trauma and narrate his testimony, and then his retelling of his and others; story to a Western audience. Eggers, writing Achak, says,

> [B]e grateful, TV boy. Have respect. Have you seen the beginning of a war? Picture your neighbourhood, and now see the woman screaming, the babies tossed into wells. Watch your brothers explode. I want you there with me. (72)

The final sentence sums up both didactic purpose and the implicit comprehensibility of the events Eggers is describing.[23]

The reasons for this significant difference are hard to pin down. Of course, if the traumatic events were discussed as incomprehensible, as the Holocaust often is, then the books would undermine themselves: Iweala's novel would be trapped in an aporia; Eggers' method would seem futile (and, like Pierre in Delbo's work, rather insulting); and all Beah's work

---

[21] Sarah Kofman, *Smothered Words*, trans. Madeleine Dobere (Evanston: Northwestern University Press, 1998).

[22] Kertész, *Fateless*, p. 250.

[23] For a useful dissection of this trope, see Thomas Trezise, 'Unspeakable', *The Yale Journal of Criticism* 14:1 (2001), 39–66.

would seem to be wasted. As in Holocaust narrative, there is a sense that the story 'must be told'. But perhaps here there is also a more burning political need, too. As the news reminds us daily, and notwithstanding the view of Africa which Wainaina criticizes, many of these sorts of events are continuing. Without grasping them, perhaps nothing can be done: these works are 'engaged literature' in a renewed Sartrean sense. That is, they are not simply affective works; they are also aimed explicitly at pricking Western consciences.

Holocaust texts often have moments of epiphany. Perhaps the most celebrated of these occurs in Levi's testimony: reaching for an icicle to quench his thirst, a guard snatches it away: '"Warum?" I asked him in my poor German. "Hier ist kein warum" ("there is no why here")'.[24] This moment reveals to Levi the unreasoning and irrational nature of the death camps. Like Holocaust testimony, these texts make use of similar tropes. The protagonist's first killing in *Beast of No Nation* marks one such event, and Beah's testimony is full of worse and worse horrors that reveal Beah's condition to himself. [25] *What is the What* sounds as if it is built around an epiphany (the what) but in fact, the what constantly escapes. It might be the return of Dinkaland to itself (126) or the protagonists' growth and success (456) but it is never really clear. Indeed, just as Eggers avoids a redemptive conclusion, so he avoids a cliché of discovery: just as in his first book, the process—open-ended, painful, often filled with delusion and error—is the focus of the narrative. While there are many moments of terror and showing, there is no one unifying vision.

Many Holocaust testimonies feature interruptions or slips in the diegetic of the text: there are analepses and prolepses, disruptions to the narrative flow in the form of historical accounts and interludes, things the protagonist could not have known at the time but learnt later, explanations, and so on. These are reproduced in all these texts and are so prevalent that they might be considered almost ubiquitous in texts that deal with traumatic events. *Beasts of No Nation* begins *in medias res*, then flashes backwards to cover the past. Both Eggers' and Beah's books begin, in terms of form, in the USA, and then flash back to the past. Beah's use of flashback is especially interesting: the most vivid accounts of the atrocities in which he participated are offered during the narrative when he is recounting precisely his recovery from the psychological damage of being a boy soldier. In this way, the text echoes the accounts of trauma that stress that the events are not experienced as they happen, but only

---

[24] Primo Levi, *If This Is a Man*, trans. Stuart Woolf (London: Abacus, 1979), p. 35.
[25] Iweala, *Beasts of No Nation*, pp. 25–6. Further page references to this volume are given in parentheses in the text.

afterwards, in fragmentary and broken ways, as the self struggles to work through and reintegrate itself. Rusesabagina, too, moves about in time, as the text covers the genocide and its context in relation to his own life narrative.

CONCLUSION

These five texts share, among others, several formal characteristics of Holocaust testimony. This is not a full taxonomy and, more importantly, it is not meant to suggest these texts are written in imitation of Holocaust testimonies. More, this chapter has not focused attention on the many characteristics of postcolonial and contemporary fiction shared by these African accounts. It does suggest, though, that the cultural tools for representing terrible atrocities to and in the West, in English, echo or parallel each other. Some psychologists argue that these tools or codes stem from the experience of trauma itself: it seems more likely that they are the conventions by which trauma is recognized through literary representation in the West.[26]

Despite being about genocide and atrocity, these texts do not rely on the Holocaust for their affective power, nor do they seem competitive. However, there are illuminating congruencies between discourses about the Holocaust and about genocide, atrocity, and trauma in Africa. Post-colonial texts offer ways to understand how 'colonialism was experienced, or analysed, by those who suffered its effects'.[27] These five texts, which witness awful events taking place in the aftermath of colonialism and empire, certainly do this. However, as scholars have learnt from Holocaust studies, such witnessing is complex, positioned, structured by generic concerns, and interwoven with a range of other discourses. Moreover, these texts are already problematic in terms of the politics of representation: they are about Africa, but all directly address the West, and especially the USA. A harsh critic might easily accuse them of offering a voyeuristic opportunity, or of colonizing atrocity. It is true that they criticize the West: Rusesabagina's and Courtemanche's texts both offer a clear-sighted view of colonial history; Eggers' makes it clear that the USA is no safe haven and the global indifference to Sudanese disasters is enacted on the level of personal interactions. However, these critiques are located in an

---

[26] See, among others, Gadi BenEzer, 'Trauma Signals in Life Stories', in *Trauma and Life Stories*, ed. Kim Lacy Rogers et al. (London: Routledge, 1999), 29–44; Judith Lewis Herman, *Trauma and Recovery* (London: Routledge, 1992).

[27] Young, *Postcolonialism: An Historical Introduction*, p. 18.

English-speaking, Western-facing context, which reduces the force of the critique.

The same harsh critic might also suggest that the focus on the personal reduces a wider engagement with political and global issues. Perhaps this view of these testimonies misses the point: the texts are forms of engaged literature which seek to influence, explain, and educate. This is why they share the implicit conception that the events, the 'what', is communicable and can be put into narrative. In these complexities—the need to speak, the immediate difficulties that this raises—these texts further echo Holocaust testimony. One key area where they differ is that many of the scandals they discuss—the atrocities in Sudan, for example—are continuing, which makes both their need to communicate and their engagement even more vital.

In his study of the intertwining of Jewish and postcolonial writing, Bryan Cheyette stresses the need to move beyond what he names 'disciplinary thinking—whether it be in relation to nation, community of the literary canon', so that thought—literary, political, philosophical—can better 'connect with dissimilarities': this move, he writes, is 'not without risks'.[28] This chapter and Chapter 4 have tried, while attempting to be aware of these risks, to see what links can be found by placing together these texts and these disoriented histories.

---

[28] Cheyette, *Diasporas of the Mind*, p. 264.

6

Post-Holocaust Kitsch

INTRODUCTION

From the sixties to the present, a recurring theme in discussions of the Holocaust by survivors, historians, and many others has been the ways in which understanding what happened falls prey to what Primo Levi called 'simplification and stereotype'.[1] This gap between the events and their representation is understood in different ways and at different levels. Most profoundly, many think it is existentially impossible to comprehend the Holocaust unless one is a survivor, that there is an abyss between history and memory. Certainly, there are many ways in which this is so.

But other, less profound, versions of this gulf exist, not least because any representation involves some degree of simplification and shaping: the work of historians is shaped by their metahistorical commitments, for example. Pedagogy, too, inescapably begins with broader strokes which provide the foundation for a more detailed, fine-brush picture, and so simplifies events. But the most contentious version of this gulf is the divide between the horrors and their artistic representations. (Recall how the historian and survivor Otto Dov Kulka, discussed in Chapter 3, avoided artistic accounts of the genocide because 'I cannot find in them what they seek to convey'.[2]) Very many survivors and others have expressed the gravest misgivings about Holocaust art in general and its sometimes irresponsible freedom. Indeed, works of art—novels, films, visual art— are not obviously constrained by the 'genre rules' or language game of the discipline of history or forms of testimony. However, for some, this is precisely one reason for their importance in our understanding of the Holocaust, because they can illumine areas that history cannot: this book has been dedicated to the proposition that in the 'broken voice' of post-Holocaust art, some forms of deep understanding or response can properly be discerned. Works of art, too, usually have a wider popular reach than

---

[1] Primo Levi, *The Drowned and the Saved*, trans. Raymond Rosenthal (London: Abacus, 1988), p. 129.
[2] Kulka, *Landscapes of the Metropolis of Death*, p. 80.

works of historical scholarship, and so, for better or worse, shape public memory.

But not all works of art are the same. Some offer a dayglow popularization, which encompasses not only the glamour of evil I discussed in Chapter 2 but also simplistic explanations and crude responses: much of this art can be described, despite its subject matter, as kitsch. This post-Holocaust kitsch is the inevitable result of the growth of Holocaust consciousness. A fungus on the memory of the Holocaust, it cannot be banned or prevented. But it can be the focus of critical commentary, analysed and shown for what it is and for what it might mean. This chapter takes as its focus a celebrated narrative sculpture, *Hell* by Jake and Dinos Chapman (the 'best art of our age' wrote *The Guardian*'s chief art critic), and a very well-known novel for children, John Boyne's *The Boy in the Striped Pyjamas*.[3] I will argue explicitly that, despite their apparent differences, both are examples of contemporary post-Holocaust kitsch.

Post-Holocaust works are Janus-faced. While they look back to the past and can, as Friedländer suggests, 'reveal previously unsuspected aspects', they are also of the present and tell us about contemporary life. Kitsch post-Holocaust art, in this context, is an issue of especial concern. At a straightforward level it can obscure, rather than reveal, the events in the past with which it purports to engage or create ideas that are not merely simplistic but wrong. In the case of *The Boy in the Striped Pyjamas*, this is significant because it is very widely used for teaching school students about the Holocaust. But post-Holocaust kitsch is also a matter of concern because of what it tells us about contemporary life in relation to the questions framed by the Holocaust and genocide more widely. As Sianne Ngai argues, in the 'hypercommodified, information-saturated, performance-driven conditions of late capitalism', the constellations of our aesthetic categories are changing and shifting: more traditional aesthetic categories (say, the sublime and the beautiful) are less helpful to our orientation in the world.[4] Instead, she suggests, we better understand our times and our world through less dramatic and demanding but more pervasive aesthetic categories: she focuses on the cute (which has 'close ties' (59) to kitsch), the interesting, and the zany. These categories also give us insights into 'major problems in aesthetic theory' (2), politics, and the contemporary. These categories cannot be understood in the abstract and need to be explored with

---

[3] https://www.theguardian.com/artanddesign/jonathanjonesblog/2009/feb/23/chapman-hell-art.

[4] Sianne Ngai, *Our Aesthetic Categories: Zany, Cute, Interesting* (Harvard: Harvard University Press, 2012), p. 1. Further page references to this volume are given in parentheses in the text.

reference to specific works, so the aim of this chapter, then, following Ngai and focusing on two works in particular, is to ask what post-Holocaust kitsch means for how we understand the Holocaust and the present.

Kitsch, its more Anglophone relative 'camp' and Ngai's 'cute' are very hard words to define precisely and exist in a diffuse tradition in aesthetics and in cultural theory. Adorno and others have analysed kitsch's relation to the Nazis and to other totalitarian regimes in general, and Lisa Saltzman sums up kitsch as

> easy, sentimental, commercial. Coupled with a representation of history, it transforms its traumas into fictional melodramas, renders its catastrophes sites of catharsis. It forgoes the reflective and enduring encounter demanded by avant-garde culture and offers in it is place instant gratification. Kitsch, when coupled with a representation of history, a history of fascism, of the Holocaust, of genocide, makes that history all too assimilable, digestible, consumable.[5]

Here, 'assimilable, digestible, consumable' means that the Holocaust has been mythologized and is no longer an issue of concern. By catharsis, here, Saltzman means that kitsch purges the memory of the genocide, and that mass murder is no longer an emotional, intellectual, or political problem: crucially, that the connection between the Holocaust and our world, which should pull on us, has been severed. Kertész put this same idea in a much starker form:

> I regard as kitsch any representation of the Holocaust that is incapable of understanding or unwilling to understand the organic connection between our own deformed mode of life (whether in the private sphere or on the level of 'civilization' as such) and the very possibility of the Holocaust.[6]

That is, kitsch is that which separates the world of the Holocaust from our world in the very act of representing the Holocaust.[7]

Saul Friedländer's *Reflections on Nazism: An Essay on Kitsch and Death* (1982 French, 1984 English), explores further how, counter-intuitively, works which represent the Holocaust 'break the link' between that world and the present. Friedländer argues that for some artists, film-makers, and authors, the 'transformation of the past is deliberate; for

---

[5] Lisa Saltzman, 'Avant-Garde and Kitsch Revisited', in *Mirroring Evil: Nazi Imagery/ Recent Art*, ed. Norman Kleeblatt (New York: The Jewish Museum and New Brunswick: Rutgers University Press, 2001), 53–64, p. 55.

[6] Imre Kertész, 'Who Owns Auschwitz?', trans. John MacKay, *The Yale Journal of Criticism* 14:1 (2001), 267–72, p. 270.

[7] Ibid.

others, it is a free play of phantasms'.[8] Rather than simply condemning these, Friedländer argues that because Nazism's attraction lay 'less in any explicit ideology than in the power of emotions, images and phantasms' (14) coming to understand more contemporary versions of these in art, grasping what he calls, with a nod to psychoanalysis, their 'latent discourse' (15), would help clarify their logic. More than this, 'it is precisely their evocation and reinterpretation of the past that helps us better to understand the past itself' (17–18). This is of particular importance because Friedländer senses, responding to George Steiner's novel *The Portage to San Cristóbal of A. H.* and to Hans-Jürgen Syberberg's *Hitler, a Film from Germany*, that a new discourse has arisen, some kind of barrier 'has been overstepped and uneasiness appears' (21), and he wants to draw a boundary. He names this new discourse 'kitsch'. The choices of texts which made Friedländer uneasy in 1982 reveal something significant about post-Holocaust kitsch. Neither Steiner's novel nor Syberberg's film, for all their problematic issues, would be easily categorized as kitsch today: perhaps at root what Friedländer is responding to is not the content of the artworks per se but the sense that they are 'overstepping' a barrier, breaking a taboo set by their context. Because aesthetic boundaries (of taste, of what can be shown) change with time, what is at issue in post-Holocaust kitsch is less the content for itself and more the idea that the artwork gives the impression of breaking some kind of boundary, which in turn reflects on the context which sets that boundary. But this shifting boundary also marks the link between the world of the Holocaust and the present.

Friedländer argues that kitsch is not simply the 'pinnacle of good taste in the absence of taste' (25) but is also the 'anti-modern face of modernity' (30). Post-Holocaust kitsch, he suggests, is made up of two contradictory forces:

> [on] the side of the affirmation of order, the kitsch vision reinforces the aesthetic criteria of a submissive mass, serene in its quest for harmony, always partial to sentimentality.... But facing the kitsch aesthetic is the unfathomable world of myths; facing the visions of harmony, the lights of the apocalypse; facing the young girl's cape with flowers and the snow-capped peaks of the Bavarian alps, the call to the dead of the *Feldherrnhalle*, the ecstasy of the Gotterdammerung, the vision of the end of the world. (130–1)

---

[8] Saul Friedländer, *Reflections on Nazism*, p. 12. Further page references to this volume are given in parentheses in the text. See also: Joanne Devine, 'On Kitsch: A Symposium', *Salmagundi: A Quarterly of the Humanities & Social Sciences* 187 (2015), 347–402, pp. 404–31, 634–7.

It is precisely the union of these two, the sentimental or domestic with the destructive or chaotic, that makes Nazi kitsch. For Friedländer, drawing on Freud, this is a fundamental problem in civilization itself: that this, the perception of society as both 'an accomplishment and an unbearable yoke' in which 'submission' to the social 'nourishes fury' and 'fury clears its conscience in the submission' (135). He argues that while other Western societies keep these two currents separate, Nazism was the 'expression of these opposing needs' (135). One does not have to accept the conclusion of the fuller, Freudian argument that Friedländer makes in order to use and develop his account of kitsch.

Saltzman, Kertész, and Friedländer, then, together identify some complex characteristics of Holocaust kitsch. Holocaust kitsch exists as sentimental and as appalling, but both aspects eschew reflection, and offer instead instant mawkish emotional gratification. Rather than being the sort of art that can help us rethink or re-envision the events, kitsch is a transformation of the past into something meant to titillate or offer a saccharine ease. Despite having some indexical link to the Holocaust, these artworks prevent or diminish our fuller engagement with that world.

PEEPING AT MONSTERS IN A GLASS CASE

The sculpture *Hell* (1999–2000) by Jake and Dinos Chapman was located in the last gallery, as the closing act, of the *Apocalypse: Beauty and Horror in Contemporary Art* exhibition at the Royal Academy in London in 2000. The sculpture comprised nine cases, eight rectangular (182.9cm × 121.9cm × 121.9cm) and one square (121.9cm × 121.9cm × 121.9cm): the square case was at the centre, and the others radiated from it in the shape of a reverse swastika. The cases contained over 5,000 1:32 scale model toy soldiers, buildings, and vehicles in nine different landscapes made of glass fibre, plastic, and mixed media. The artwork was subsequently destroyed by fire on 26 May 2004 while in storage. It was rebuilt as *Fucking Hell* and shown at London's White Cube Gallery in 2008.[9] The artists claim that 'you can take nothing from it': however, I will suggest that *Hell* and its remake *Fucking Hell* reveal a great deal about our engagement with the memory of the Holocaust.[10]

Many images of the sculpture and the scenes it depicts (a massive pit of bodies, a church with a huge ape preaching, a Greek temple hung with

---

[9] https://www.theguardian.com/artanddesign/2008/may/30/art.
[10] 'Sheer Hell', *TimeOut* (Apocalypse Supplement), 2000, 12–14, p. 13.

swastikas) exist online, and these images make the comparison with Bosch and to church murals depicting hell very clear. However, a better point of comparison is a military monument, the Column of Trajan, because the work is a *narrative* sculpture. That is, it shows a process which can be analysed as a narrative. The altered toy soldiers and others enact a journey of suffering as they travel from the central case along the cases that make up the arms of the swastika. To complement and contextualize the easily available internet images, I will briefly describe that journey.

The central case houses a volcano which belches a mushroom cloud. Emerging from the crater, an avernal mouth of hell, and fleeing down the steep sides of the volcano are four columns of SS troops: I will describe these as the north, south, east, and west columns. They are in disarray. Some are naked, some are in tattered uniforms; some, as in a horror film, are mutilated beyond death but still moving. Some are helping each other and some are fighting amongst themselves. At the base of the volcano they find themselves in a grim landscape littered with corpses and hundreds of mounted heads (a recurring motif), crucifixions, and Goya-like bodies on poles. The columns stream to the edge of the case and the story of each is told in the different arms of the swastika cases. This is not, as Bosch, say, a universal hell for all humanity but a particular modern hell for the crimes of the Third Reich.

The northern column flees from the volcano into the next case in which there is a huge polluted lake: the water kills the soldiers or makes their heads explode. Fully dressed SS men with science fiction purple skulls throw things and jeer from the bridge crossing the middle of the case. Monsters in anti-pollution suits collect the heads and bodies of the dead from the lake and take them to a factory. The factory seems to make two things: purple skulls and saluting Hitlers. Carnivorous plants grow skulls, and heads lie fermenting in barrels. Finally these are taken to a collection yard where SS men go to have their heads replaced with purple skulls and become laughing monsters. Meanwhile, the column, now mutants and monsters, goes on to the next case. In tanks and assorted military vehicles, a demonic column emerges from the sea: one bears the image of the reversed swastika in spray paint (this image recurs elsewhere, too). There is a desert island inhabited by three people. Two are naked but their genitals are covered with fig leaves: perhaps they are Adam and Eve and the island an atrocious Eden. The man eats a plate of skulls and has a soft drink: the woman is having sex with a crippled figure in a caterpillar wheelchair (possibly Stephen Hawking, a previous Chapmans' subject). Meanwhile, a ramshackle little wooden chapel has a service of the dead, reanimated and maimed, led by a gorilla in the pulpit.

After leaving the central volcano case, the southern column finds itself moving amongst the remains of trucks, half-tracks, and tanks. Herded and tormented by helmeted skeletal storm troopers and by 'Dinos Mutants' (naked male and female human bodies often welded together at the chest or stomach, recognizable from the brothers' earlier work), they rush headlong through a landscape in which books are burnt in a pyre, hundreds of heads top stakes, and corpses hang from trees. A few of them are being dropped into a creek. Most run, with heads cracked open, past rotting and sometimes mutated military machinery. As they advance to the next case along the arm, they find themselves at a huge death pit where two squads of mutants kill them and fling them in, or empty trucks of these living dead. However, here, there is no real death: the toy soldiers lie in huge piles, kicking and screaming, until they rot and emerge as skeletons. (A pair, buried deep, touch each other's hands: hope in hell, a mistake, or mere chance?) A monster eats the heads of those in the pit. Next to the pit is a puppet theatre, where mutants make four soldiers dance and a small crowd of maimed and bleeding, but still animated SS men watch, smiling and applauding.

From the central volcano, the eastern column finds itself on gangways over mountainous land. Harried and directed by mutants they flee along the creaky paths: those that fall lie rotting or are eaten by sheep. Again, there are crucifixions, bodies hanging from telegraph poles, and heads on sticks. Some of the gangways lead to mass gallows, where mutants hang them. Some have escaped from the gangway and down into the valley, but they discover the glass of the case and are thrown against it: hell has its limits (for them) and prevents their exit. They are suddenly in some twisted Hans Christian Anderson story, living toys, trapped behind glass. The main body of the column makes its way down a track into the next case. And this one is perhaps the most ghastly: it is a death camp, made with great attention to detail. Over the gateway is the slogan 'Kunst Macht Frei' ('art makes you free'). The camp has the full roster of horrors: watchtowers, a courtyard with an inspection, a gallows, a murderous hospital, offices, people in cages, a *kanada* where looted possessions stack up (but from where? The dead SS from the volcano have nothing), a crematorium with a pile of corpses and a *Sonderkommando*, a shower room, and a gas chamber. In the corner another figure flings him self against the glass case: but again there is no escape from the artwork. 'Peeping into these nooks and crannies is like peeping through a key hole' writes a reviewer, and there is something voyeuristic about looking at all this fetishistic detail: the viewer's participation is made explicit in the act of looking down through the cutaway sections of the buildings.[11]

---

[11] Ibid., p. 14.

Finally, the west column is directed by mutants and horse-mounted skeletal troopers with pikes down to the shore past a pyre of bodies, stakes, Goya-like medieval torture machines, and another book-burning. The water is full of bodies and red with blood: a huge mutant—seven or eight bodies merged together—stands on a jetty close to a large contraption for sawing up bodies. But the column goes on to the next case. Here there is a forest of heads on stakes and many maimed or killed: trees grow through their bodies. Corpses and living skeletons line the foothills which rise to a ruined Greek temple decorated with tattered Nazi regalia, a reminder of Germans' obsession with Ancient Greece. Inside is a huge orgy of destruction: a man disputes with heads on poles while performing a sexual act, a woman kisses a corpse, while to the side a skeleton holds its head in fleshless despair. Here bodies are merged, perhaps to form the mutants in a Dionysian frenzy. Mutants and skeletons roam the hills attacking any who have escaped. Dante's journey through the inferno leads eventually to redemption; the narrative of Trajan's column is one of victory. In contrast, *Hell* offers a narrative with no point: the suffering is 'useless'.

The clue to unravelling this work, and why, as a starting point of analysis, Friedländer's understanding of kitsch is so useful, lies in the deformed but recognizable toy soldiers that make up the narrative. The toy soldier is, in Freudian terms, an ideal fetish object: we look at it and see that it is both horrific and excessive, and that at the same time it is only a toy. This means that the horror of *Hell* is not really horror but only a 'game' of horror, like a horror film with its predetermined steps and clichés. ('September 11th is the new Friday the thirteenth' (*sic*) writes Jake Chapman in his Deleuze-influenced artwork/book, *Meatphysics*).[12] The evil here has become 'free floating' from the actual events of 1933–45.[13]

Significantly, the very use of toys reveals a core and rarely discussed enactment of British collective memory of the Second World War. There was a supplement to the official and public memories, and the other technologies of memory (the 'Second World War combat film was a staple of the principal Allied national cinemas . . . until the late 70s' and now several bestselling computer games are set in the Second World War).[14] A crucial vector of memory lay in the endless masculine childhood games

---

[12] Chapman, *Meatphysics* (London: Creation Books, 2003), n.p.

[13] On the Holocaust as a 'free-floating symbol', and reflections on this, see Jeffrey Alexander and others, *Remembering the Holocaust* (Oxford: Oxford University Press, 2009), pp. 123–34.

[14] Barry Langford, *Film Genre: Hollywood and Beyond* (Edinburgh: Edinburgh University Press, 2005), p. 117. On British collective Holocaust memory, see Andy Pearce, *Holocaust Consciousness in Contemporary Britain* (London: Routledge, 2014); Mark Rawlinson,

of 'English and Germans' and the toys that service these games (toy guns, and of course the toy soldiers that the Chapman brothers used). Paul Gilroy, for example, writes that he

> spent much of my childhood re-enacting the glories of the Second World War. The leafy fringes of north London provided the imaginary battle-grounds across which I marched my troops and flew my imaginary Battle of Britain aircraft. We preferred these games to alterative pastimes like cowboys and Indians because we savoured the fact that we always had right on our side. Our faceless, unremittingly evil enemies were Hitler's Nazis and, inspired by what we read in comics like *Eagle* and *Swift*, as well as the stronger fare to be found in places like the barbershop, we harried and slaughtered them wherever they could be located.[15]

The Nazis were simply evil, childlike enemies to be machine-gunned down. (That this was a very widespread experience is shown by Gilroy's note that while this 'may seem to be an eccentric pursuit for a black boy...it was entirely unproblematic'.) The Chapman brothers' *Hell* is akin to this, a child's game taken to its ultimate conclusion. However, it makes the baddies the victims of a horrific cartoon and so strips them of the real complexities of evil. This is part of what the sculpture reveals about contemporary British memory.

This focus on the perpetrators is also in line with other aspects of British collective memory. Tony Kushner and many others have demonstrated that the British reaction to pre- and post-war migrants, survivors, and displaced persons shows them in a less favourable light.[16] Better, instead, as Gilroy suggests, to recall having right unquestioningly on one's side and focus on harrying and slaughtering the enemy. Again, this is childlike, passing over complex shadings of guilt and innocence. *Hell* focuses on the visible and well-recognized tropes of Holocaust memory (camps, chambers, experiments) that are recycled from films, comics, and popular culture: this focus too reflects a British collective public memory, traditionally unaware of the killing actions and ghettos. This focus on the perpetrators in the sculpture repeats the untrue idea that only the 'hard core' of Nazi SS men were implicated in the Holocaust and this diverts attention from the less reassuring thesis that the perpetrators of the Holocaust were ordinary men and women or that, as I discussed in Chapter 1, complicity and secrecy pervaded the whole Reich. Conversely,

---

'This Other War: British Culture and the Holocaust', *Cambridge Quarterly* 25:1 (1996), 1–25.

[15] Gilroy, *Between Camps*, p. 2.

[16] See Tony Kushner, *The Holocaust and the Liberal Imagination* (Oxford: Blackwell, 1994).

it also childishly implies that the Allies—lacking fanatical and monstrous SS divisions—would never stoop to torture or to carry out war crimes. This focus on the evil of the SS, and the implication of a special punishment for them in *Hell*, serves then to create precisely the sort of 'impermeable barrier' that Kertész discusses between 'them' and 'us' and so to isolate the audience from the processes of the Holocaust in particular and genocide more generally.

Finally, as many reviewers suggested, the way that this sculpture makes the viewer 'peep about', bend over, and peer at details makes the audience identify with the bystanders—looking around in fascination at the horrific events. Again, this reproduces a British bystander memory of the Holocaust itself: the British are not directly involved with the genocide and only witness it from a distance of time and space.

The very nature of the punishment, too, reveals something important about post-Holocaust kitsch. As is well known, many people had reservations about the Nuremburg legal processes. Hannah Arendt, in her letters to Karl Jaspers, doubted that any law was adequate:

> [the] definition of Nazi policy as a crime ('criminal guilt') strikes me as questionable. The Nazi crimes, it seems to me, explode the limits of law; and that is precisely what constitutes their monstrousness. For these crimes, no punishment is severe enough. It may well be essential to hang Goring, but it is totally inadequate... this guilt, in contrast to all criminal guilt, oversteps and shatters any and all legal systems. That is the reason why the Nazis in Nuremburg are so smug. They know that, of course... We are simply not equipped to deal, on a human level, political level, with a guilt that is beyond crime and an innocence that is beyond goodness and virtue.[17]

The Chapman sculpture seems to take this sort of idea at its word: the figures' satanic punishment is beyond earthly legal norms. But actually *Hell* is still a child's idea of punishment. The satanic rules through which the SS are punished are simply beefed-up versions of human rules, the 'beyond human' drawn down to the human. The sculpture implies that as it does not suffice to hang Göring once, one could hang him a thousand times, a million. But it is surely, as Arendt argues, the impossibility of a punishment for a crime that 'explodes the limits of law' that is the issue. To extend human finitude to the undying suffering of the SS men is a child's answer to what suffering involves, based on a simplistic accountant-style answer to the problem of guilt: measuring up suffering and doling out the 'right amount'. Thus, in *Hell*, which seems to indulge all kinds of excess, we find quite the opposite: the seeming excess (heads on stakes and

---

[17] Arendt and Jaspers, *Correspondence*, p. 54.

so on) turn out to be only a sort of rather crude, puerile equation. Far from making a sculpture that draws on Bataille, the Chapman brothers have made one that would better suit a playground. This again serves to encapsulate and delimit our thoughts about the Holocaust, rather than to open them up. The 'conclusive' punishment enacted in *Hell* implies, then, not only a finished punishment, but in the same gesture a finished chapter, an end, a disassociation between the past events and the present. The war and the Holocaust are over, and however horrific, the books are closed and they are in a glass case, far from us. Following Kertész and Friedländer, in bringing together the sentimental and the 'unfathomable world of myths', here, in graphic form as satanic myths, post-Holocaust kitsch separates 'our' world from the world of the Holocaust and works to prevent reflection and engagement.

In conclusion, then, this sculpture with its childish images and form is saturated with a dated version of British collective Holocaust memory, which it rearticulates rather than critiques in the form of post-Holocaust kitsch. Threats to British public memory are covered up (the literally 'beastly Hun' which implies 'our heroic boys'; the unremitting evil which then implies a British or Allied unquestioned good); barriers between the monstrous SS and Holocaust perpetrators and the modern world are enforced; Holocaust clichés gained from popular culture are used as quick reference points; and the seeming excess of the events in fact turns out to be a simplistic child's view of punishment.

This is even more apparent if this sculpture is contrasted with other similar artworks. Using toys to engage with the Holocaust is not new: indeed, this gesture itself has attracted a critical bibliography.[18] David Levinthal's series *Mein Kampf* (1993–4) and *Hitler Moves East* (1975–7) use photographs of toy soldiers and are clearly a source for the Chapman brothers; Ram Katzir created 'Your Colouring Book' (1996) with images of the Holocaust to colour in. However, perhaps most strikingly different are the Lego concentration camp box sets by Zbigniew Libera which include inmates, a barracks, SS officers, a hanging, medical experiments, a *kanada* block and a crematorium. These boxes do not fetishize the events: they shock rather than fascinate. Because of the limitations of Lego, the horrors cannot be represented very exactly or in the manner of a hyperbolic 'horror film', as in the Chapman brothers' work: rather they are hinted at. However, the ubiquitous existence of Lego the world over, highlighted on the box with the company's logo, connects the normality

[18] See Norman L. Kleeblatt (ed.), *Mirroring Evil: Nazi Imagery/Recent Art* (New York: The Jewish Museum and New Brunswick: Rutgers University Press, 2001), esp. Ernst van Alphen's 'Playing the Holocaust', pp. 65–83.

of present-day existence with the camps. The word 'system' in the phrase 'Lego system' is suddenly given a very ominous ring.[19] This uncanny exposure of the hidden complicities of modern life with the Holocaust contrasts with the 'out of this world' horror of *Hell*.

In the same Apocalypse exhibition as *Hell* was a much more restrained installation by Darren Almond, called *Bus Stop (2 Bus Shelters)*. It consisted, as the name suggests, of two bus shelters from Oświęcim and is the cover image for this book. The shelters were the focus of a previous work by Almond, *Oświęcim, March 1997* (two 8mm parallel films) which also features people 'who have perhaps visited the camp and are about to make the return journey' and those who are waiting 'for a bus to take them further'.[20] Like Kertész's suggestion of the 'broken voice' of Holocaust art, this installation approaches the Holocaust indirectly, avoids any attempt at a representation of the past, and does not offer any instant moment of easily assimilated gratification (what could be less titillating or glamorous than a bus stop?). Instead, the installation, at first opaque in its potential meaning, stimulates reflection. The bus shelters are tied into a mundane contemporary political in the present-day world in Oświęcim (mass transport, timetables, commuting, civic responsibility) but, as art, they begin to evoke ideas of terminus, of system and transport which, given their geographical specificity, draw associations to Nazi Auschwitz. More, this very banal normality reminds us that that for its enormity and atrocity the Holocaust was not committed by mutants or monsters using satanic magic but by people. In this, the shelters make an allusive and powerful connection between 'then' and 'now': an awareness of the past which roots it in the present and so both admits the movement of time and our ties to the past. In doing this, rather than offering an obvious dayglow representation of the past, which is simply a shallow version of the present, this artwork, because its meaning is opaque, also points to the risk of a lack of engagement with history: a bus shelter might simply be a bus shelter, and one can simply walk past the most impressive monuments. As Almond says: 'I'm outside waiting at a bus stop. I can choose to go in and get involved with the history and look at the relics and try to come to terms with that moment in history, or I can get on that bus and carry on.'[21] But this chance to decide, consciously or not, to engage with the past or not, is meaningful. A refusal to engage with the past is, of course, precisely one

---

[19] Stephen C. Feinstein, 'Zbigniew Libera's Lego Concentration Camp: Iconoclasm in Conceptual Art About the Shoah', *Other Voices*, 2:1 (2000), http://www.othervoices.org/2.1/feinstein/auschwitz.php.

[20] Cited in Norman Rosenthal, *Apocalypse: Beauty and Horror in Contemporary Art: Catalogue* (London: Royal Academy of Arts, 2000), p. 184.

[21] Ibid.

form of engagement with the past: one which problematically declines thought because 'thinking of past matters means moving in the dimension of depth' as Arendt puts it.[22] Understated, unsensational, this installation links the past and the present in an unclichéd way. In the exhibition, the rusty and decrepit bus shelters stood as a counterpoint to the frenetic pretense of engagement with the past offered by the Chapman brothers. Despite its seeming horrors, the Chapmans' sculpture appears kitsch and parochial: rather than throwing 'into question' assumed ideas about 'the artist as a witness to history', it does not get on the bus to go any further than a stock of clichéd images in which complexities disappear.[23]

HOW THE HOLOCAUST BECAME A FABLE

Despite its shock value, the Chapman brothers' sculpture achieved only a limited impact in the public sphere. In contrast, my second example of contemporary post-Holocaust kitsch, John Boyne's 2007 *The Boy in the Striped Pyjamas*, is not only a very successful bestselling book—a multiple prize winner, translated into many languages and now very widely taught and read in schools in the UK—but is also perhaps currently the best known 'young adult' book about the Holocaust.[24] In 2008, it was turned into a successful film. For the reasons I describe below, the book and its popularity profoundly worry professional Holocaust educators in the UK: the impact of a kitsch work on issues of memory and understanding of guilt and innocence is rightly a matter of pedagogical concern.[25] Of course, introducing the Holocaust to children is a complex and challenging matter: however, this novel turns the Holocaust into a childish fable in which Auschwitz becomes as unreal as Harry Potter's Hogwarts School. It strips the genocide out from history and so prevents any sense of a relation between the world of the Final Solution and the contemporary world.

The protagonist of *The Boy in the Striped Pyjamas* is Bruno, the nine-year-old son of a leading SS officer. One evening 'The Fury' (the Führer) comes to dinner and orders his father to leave Berlin in order to take

---

[22] Arendt, *Responsibility and Judgement*, p. 95.
[23] Mark Holborn, 'Introduction', in A. Lutgens (ed.), *Jake and Dinos Chapman: Hell* (London: Jonathan Cape with the Saatchi Gallery, 2003), 11–14.
[24] John Boyne, *The Boy in the Striped Pyjamas* (London: Random House, 2006). Further page references to this volume are given in parentheses in the text.
[25] A public example: in 2012, the Holocaust Education Trust, a UK-based charity, released a DVD, 'Thinking Film, Thinking History'. Using clips from films, it aimed to encourage 'pupils to consider what they can and can't learn from films that may be historically inaccurate or fictional, such as *The Boy in the Striped Pyjamas*, based on the novel by John Boyne'. The explicit citation of this film reflects the level of concern.

command of a place called 'Out-With' (these homophones, which do not work in German, are heavily laden with significance). Bruno is sad to leave his friends, and does his best to live in his new home, a camp, where he notices all sorts of odd goings-on. Thin people in pyjamas live behind a wire fence. While exploring one day, he chances to chat through the fence to a small boy his own age called Shmuel. They become friends and, on one occasion, Shmuel is even allowed into the commandant's house. Finally, however, Bruno crawls under the fence to help Shmuel look for his father. Both boys are rounded up and taken away to be murdered and sentimentality is poured on: 'You're my best friend, Shmuel . . . My best friend for life' (213) says Bruno as they are both about to be gassed, in what is less 'a consequence of prejudice and more a bizarre health and safety incident'.[26]

The story is inaccurate and implausible: but does this matter? The issue of historical inaccuracies and implausibility in Holocaust literature is complex. Binet's *HHhH* is about the tension between writing a historical novel and its impossibility ('I refuse to write a sentence like: "Automatically they checked the release boxes and static lines of their parachute harnesses." Even if, without a doubt, they did exactly that' (section 146)). Binet wonders 'how Jonathan Littell . . . knows that Blobel had an Opel? If Blobel really drove an Opel, then I bow before his superior research. But if it's a bluff, it weakens the whole novel' (section 189). Apart from a concern for detail, the real issue is not inaccuracies per se, but what they mean for the work as a whole, and so in turn what they mean for thinking about the Holocaust and the post-Holocaust. In a dense, detailed novel like *The Kindly Ones*, the make of car a minor character drives might be important. But in the case of a 'fable' like *The Boy in the Striped Pyjamas*, it might not matter that the fences of camps were guarded and often electrified, or that, because Bruno's paternal grandmother is Irish, his father would not be able to join the SS. Indeed, some simple implausibilities just stem from bad writing: Shmuel speaks German fluently—his mother is a language teacher—and yet he asks Bruno where Berlin is (111). It may not matter that the real 'Auschwitz' ('Out-with') was, in fact, a complex of camps and the commandant's house and the gas chambers were not really where the author imagines them. However, these inaccuracies reveal that the novel has no concern with the history of the Holocaust. Indeed, there are almost no historical facts or references in the novel at all: Boyne's Shmuel is from 'Cracow' and experienced the liquidation ('Then one day soldiers came in huge trucks . . . And everyone

---

[26] David Cesarani, *The Literary Review*, http://holocaustcentre.com/cms_content/upload/PDFs/Cesarani%20Review%20Striped%20Pyjamas.pdf.

was told to leave the houses. Lots of people didn't want to and they hid where they could find a place' (129)). Interestingly, in *Schindler's List*, the Jews are taken from the Kraków ghetto (the ghetto was finally 'liquidated' on 13–14 March 1943) to the labour camp at Płaszów, and some, thence to Auschwitz. In *Schindler's List*, Schindler claims he needs the children's tiny fingers to reach inside shells; in *The Boy in the Striped Pyjamas*, an SS officer claims to need Shmuel's 'tiny fingers' (167) to polish glasses (as if normal fingers would not do). The same SS lieutenant beats up a Jewish waiter at a party: a similar scene occurs in *Schindler's List*. The inaccuracies also show that the novel is not really being told from the child's point of view (the 'What Maisie Knew' genre) because an electrified fence is electrified whether the protagonist knows it or not. But what they reveal most significantly is that the world of the Holocaust is being reduced to a fable, to kitsch.[27]

In his 'Author's Note', John Boyne writes that he was trying to tell the 'emotional truth' of the events. This is easy, sentimental rhetoric. What is the 'emotional truth' of the Holocaust? While some underaged boys got away with pretending to be sixteen (Elie Wiesel was fifteen), younger Jewish children from Poland—like Shmuel—were gassed on arrival at Auschwitz-Birkenau (the 'twenty minutes' Kertész talks about). To pretend this is not so is to misunderstand and so misrepresent the nature of the genocidal operation both in terms of its aim and in terms of its utterly ruthless execution: it is precisely not telling the emotional truth about the victims.

Nor does *The Boy in the Striped Pyjamas* tell the emotional truth about the perpetrators. Bruno, a nine-year-old boy, the son of a leading SS officer, would certainly be looking forward to joining the *Deutsches Jungvolk* (the younger subdivision of the Hitler Youth) at ten. At school he would be bombarded with anti-Semitic propaganda; on the street he would see the very many signs banning Jews from most places and activities; at home he would be playing board games in which the aim was to round up Jews (one of these games is on display at the Wiener Library in London). Ruth Kluger writes of how

> on the street...the Nazi boys were singing the song about Jewish blood spurting from their knives.... And they were carrying sharp little daggers... You didn't have to be very smart to get their meaning; on the contrary, it required some mental agility to ignore it.[28]

[27] This is not at all to suggest that only realism is a suitable form for Holocaust fiction: see, for example, the insightful study by Jenni Adams, *Magic Realism in Holocaust Literature: Troping the Traumatic Real* (Basingstoke: Palgrave Macmillan, 2011).

[28] Ruth Kluger, *Landscapes of Memory: A Holocaust Girlhood Remembered* (London: Bloomsbury, 2003), p. 6.

Bruno would not ask his sister 'Are we Jews?' (182). Setting out to tell the emotional truth of the events, *The Boy in the Striped Pyjamas* fails because it does not show how a nation-state was turned into a genocidal state, precisely how boys Bruno's age—nearly old enough to read Gustav Frenssen's *Peter Moor's Fahrt nach Sudwest*—would have been corrupted. Kluger describes a colleague who showed her the knife he used to own as a member of the Hitler Youth: 'I would have preferred a real weapon', he reminisces, then adds, 'Our knives carried the legend "Blood and Honor".'[29]

However, the book goes further. The 'Author's Note' in the US edition describes what Henry James would call the 'donnée', the image

> of two boys sitting on either side of a fence . . . taken away from their homes and friends and brought, separately, to a terrible place. Neither of them knew what they were doing there, but I did, and it was the story of these two boys, who I named Bruno and Shmuel, that I wanted to tell.

This, too, betrays the emotional truth of the Holocaust by creating a totally false equivalence between the victims and the perpetrators, akin to Ronald Reagan's suggestion at the Bitburg war cemetery.[30] In the last pages of the book, the writing encourages sympathy even for Bruno's father, the commandant of Auschwitz, no less, as he realizes what has happened to his son: 'he ended up sitting on the ground in almost exactly the same position as Bruno had' (215–16) and when he is later arrested (perhaps by the Red Army, but it is, of course, unclear), 'he went without complaint and he was happy to do so because he really didn't mind what they did to him any more' (216). The film foregrounds this moment of sympathy, closing on the face of the commandant, played by David Thewlis, crying out in realization that his son has been murdered by his own genocidal machinery.

Art can shape meaning by creating a framework within which events are to be understood. This activity is neither telling the truth nor lying but rather presenting a world. In the case of Holocaust education, this framing is clearly very important. The risk is that if *The Boy in the Striped Pyjamas* is too often used in schools, it will begin to solidify a very dubious

---

[29] Ibid.

[30] Reagan said: 'These [SS troops] were the villains, as we know, that conducted the persecutions and all. But there are 2,000 graves there, and most of those, the average age is about 18. I think that there's nothing wrong with visiting that cemetery where those young men are victims of Nazism also, even though they were fighting in the German uniform, drafted into service to carry out the hateful wishes of the Nazis. They were victims, just as surely as the victims in the concentration camps.' (http://en-tanz.annysings.com/ar tikeldetails/Bitburg.html.)

understanding of the Holocaust.[31] The success of the novel also demonstrates a desire to avoid complexity and have, instead, a simplistic picture of 'good' and 'evil', more suited to a playground than a classroom. It also suggests a 'culture of victimhood', the sense we are all—even the commandant of Auschwitz—victims of something. This reassures us of our lack of complicity in other horrors and reaffirms a sense of our own innocence.

CONCLUSION

From the reflections of Kertész, Friedländer, and Saltzman, it is clear that Holocaust kitsch prevents a consideration of the relationship between our ('deformed' for Kertész) world and the world of the Holocaust, including contemplation on the possibilities for future genocide (the fable world of Boyne is not our world, nor could the monsters of *Hell* have anything to do with us). It combines both the sentimental and the mythical or excessive, and in so doing domesticates the excess (the model soldiers are turned into monsters, but then become just models of monsters; the boys murdered at Auschwitz become just a fable); it is simplistic and easy to grasp or consume (it is a children's story; a sculpture which requires little work to understand). Ngai's work argues that categories can change and develop: the two works this chapter has examined have expanded or shifted the category of post-Holocaust kitsch.

First, it is clear that kitsch is less about the content per se, but rather the relationship between that content and socially constituted aesthetic boundaries. Holocaust kitsch gives the impression of breaking taboos (shocking models of monsters; a missing child) but in fact does not really threaten them. Second, post-Holocaust kitsch is pious. Matthew Boswell argues that there has been a generational shift from what he names, following Gillian Rose, 'Holocaust piety', the mystification of the Holocaust as ineffable. In its place is Holocaust impiety, the 'flagrant articulation of the friction that is produced by the coming together of fact and fiction, experience and the imagination, history and culture': he suggests that 'challenging aesthetic gestures' are used to 'to engineer a response from those who feel increasingly disengaged from the events... as

---

[31] See also Ruth Gilbert, 'Grasping the Unimaginable: Recent Holocaust Novels for Children by Morris Gleitzman and John Boyne', *Children's Literature in Education* 41:4 (2010), 355–66; Michael Gray, '*The Boy in the Striped Pyjamas*: A Blessing or Curse for Holocaust Education?', *Holocaust Studies* 20:3 (2015), 109–36.

chronological, genealogical and emotional ties loosen'.[32] The kitsch works I have looked at are pious: *Hell*, for all its apparent shock, does not offer any history, but just devilish punishment. Boyne ends his 'Author's Note' in the schmaltz of easily won Holocaust piety:

> I hope that the voices of Bruno and Shmuel will continue to resonate with you as they have with me. Their lost voices must continue to be heard; their untold stories must continue to be recounted. For they represent the ones who didn't live to tell their stories themselves. (n.p.)

Of course, his novel has just told the story of Bruno and Shmuel, such as it is, and I've suggested that it is rather a stretch to suggest that they 'represent' the dead when they so clearly fail to tell what Boyne calls the 'emotional truth' of the Holocaust.

Third, despite all the movement in *Hell* and the plot in *The Boy in the Striped Pyjamas*, there is no sense of development or engagement. Indeed, *Hell*—an eternity of suffering—is based on the lack of change in endless punishment. Ngai suggests that the apparent powerlessness of the cute can inspire a complex (and often aggressive) reaction in us.[33] The kitsch starts no process in this way. Rather, it gives back to us the simple pieties with which we began and, unlike many of the novels this book has examined, invites us into easy acts of identification (with the onlooker in the case of *Hell*, with Bruno, the protagonist of the novel). Adorno writes that 'one of its [kitsch's] most tenacious characteristics is the prevarication of feelings, fictional feelings in which no one is actually participating, and thus the neutralisation of the feelings. Kitsch parodies catharsis.'[34]

Fourth, these kitsch texts offer a simple, apolitical, oddly ahistorical world. There are no complexities or difficulties: people are 'good' or 'bad'. These texts remove the audience from the possibility of judgement. This is not an intrinsic quality of children's books. By contrast, for example, the classic children's book by Anne Holm, *I am David* (1963 Danish, 1965 English), about post-war displaced persons, as well as more recent young adult Holocaust fiction like Morris Gleitzman's *Once* (2005) and Michael Morpurgo's *The Mozart Question* (2006) manage to offer more complex views of characters and events.[35] The apolitical ahistorical world is a

---

[32] Matthew Boswell, *Holocaust Impiety in Literature, Popular Music and Film* (Basingstoke: Palgrave Macmillan, 2012), p. 33.

[33] Ngai, *Our Aesthetic Categories*, pp. 59ff.

[34] Theodore Adorno, *Aesthetic Theory* (London: The Athlone Press, 1997), p. 239.

[35] Anne Holm, *I am David*, trans. L. W. Kingsland (London: Egremont, 2000); Morris Gleitzman, *Once* (Melbourne: Puffin, 2005); Michael Morpurgo, *The Mozart Question* (London: Walker Books, 2006).

retreat from the public sphere, from dialogue and argument, to a sort of infantilism.

The final characteristic then, is that these kitsch texts are childish. Using model soldiers and the legal theory of the playground, both *Hell* and *The Boy in the Striped Pyjamas* are not just taken from a child's point of view but exist in a child's universe: the fences are not electrified; there is 'extra' punishment if you have been 'extra' bad. These characteristics seem to mark off new developments of post-Holocaust kitsch. Adorno, again, warns that kitsch is not the 'refuse' of art but rather that no boundaries can be drawn between art and kitsch. Instead kitsch is a 'poison admixed to all art' and so varies over time and place.[36] The aim of this chapter is not to police post-Holocaust kitsch—although, if culture is in part contestation, kitsch can be described as kitsch—but rather, to discover what this kitsch means and what it reveals about contemporary cultural views on the Holocaust.

---

[36] Theodor Adorno, 'Avant-Garde and Kitsch Revisited', in Kleeblatt (ed.), *Mirroring Evil*, 53–64, p. 55.

7

Conclusion

What good is literature? 'Perhaps', wrote Sebald, 'only to help us to remember, and teach us to understand that some strange connections cannot be explained by causal logic.'[1] This book has followed Kertész's suggestion that the 'broken voice' of the Holocaust will remain through culture: it has also explored the role of literature in memory and analysed some of the strange links between the past and the present which shape the meaning of both. Some themes have recurred.

One of these, throughout, is the complex issue of complicity. In his memoir of playing Primo Levi, Anthony Sher describes his visit with friends to Auschwitz. Afterwards,

> Greg can't stop crying. He says: 'I felt so angry in that place. I hate what we did to ourselves there.'
>
> I say, 'who's we?'
>
> He and Richard answer in unison: 'We—us—human beings.'[2]

Through the reflexive phrase 'what we did to ourselves', this voices a common feeling not only of a passionate sympathy for the victims of the Holocaust but also of an uncomfortable complicity with the perpetrators. This feeling may not be explicable through causal logic but it exists and persists. Perhaps it arises from an awareness of our shared humanity, an awareness that the perpetrators 'are men like ourselves', as Arendt points out.[3] Certainly, this sentiment, if taken too far, implies a false equivalence between victims and murderers: in his essay, 'The Memory of the Offence', Levi writes that he does not wish to

> abet confusions, small-change Freudianism, morbidities and indulgences. The oppressor remains what he is, and so does the victim. They are not

---

[1] W. G. Sebald, *Campo Santo*, ed. Sven Meyer, trans. Anthea Bell (London: Penguin Books, 2006), pp. 213–14.

[2] Antony Sher, *Primo Time* (London: Nick Hern Books, 2005), p. 87. With thanks to Poppy Corbett for this example.

[3] Arendt, *Essays in Understanding*, p. 134.

interchangeable, the former is to be punished and execrated (but if possible understood), the latter is to be pitied and helped.[4]

But Levi himself tempers this in an astonishing passage where he goes on to say that 'both, faced by the indecency of the act which has been irrevocably committed, need refuge and protection, and instinctively search for them'.[5] In their need for refuge and protection, Levi recognizes the shared humanity—but clearly not shared blame—of victims and the perpetrators after the irrevocable acts.

This feeling of unfocused complicity is akin, but not identical, to guilt. In her essay, 'Personal Responsibility under Dictatorship' (1964), Arendt gave a stern warning about this. It is, she writes,

> only in a metaphorical sense that we can say we *feel* guilty for the sins of our fathers or our people or of mankind, i.e. for deeds and misdeeds we have not done. Morally speaking, it is as wrong to feel guilty without having done something specific as it is to feel free of all guilt if one actually is guilty of something... There are no such things as collective guilt or collective innocence; these terms make sense only if applied to individuals.[6]

Here, despite her claims that she is 'speaking morally' and her allowance of a 'metaphorical sense' for the word, Arendt relies on a legalistic sense of guilt and not the experience of guilt, as her italicization of 'feel' suggests. Indeed, as a result of the Nuremberg trials the juridical categories of guilty perpetrator and innocent victim became part of the discourse through which we understand the horrors of the Second World War and genocide, and these legal terms have proved very powerful hermeneutic tools for historians and others. However, as Shoshana Felman argues, the 'law is a straightjacket to tame history'.[7] She advocates that while 'we needed law to totalize the evidence, to totalize the Holocaust and, through totalization, to start to apprehend its contours and its magnitude... we needed art to start to apprehend and to retrieve what the totalization has left out'.[8] The legalistic categories (innocent/guilty, bystander/perpetrator, and so on) do not capture the many shades and complexities of complicity, knowing, and not wishing to know: the complexities of the public secret,

[4] Levi, *The Drowned and the Saved*, p. 13.   [5] Ibid.

[6] Hannah Arendt, 'Personal Responsibility under Dictatorship', *The Listener*, 6 August 1964, 185–7, p. 185. The full version published in 2003 has some minor changes: see Arendt, *Responsibility and Judgement*, pp. 28–9.

[7] Shoshana Felman, *The Juridical Unconscious* (Cambridge, MA: Harvard University Press, 2002), p. 146.

[8] Shoshana Felman, 'Theaters of Justice: Arendt in Jerusalem, the Eichmann Trial, and the Redefinition of Legal Meaning in the Wake of the Holocaust', *Critical Inquiry* 27:2 (2001), 201–38, p. 202.

for example. Nor do they come close to the affective senses of guilt, still felt today by, for example, Sher's legally blameless friends. Instead, it is in works of culture, and centrally literature, that this affective dimension of meaning is explored.

Similarly, complicity is also close (but again, not identical) to responsibility, and because complicity must involve at least two, some form of collective responsibility. For Arendt, collective responsibility gives us 'vicarious responsibility for things we have not done', and exists because it is 'the price we pay for the fact we live our lives not by ourselves but among our fellow men'.[9] It has two conditions: that someone is held responsible, and that they are part of a group with which they cannot dissolve their membership. This is close to the view suggested by Sebald's work: the various narrators are held by responsibility, by—something like—complicity as a German, and attempts to 'work through' this are in vain. These conditions lead Arendt to a further claim. Because collective responsibility stems from being in a community, then refugees and stateless people, cast out or exiled from communities, 'cannot be held politically responsible for anything' (150). If there was, she writes, 'such a thing as collective, namely, vicarious guilt, this would be a case of collective, namely, vicarious innocence' (150). And, with her bleak, ironic humour, she points out that while we take collective responsibility to be a 'burden and even as a kind of punishment . . . the price paid for collective nonresponsibility is considerably higher' (150). Kertész was deprived of rights not only by the fascist Hungarian government and the Nazis during the Holocaust, but again by the communist Hungarian government, especially after 1956. *Kaddish for an Unborn Child* seems to reflect this negation of community, a paradoxically responsible negation of responsibility for the collective in the present and in the future.

Evil, too, is a central theme of this book. The question of evil is often posed with the question of 'why' the Holocaust happened: yet conceptions of evil from before the Holocaust seem inadequate in answering this 'why' question. This is Arendt's view, certainly, and over her career she strove to understand and outline another form of evil, one unaccounted for in the work of previous thinkers, and only hinted at by artists (by, for example, the fear and self-loathing that Shakespeare puts into the mouth of Richard III). This other form of evil is not monstrous or satanic—it has no glamour; it is dull and unthinking, characterized by cliché in language and the incomprehension of both self and other; it is a failure of memory and a lack of rootedness. It is becoming nobody, even when one is a

---

[9] Arendt, *Responsibility and Judgement*, pp. 157–8. Further page references to this volume are given in parentheses in the text.

somebody in the eyes of the world. Literature and testimony, in this matter, can often mislead us: this evil is hard to grasp precisely because it is boring and distant from what fiction so often provides, or from the penetration of a personality seemingly offered by the accounts of perpetrators. The 'routine-ization' of evil rarely makes fascinating literature—the long descriptions of the meetings about the murder of the 'Mountain Jews' in *The Kindly Ones*, for example. (Although, by the same token, fiction does seem effective at thinking about the 'after-effects' of this evil, about 'the entire weight of the past, of the pain of life and of inalterable memory'.[10]) It is important to try not to be misled by the simpler fictional representations of evil, precisely because the question of evil is so central to the current crises in the world.

These issues of complicity and evil reach into the relationship between the West and the colonial world, the global north and south. In the wake of Aimé Césaire's polemical *Discourse on Colonialism* which claimed that the Nazis had only done in Europe what the Europeans had previously done around the world, I have argued that the Holocaust serves to foreground for the West the horrors of colonial atrocities and genocide: the action of what Michael Rothberg calls multi-directional memory. Conceptually, what we have learned about genocide from the Holocaust can give us more complex and nuanced views of these colonial atrocities and vice versa. More, it is clear that colonial genocides (and, of course, colonialism in general) provided wealth and power to the perpetrators and that there is a case that those in the West, who have come afterwards, have benefited and are, despite themselves, perhaps complicit. Just as the Nazi past calls for *Vergangenheitsbewältigung*, 'working through the past', in all its complexities, so does colonial and imperial history. This complicity may emerge in exactly the unease that *Heart of Darkness* and other texts evoke. Paul Gilroy argues that this complicity can be mediated through or hidden by the 'screen memory' of the Holocaust.[11] However, at the same time, this memory carries the risk of 'screening off' or 'over-coding' colonial genocides with the Holocaust and so failing to see them with clear eyes.[12] Clear eyes are needed too in relation to the risks of kitsch which fail to engage with the complexity and difficulty of complicity and evil through their *faux* taboo-breaking, saccharine piety, simplicity, and

---

[10] Littell, *The Kindly Ones*, p. 975.

[11] Gilroy, *After Empire*, pp. 95ff. One example is the controversy surrounding Caroline Elkins' *British Gulag: The Brutal End of Empire in Kenya* (London: Jonathan Cape, 2005) and continuing attempts by Kikuyu survivors to obtain reparations from the British government.

[12] See, *inter alia*, Rebecca Jinks, *Representing Genocide: The Holocaust as Paradigm?* (London: Bloomsbury, 2016).

easy, childish identifications. In response to these unthinking accounts it is not enough simply to retell or reshape the history of the Holocaust: more 'facts' will not dent these forms of culture. Instead, it is important to think through the latent meaning of the kitsch work and contrast that with other, more serious art and thought.

Most of the works examined in this volume have something to say about the sense of time and rupture so often invoked by those who speak or write about the Holocaust. On the one hand, the Holocaust is very often taken to mark a new epoch, a radical break with the past, an event that has changed everything. Indeed, as Alon Confino points out, this is an uncanny reflection on what the Nazis themselves thought they were doing: separating the past from the future to create a new Nazi epoch (the genocidal perpetrators in *Peter Moor* thought something like this too). This break between times is sometimes more subtly implied. Benjamin's 'weak Messianic power' of the present to redeem the past is often invoked.[13] Yet this presupposes a form of break. For example, carved into a wall at the US Holocaust Memorial Museum are words from Bill Clinton's speech, made at the dedication ceremony on 22 April 1993:

> [this] museum will touch the life of everyone who enters and leave everyone forever changed—a place of deep sadness and a sanctuary of bright hope; an ally of education against ignorance, of humility against arrogance, an investment in a secure future against whatever insanity lurks ahead. If this museum can mobilize morality, then those who have perished will thereby gain a measure of immortality.[14]

The museum offers to redeem the dead—give them a measure of immortality, give their deaths a meaning—if, through the museum, they mobilize morality. This is not to criticize an act of public oratory but to illustrate this common idea which sets the present over the past. Daniel Levy and Natan Sznaider's proposal that the Holocaust becomes a foundation for international law is, too, a version of this power.[15] Derrida implicitly, if with purposeful obscurity, critiques this view in the postscript to 'Force of Law', where he imagines Benjamin's response to the Holocaust.[16] When the Holocaust is taken as a sort of transcendental or sacred framing to

---

[13] Walter Benjamin, *Illuminations*, trans. Harry Zorn (London: Pimlico, 1999), p. 246.

[14] https://www.ushmm.org/research/ask-a-research-question/frequently-asked-questions/clinton.

[15] Levy and Sznaider, 'Memory Unbound'.

[16] Jacques Derrida, 'Force of Law: The "Mystical Foundation of Authority"', trans. Mary Quaintance, in *Deconstruction and the Possibility of Justice*, ed. Drucilla Cornell, Michael Rosenfeld, and David Gray Carlson (London: Routledge, 1992), pp. 3–67. For commentary, see Eaglestone, *The Holocaust and the Postmodern*, pp. 294ff.

memory and, because of that role in framing memory, for identity, it is put out of bounds for question or investigation. Similarly, when it is turned to kitsch it is no longer open to analysis or deeper understanding because it has fallen out of time. In both cases, it means 'that time' has nothing to do with 'our time'. The risk of this division of time, between 'that' world then and 'our' world now, done either subtly or explicitly, is that the evil events of the Holocaust are separated from us, outside of 'our' time. They are incomprehensible and no part of our world.

On the other hand, there is a sense that the Holocaust is not a break from the past but rather an emergence of longstanding and continuing historical forces: Imre Kertész's metaphor for Auschwitz as a 'dark fruit ripening' over 'centuries' waiting to drop suggests it is growing again, waiting to drop once more from the tree of history. Adorno and Bauman find the Holocaust in the modernity that we still inhabit, with its scientific and pseudo-scientific currents and demands. Dan Stone writes that the Holocaust

> chills us to the bone because its resources are ones that remain familiar to us in late modernity—censuses and the categorisation of people, technology, medicalization, 'biopower'—and because we see daily how our 'rational' lives are in fact suffused with 'magical' thinking that under the right circum-stances can be put to terrible use: fear of immigrants and disease, hygiene fetishism, body-culture obsession.[17]

In this temporality, the Holocaust is still here until its profoundest causes have been eliminated. As Kertész said, in his writing 'the Holocaust could never be present in the past tense'.[18] However, this can sometimes lead to hyperbole and a lack of discernment: not all events are like the Holocaust. Part of Arendt's point about the yardstick which judges whether events serve totalitarian domination or not is that this invalidates all other political differentiations (between types of nationalist and nativist rhetoric, for example).[19] Similarly, as Godwin's law satirically suggests, as soon as the Holocaust is invoked in some online discussion or in a more serious deliberation, distinctions made within that conversation disappear and the conversation ends.

Faced with this radical separation of past and present or its uneasy continuity, there exists a third possibility: that these times might, in a powerful but hard to define way, coexist and intertwine without merging. This coexistence of times is true for many testimonies, in which different

---

[17] Stone, *Histories of the Holocaust*, p. 287.   [18] Kertész, 'Heureka!', p. 607.
[19] Arendt, *The Origins of Totalitarianism*, p. 442.

moments collide: survivors live both in the trauma of the past and in the quotidian present. This alerts us to the idea that for individuals, trauma cannot be simply healed or the time passed through, but rather that is lived as an unresolvable aporia. There is something of this, too, in Blanchot's aphorism that 'disaster ruins everything, all the while leaving everything intact'.[20] Similarly, but on a larger scale, in his historical and philosophical analysis of state violence, Berber Bevernage draws attention to two temporalities: that of history (which works 'with what has happened and now is irretrievably gone') and that of jurisdiction ('which assumes a reversible time in which the crime is, as it were, still wholly present and able to be reversed, annulled or compensated by the correct sentence and punishments').[21] For Bevernage (and Derrida, on whom he draws), these two different times find themselves entangled in complex ways and yet are lived at the same moment. Another example of these incommensurable times lived together is given by the Galicia Jewish Museum in Kraków. Here, as close to an 'imaginary museum' as any real museum could be, the only exhibits are photographs by Chris Schwartz which instantiate ideas and a form of narrative. The first section portrays 'Jewish Life in Ruins' after the Holocaust: a deserted synagogue, a devastated Jewish cemetery. But 'in powerful contrast' the second section stresses what still stands of the 'strength and splendour of Jewish culture before its destruction during the Holocaust'.[22] The two coexist. This aporetic sense of the age, the saeculum, is close, I think, to the meaning of the 'broken voice' which characterizes the post-Holocaust era. The horrors of the past both present and absent simultaneously in a trace.

Finally, although this volume has engaged with stories and how they shape meaning, Arendt warns about their power. For Arendt, the story marks an action disclosing the 'specific uniqueness' of each person. The 'whole realm of human affairs . . . consists of the web of human relationships which exists wherever men live together' and the

> disclosure of the 'who' through speech and the setting of a new beginning through action, always falls into an already existing web where their immediate consequences can be felt. Together they start a new process which

---

[20] Maurice Blanchot, *The Writing of the Disaster*, trans. Ann Smock (Nebraska: University of Nebraska Press, 1996), p. 1.

[21] Berber Bevernage, *History, Memory and State-Sponsored Violence* (London: Routledge, 2012), p. 2.

[22] Jonathan Webber and Chris Schwarz, *Rediscovering Traces of Memory: The Jewish Heritage of Polish Galicia*, Littman Library of Jewish Civilization (Bloomington: Indiana University Press, 2009), p. 45.

eventually emerges as the unique life story of the newcomer, affecting uniquely the life stories of all those with whom he comes into contact.[23]

The 'life story' discloses the 'who' each of us are.

But 'story' for Arendt turns out to be quite problematic. She suggests that our philosophical 'vocabulary' (181) means that when we want to find out 'who somebody is', we too often end up finding out 'what' they are instead: what categories that person shares with others and so on. The consequence of this slip is that their 'specific uniqueness' (181) escapes us. Further, the primary sense of a person's story is reified into a secondary sense by being 'recorded in documents and monuments . . . told and retold and worked into all kinds of material' while the actual stories themselves 'in their living reality, are of an altogether different nature than these reifications' (184). Worse, we are further misled by the fictional story in which an author 'pulls the strings and directs the play'. This leads us to think 'real' stories are made whereas in fact the 'real story in which we are engaged as long as we live has no visible or invisible maker because it is not made' but lived and spoken: 'Life stories' are less like a traditional play and more a continually devised improvisation, perhaps hardly a story at all. Further, even literary works of genius cannot reveal the 'who', as they too are made, not lived and spoken. One way Arendt tries to resolve these problems is by turning to the 'backward glance of the historian' (192) who, as a storyteller looking over the (ended) story, is able to apprehend the actions and their meaning. The stories are 'inevitable results of action' but it is 'not the actor but the storyteller who perceives and "makes" the story' (192). However, this seems not to escape the aporia she has set up— as the inverted commas around ' "makes" ' suggests—because this story would be not the real speech but, again, another monument or reification.

More, the very *form* of a story, even a spoken one, is shaped by cultural conventions—what is written, what has gone before. In this sense, 'real' stories, built from the elements of culture, come not before but after the written, reified ones which teach us those elements: the 'real' depends on the 'reified'. An example of this occurs in her famous discussion of Isak Dinesen, which is much more complex than is usually noticed. Arendt writes that storytelling 'brings about consent and reconciliation with things as they really are'.[24] That is, it establishes meaning, and so (in the widely-cited epigram in *The Human Condition*), 'All sorrows can be borne if you put them into a story or tell a story about them' (175). (This is often

---

[23] Arendt, *The Human Condition*, pp. 183–4. Further page references to this volume are given in parentheses in the text.

[24] Arendt, *Reflections on Literature and Culture*, p. 271.

taken as a declaration that by turning an event into narrative, the event is mastered and a 'trauma' is resolved. This is clearly not the case for Holocaust survivors who tell and retell their narratives: a 'genocide is not just any kind of story, with a beginning and an end between which more or less ordinary events take place'.)[25] But Arendt turns out to be very wary of this. She goes on:

> And yet, if we listen to Isak Dinesen's 'philosophy' of storytelling and think of her life in the light of it, we cannot help becoming aware of how the slightest misunderstanding, the slightest shift of emphasis in the wrong direction will inevitably ruin everything. If it is true, as her 'philosophy' suggests, that no one has a life worth thinking about whose life story cannot be told, does it not follow that life could be, even ought to be, lived as story, that what one has to do in life is to make the story come true . . . From what we now know of her early life it seems quite clear that this is what she herself had tried to do when she was a young girl, to 'realise' an 'idea' and to anticipate her life's destiny by making an old story come true.[26]

Arendt is warning that holding to a story too strongly can mislead a life: a 'reified' story is not a living story but forms, perhaps, too inflexible a rule to respond to the world. (There is a development here, too, of her description of ideology in *The Origins of Totalitarianism*, which I discussed Chapter 2. An inflexible story, or ideology, makes it impossible to experience the events of the world.)

Arendt cautions that stories can fail to 'disclose' the 'who' each of us is, and that they can be a malign influence on us because of the way they shape meaning. The most effective response to this warning lies, counter-intuitively, in the very intangibility of thinking. Thinking, for Arendt, unlike knowledge, produces nothing, no final answers; the need to think cannot be stilled by results or the answers of previous generations. Instead, it is the constant process of understanding, bringing past, present, and future together in different and shifting ways. The danger of stories is avoided in the same manner: they are to be thought about, discussed, recast, and retold. This is how we best attend to the 'broken voice' of the Holocaust.

---

[25] Diop, *Murabi, The Book of Bones*, p. 178.
[26] Arendt, *Reflections on Literature and Culture*, p. 271.

Bibliography

Achebe, Chinua, 'An Image of Africa: Racism in Conrad's *Heart of Darkness*', *Massachusetts Review* 18:4 (1977), 782–94.

Adams, Jenni, *Magic Realism in Holocaust Literature: Troping the Traumatic Real* (Basingstoke: Palgrave Macmillan, 2011).

Adams, Jenni, 'Reading Violence in Jonathan Littell's *The Kindly Ones*', in Jenni Adams and Sue Vice (eds.), *Representing Perpetrators in Holocaust Literature and Film* (London: Valentine Mitchell, 2013).

Adams, Jenni (ed.), *The Bloomsbury Companion to Holocaust Studies* (London: Bloomsbury, 2014).

Adorno, Theodor, *Negative Dialectics*, trans. E. B. Ashton (London: Routledge, 1973).

Adorno, Theodor, *Aesthetic Theory* (London: The Athlone Press, 1997).

Adorno, Theodor, 'The Meaning of Working through the Past', in *Critical Models: Interventions and Catchwords*, trans. Henry W. Pickford (New York: Colombia University Press, 1998).

Albahari, David, *Götz and Meyer*, trans. Ellen Elias-Bursać (London: Vintage, 2005).

Alexander, Jeffrey and others, *Remembering the Holocaust* (Oxford: Oxford University Press, 2009).

Aly, Götz, *Hitler's Beneficiaries: Plunder, Racial War and the Nazi Welfare State*, trans. Jefferson Chase (New York: Metropolitan Books, 2005).

Améry, Jean, *At the Mind's Limits*, trans. Sidney Rosenfeld and Stella P. Rosenfeld (London: Granta Books, 1999).

Anonymous, 'A Complete Congo Controversy Illustrating the Controversial Methods of Mr Morel' (Edinburgh: Oliver and Boyd, 1905).

Anonymous, 'Dr Guinness Self-Refuted: Inconsistency of the Congo Balido Missionaries' (Edinburgh: Oliver and Boyd, 1905).

Arendt, Hannah, *The Origins of Totalitarianism* (London: Harvest, 1958).

Arendt, Hannah, 'Personal Responsibility under Dictatorship', *The Listener*, 6 August 1964, 185–7.

Arendt, Hannah, *The Life of the Mind* (London: Harcourt, 1978).

Arendt, Hannah, *Eichmann in Jerusalem* (London: Penguin, 1994).

Arendt, Hannah, *Essays in Understanding* (New York: Schocken Books, 1994).

Arendt, Hannah, *The Human Condition*, 2nd edn. (Chicago: University of Chicago Press, 1998).

Arendt, Hannah, *Responsibility and Judgement*, ed. Jerome Kohn (New York: Schocken Books, 2003).

Arendt, Hannah, *The Jewish Writings*, ed. Jerome Kohn and Ron H. Feldman (New York: Schocken Books, 2007).

Arendt, Hannah, *Reflections on Literature and Culture* (Stanford: Stanford University Press, 2007).

Arendt, Hannah and Karl Jaspers, *Correspondence, 1926–1969*, ed. Lotte Kohler and Hans Saner, trans. Robert and Rita Kimber (New York: Harcourt Brace Jovanovich, 1992).

Ascherson, Neal, *The King Incorporated: Leopold the Second and the Congo* (London: Granta Books, 1999).

Ashcroft, Bill and Pal Ahluwalia, *Edward Said: The Paradox of Identity* (London: Routledge, 1999).

Bailey, James, 'Repetition, Boredom, Despair: Muriel Spark and the Eichmann Trial', in Jenni Adams and Sue Vice (eds.), *Representing Perpetrators in Holocaust Literature and Film* (London: Valentine Mitchell, 2013).

Banham, Gary, *Kant's Practical Philosophy: From Critique to Doctrine* (Basingstoke: Palgrave Macmillan, 2003).

Bankier, David, *The Germans and the Final Solution: Public Opinion Under Nazism* (Oxford: Basil Blackwell, 1992).

Bauer, Yehuda, *Rethinking the Holocaust* (New Haven: Yale University Press, 2002).

Beah, Ishmael, *A Long Way Gone* (London: Fourth Estate, 2007).

Bechhofer, Susi, *Rosa's Child: One Woman's Search for Her Past* (London: I.B. Tauris, 1996).

BenEzer, Gadi, 'Trauma Signals in Life Stories', in *Trauma and Life Stories*, ed. Kim Lacy Rogers et al. (London: Routledge, 1999), 29–44.

Benhabib, Selya, 'Hannah Arendt and the Redemptive Power of Narrative', *Social Research* 57 (1990), 167–96.

Benhabib, Selya, *The Reluctant Modernism of Hannah Arendt* (London: Sage, 1996).

Benhabib, Seyla, 'Who's On Trial, Eichmann or Arendt?', 21 September 2014: http://opinionator.blogs.nytimes.com/2014/09/21/whos-on-trial-eichmann-or-anrendt/?_r=0.

Benjamin, Walter, *Illuminations*, trans. Harry Zorn (London: Pimlico, 1999).

Bergmann, Peter, 'Kertész among the Germans', *Hungarian Studies* 18:2 (2004), 235–42.

Bernstein, Richard J., *Hannah Arendt and the Jewish Question* (Cambridge MA: MIT Press, 1996).

Bernstein, Richard J., *Radical Evil: A Philosophical Interrogation* (Cambridge: Polity, 2002).

Bevernage, Berber, *History, Memory and State-Sponsored Violence* (London: Routledge, 2012).

Bigsby, Christopher, *Remembering and Imagining the Holocaust: The Chain of Memory* (Cambridge: Cambridge University Press, 2006).

Binet, Laurent, *HHhH*, trans. Sam Taylor (London: Harvill Secker, 2012).

Blanchot, Maurice, *The Writing of the Disaster*, trans. Ann Smock (Nebraska: University of Nebraska Press, 1996).

Bloxham, Donald, *The Final Solution: A Genocide* (Oxford: Oxford University Press, 2009).

Boswell, Matthew, *Holocaust Impiety in Literature, Popular Music and Film* (Basingstoke: Palgrave Macmillan, 2012).

Boyne, John, *The Boy in the Striped Pyjamas* (London: Random House, 2006).

Brooks, Peter, *Reading for the Plot* (Oxford: Clarendon Press, 1984).

Browning, Christopher, *Ordinary Men: Reserve Police Battalion 101 and the Final Solution* (London: HarperCollins, 2nd edn., 1998).

Burleigh, Michael, *Death and Deliverance* (London: Pan, 1994).

Caruth, Cathy (ed.), *Trauma: Explorations in Memory* (Baltimore: Johns Hopkins University Press, 1995).

Cavell, Stanley, *The Claim of Reason* (Oxford: Oxford University Press, 1979).

Césaire, Aimé, *Discourse on Colonialism*, trans. Joan Pinkham (New York: Monthly Review Press, 1972).

Cesarani, David, *Eichmann: His Life and Crimes* (London: Heinemann, 2004).

Cesarani, David, *The Final Solution: The Fate of the Jews 1933–1949* (London: Palgrave Macmillan, 2016).

Cesarani, David, *The Literary Review*, http://holocaustcentre.com/cms_content/upload/PDFs/Cesarani%20Review%20Striped%20Pyjamas.pdf.

Chapman, Jake, *Meatphysics* (London: Creation Books, 2003).

Cheyette, Bryan, 'Frantz Fanon and Jean-Paul Sartre: Blacks and Jews', *Wasafiri: The Transnational Journal of International Writing* 44 (Spring 2005), 7–12.

Cheyette, Bryan, *Diasporas of the Mind: Jewish and Postcolonial Writing and the Nightmare of History* (New Haven: Yale University Press, 2013).

Chrisman, Laura, *Rereading the Imperial Romance: British Imperialism and South African Resistance in Haggard, Schreiner, and Plaatje* (Oxford: Oxford University Press, 2000).

Cohen, Stanley, *States of Denial* (London: Polity, 2001).

Confino, Alon, *Foundational Pasts: The Holocaust as Historical Understanding* (Cambridge: Cambridge University Press, 2012).

Confino, Alon, *A World without Jews* (New Haven: Yale University Press, 2014).

Conrad, Joseph, *Heart of Darkness with The Congo Diary*, ed. Robert Hampson (London: Penguin, 1995).

Cornwell, Gareth, 'J. P. Fitzpatrick's "The Outspan": A Textual Source of "Heart of Darkness"', *Conradiana* 30:3 (1998), 203–12.

Courtemanche, Gil, *A Sunday at the Pool in Kigali* (Edinburgh: Canongate, 2003).

Craps, Stef, *Postcolonial Witnessing: Trauma out of Bounds* (Basingstoke: Palgrave Macmillan, 2013).

Crownshaw, Richard, *The Afterlife of Holocaust Memory in Contemporary Literature and Culture* (London: Palgrave Macmillan, 2010).

Currie, Mark, 'The Expansion of Tense', *Narrative* 17:3 (2009), 353–67.

De Mul, Sarah, 'The Holocaust as a Paradigm for the Congo Atrocities: Adam Hochschild's *King Leopold's Ghost*', *Criticism* 53:4 (2011), 587–606.

Delbo, Charlotte, *Days and Memory*, trans. Rosemary Lamont (Marlboro, VT: Marlboro Press, 1990).

Derrida, Jacques, 'Canons and Metonymies: An Interview with Jacques Derrida', in *Logomachia: The Contest of the Faculties*, ed. Richard Rand (Lincoln: University of Nebraska Press, 1992).

Derrida, Jacques, 'Force of Law: The "Mystical Foundation of Authority"', trans. Mary Quaintance, in *Deconstruction and the Possibility of Justice*, ed. Drucilla Cornell, Michael Rosenfeld, and David Gray Carlson (London: Routledge, 1992), pp. 3–67.

Dews, Peter, *The Idea of Evil* (Oxford: Blackwell, 2008).

Diop, Boubacar Boris, *Murabi, The Book of Bones*, trans. Fiona McLaughlin (Bloomington: Indiana University Press, 2006).

Disch, Lisa Jane, *Hannah Arendt and the Limits of Philosophy* (Ithaca: Cornell University Press, 1994).

Donovan, Stephen, 'Figures, Facts, Theories: Conrad and Chartered Company Imperialism', *The Conradian* 24:2 (2000), 31–60.

Drechsler, Horst, *'Let Us Die Fighting': The Struggle of the Herero and Nama against German Imperialism* (London: Zed Press, 1980).

Dryden, Linda, 'Heart of Darkness' and *Allan Quartermain*: Apocalypse and Utopia', *Conradiana* 31:3 (1999), 173–97.

Dryden, Linda, *Joseph Conrad and the Imperial Romance* (Basingstoke: Palgrave Macmillan, 2000).

Eaglestone, Robert, 'Against the Metaphysics of Comprehension', *The Cambridge Companion to Postmodernism*, ed. S. Connor (Cambridge: Cambridge University Press, 2004).

Eaglestone, Robert, *The Holocaust and the Postmodern* (Oxford: Oxford University Press, 2004).

Eaglestone, Robert, 'The "Subterranean Stream of Western History": Arendt and Levinas after Heidegger', in *Hannah Arendt, Imperialism, and Genocide*, ed. Richard King and Dan Stone (Oxford/New York: Berghahn, 2007).

Eaglestone, Robert, 'Holocaust Theory?', in *Teaching Holocaust Literature and Film*, ed. Robert Eaglestone and Barry Langford (London: Palgrave Macmillan, 2008), 28–36.

Eggers, David, *What is the What: The Autobiography of Valentino Achak Deng* (London: Hamish Hamilton, 2007).

Elkins, Caroline, *British Gulag: The Brutal End of Empire in Kenya* (London: Jonathan Cape, 2005).

Eshel, Amir, 'Against the Power of Time: The Poetics of Suspension in W. G. Sebald's "Austerlitz"', *New German Critique* 88 (2003), 71–96.

Fabian, Johannes, *Language and Colonial Power: The Appropriation of Swahili in the Former Belgian Congo, 1880–1938* (Cambridge: Cambridge University Press, 1986).

Feinstein, Stephen C., 'Zbigniew Libera's Lego Concentration Camp: Iconoclasm in Conceptual Art about the Shoah', *Other Voices*, 2.1 (2000), http://www.othervoices.org/2.1/feinstein/auschwitz.php.

Felman, Shoshana, 'Theaters of Justice: Arendt in Jerusalem, the Eichmann Trial, and the Redefinition of Legal Meaning in the Wake of the Holocaust', *Critical Inquiry* 27:2 (2001), 201–38.

Felman, Shoshana, *The Juridical Unconscious* (Cambridge, MA: Harvard University Press, 2002).

Fest, Joachim, *Speer: The Final Verdict* (London: Weidenfeld and Nicolson, 2001).

Finch, Helen and Lynn L. Wolff (eds.), *Witnessing, Memory, Poetics: H. G. Adler and W. G. Sebald* (New York: Camden House, 2014).

Firchow, Peter Edgerly, *Envisioining Africa* (Kentucky: University Press of Kentucky, 2000).

Foley, Barbara, 'Fact, Fiction, Fascism: Testimony and Mimesis in Holocaust Narratives', *Comparative Literature* 34 (1982), 330–60.

Foucault, Michel, *Language, Counter-Memory, Practice*, ed. Donald Bouchard (New York: Cornell University Press, 1977).

Frenssen, Gustav, *Peter Moor: A Narrative of the German Campaign in South-West Africa*, trans. Margaret May Ward (London: Constable & Co., 1914).

Freud, Sigmund, 'Remembering, Repeating and Working-through', *Standard Edition*, 1914, vol 12.

Friedländer, Saul, *The Counterfeit Nazi: The Ambiguity of Good*, trans. Charles Fullman (London: Weidenfeld and Nicholson, 1969).

Friedländer, Saul, *When Memory Comes*, trans. Helen R. Lane (New York: Discus Books, 1980).

Friedländer, Saul, 'Trauma, Transference and "Working through" in Writing the History of the "Shoah"', *History and Memory* 4 (1992), 39–59.

Friedländer, Saul, *Reflections on Nazism: An Essay on Kitsch and Death*, trans. Thomas Weyr (Bloomington: Indiana University Press, 1984).

Fulbrook, Mary, *A Small Town near Auschwitz: Ordinary Nazis and the Holocaust* (Oxford: Oxford University Press, 2012).

Gilbert, Ruth, 'Grasping the Unimaginable: Recent Holocaust Novels for Children by Morris Gleitzman and John Boyne', *Children's Literature in Education* 41:4 (2010), 355–66.

Gilroy, Paul, *Between Camps* (London: Allen Lane, 2000).

Gilroy, Paul, *After Empire: Melancholia or Convivial Culture?* (London: Routledge, 2004).

Golding, William, *The Hot Gates and Other Occasional Pieces* (London: Harvest/HBJ, 1985).

Gourevitch, Philip, *We Wish To Inform You That Tomorrow We Will Be Killed With Our Families* (London: Picador, 2000).

Grethlein, Jonas, 'Myth, Morals and Metafiction in Jonathan Littell's *Les Bienveillantes*', *PMLA* 127:1 (2012), 77–93.

Griffin, Gabrielle, 'Science and the Cultural Imaginary: The Case of Kazuo Ishiguro's *Never Let Me Go*', *Textual Practice* 23:4 (2009), 645–63.

Grossman, David, *See Under: Love*, trans. Betsy Rosenberg (New York: Farrar, Strauss and Giroux, 1989).

Gumbrecht, Hans Ulrich, *After 1945: Latency as the Origin of the Present* (Stanford: Stanford University Press, 2013).

Hájková, Anna, 'Otto Dov Kulka Tells Auschwitz Story of a Czech Family That Never Existed', 30 October 2014, *Tablet*: http://www.tabletmag.com/jewish-arts-and-culture/books/186462/otto-dov-kulka.

Hampson, Robert, 'Conrad and the Idea of Empire', in Gail Finham and Myrtle Hooper (eds.), *Under Postcolonial Eyes: Joseph Conrad after Empire* (Cape Town: UCT Press, 1996), 65–71.

Harms, Robert, *River of Wealth, River of Sorrow: The Central Zaire Basin in the Era of the Slave and Ivory Trade 1500–1891* (New Haven: Yale University Press, 1981).

Hawkins, Hunt, 'Joseph Conrad, Roger Casement and the Congo Reform Movement', *Journal of Modern Literature* 9:1 (1981–2), 65–80.

Heidegger, Martin, *Being and Time*, trans. John Macquarrie and Edward Robinson (Oxford: Blackwell, 1962).

Heller, Agnes, 'Hannah Arendt on Tradition and New Beginnings', in Steven Aschheim (ed.), *Hannah Arendt in Jerusalem* (Berkeley: University of California Press, 2001), pp. 19–32.

Herman, Judith Lewis, *Trauma and Recovery* (London: Routledge, 1992).

Hilberg, Raul, *Perpetrators Victims Bystanders: The Jewish Catastrophe 1933–1945* (London: Harper Perennial, 1992).

Hirsch, Marianne, 'The Generation of Postmemory', *Poetics Today* 29:1 (2008), 103–27.

Hirsch, Marianne, *The Generation of Postmemory: Visual Culture After the Holocaust* (New York: Columbia University Press, 2012).

Hochschild, Adam, *King Leopold's Ghost: A Story of Greed, Terror and Heroism in Central Africa* (London: Papermac, 1984).

Hochschild, Adam, 'Dealt an Unlucky Hand', *Times Literary Supplement*, 28 July 2000, 3.

Hoess, Rudolf, *Commandant of Auschwitz*, trans. Constantine Fitzgibbon (London: Pan Books, 1959).

Holm, Anne, *I am David*, trans. L. W. Kingsland (London: Egremont, 2000).

Hungerford, Amy, *The Holocaust of Texts: Genocide, Literature and Personification* (Chicago: University of Chicago Press, 2003).

Hutcheon, Linda, *A Poetics of Postmodernism: History, Theory, Fiction* (London: Routledge, 1988).

Hutton, Margaret-Anne, 'Jonathan Littell's *Les Bienveillantes*: Ethics, Aesthetics and the Subject of Judgement', *Modern and Contemporary France* 18:1 (2010), 1–15.

Ishigoru, Kazuo, *Never Let Me Go* (London: Faber and Faber, 2005).

Iweala, Uzodinma, *Beasts of No Nation* (London: John Murray, 2005).

Jacobs, Carol, *Sebald's Vision* (New York: Columbia University Press, 2015).

Jinks, Rebecca, *Representing Genocide: The Holocaust as Paradigm?* (London: Bloomsbury, 2016).

Judt, Tony, *Postwar* (London: Heinemann, 2005).

Kansteiner, Wulf, 'Genealogy of a Category Mistake: A Critical Intellectual History of the Cultural Trauma Metaphor', *Rethinking History* 8 (2004), 193–221.

Kansteiner, Wulf with Harald Weilnböck, 'Against the Concept of Cultural Trauma or How I Learned to Love the Suffering of Others without the Help of Psychotherapy', in Astrid Erll and Ansgar Nünning (eds.), *Cultural Memory Studies: An International and Interdisciplinary Handbook* (New York: de Gruyter, 2008), 229–40.

Kershaw, Ian, *Popular Opinion and Political Dissent in the Third Reich: Bavaria 1933–1945* (Oxford: Clarendon Press, 1983).

Kertész, Imre, 'Who Owns Auschwitz?', trans. John MacKay. *The Yale Journal of Criticism* 14:1 (2001), 267–72.

Kertész, Imre, 'Heureka!', *PMLA*, 118:3 (2003), 604–14.

Kertész, Imre, *Kaddish for an Unborn Child*, trans. Tim Wilkinson (New York: Vintage International, 2004).

Kertész, Imre, *Fateless*, trans. Tim Wilkinson (London: Vintage Books, 2006).

Kertész, Imre, *The Union Jack*, trans. Tim Wilkinson (New York: Melville House, 2010).

Kertész, Imre, *Fiasco*, trans. Tim Wilkinson (New York: Melville House, 2011).

Kertész, Imre, *The Holocaust as Culture*, trans. Thomas Cooper (London: Seagull, 2011).

Kilby, Jane, *Violence and the Cultural Politics of Trauma* (Edinburgh: Edinburgh University Press, 2007).

King, Richard, *Arendt and America* (Chicago: University of Chicago Press, 2015).

Kleeblatt, Norman L. (ed.), *Mirroring Evil: Nazi Imagery/Recent Art* (New York: The Jewish Museum and New Brunswick: Rutgers University Press, 2001).

Klemperer, Victor, *The Language of the Third Reich*, trans. Martin Brady (London: Continuum, 2000).

Kluger, Ruth, *Landscapes of Memory: A Holocaust Girlhood Remembered* (London: Bloomsbury, 2003).

Kofman, Sarah, *Smothered Words*, trans. Madeleine Dobere (Evanston: Northwestern University Press, 1998).

Kouvaros, George, 'Images that Remember Us: Photography and Memory on Austerlitz', *Textual Practice* 19:1 (2005), 173–93.

Kühne, Thomas, 'Colonialism and the Holocaust: Continuities, Causations and Complexities', *Journal of Genocide Research* 15:3 (2013), 339–62.

Kulka, Otto Dov, *Landscapes of the Metropolis of Death* (London: Penguin, 2013).

Kulka, Otto Dov, Eberhard Jackel, and William Templer, *The Jews in the Secret Nazi Reports on Popular Opinion in Germany 1933–1945* (New Haven: Yale University Press, 2010).

Kushner, Tony, *The Holocaust and the Liberal Imagination* (Oxford: Blackwell, 1994).

LaCapra, Dominick, *Writing History, Writing Trauma* (Baltimore: Johns Hopkins University Press, 2001).

Lacoue-Labarthe, Philippe, *Heidegger, Art and Politics: The Fiction of the Political*, trans. Chris Turner (Oxford: Blackwell, 1990).

Langer, Lawrence, *Pre-empting the Holocaust* (New Haven: Yale University Press, 1998).

Langford, Barry, *Film Genre: Hollywood and Beyond* (Edinburgh: Edinburgh University Press, 2005).

Leavis, F. R., *The Great Tradition* (London: Penguin, 1962).

Lescourret, Marie-Anne, *Emmanuel Levinas* (Paris: Flammarion, 1994).

Levi, Primo, *If This Is a Man*, trans. Stuart Woolf (London: Abacus, 1979).

Levi, Primo, *The Drowned and the Saved*, trans. Raymond Rosenthal (London: Abacus, 1988).

Levinas, Emmanuel, *Totality and Infinity*, trans. Alphonso Lingis (London: Kluwer Academic Publishers, 1991).

Levinas, Emmanuel, *Alterity and Transcendence*, trans. Michel B. Smith (London: Athlone Press, 1999).

Levinas, Emmanuel, 'Loving the Torah more than God', in Zvi Kolitz, *Yosl Rakover Talks to God*, trans. Carol Brown Janeway (London: Jonathan Cape, 1999), 79–88.

Levy, Daniel and Natan Sznaider, 'Memory Unbound: The Holocaust and the Formation of Cosmopolitan Memory', *European Journal of Social Theory* 5:1 (2002): 87–106.

Lifton, Robert, *The Nazi Doctors* (London: Papermac, 1987).

Lipstadt, Deborah, *Denying the Holocaust: The Growing Assault on Truth and Memory* (London: Penguin, 1994).

Littell, Jonathan, Interview by Samuel Blumenfeld: http://thekindlyones. wordpress.com/littell-interview-with-samuel-blumenfeld/. Article published in 17 November 2006 edition of *Le Monde des Livres*.

Littell, Jonathan, *The Kindly Ones*, trans. Charlotte Mandell (London: Chatto and Windus, 2009).

Long, J. J. in *W. G. Sebald: Image, Archive, Modernity* (New York: Columbia University Press, 2008).

Long, J. J. and Anne Whitehead (eds.), *W. G. Sebald—A Critical Companion* (Edinburgh: Edinburgh University Press, 2004).

Longerich, Peter, *Heinrich Himmler*, trans. Jeremy Noakes and Lesley Sharpe (Oxford: Oxford University Press, 2012).

Luban, David, 'Explaining Dark Times: Hannah Arendt's Theory of Theory', *Social Research* 50:1 (1983), 215–48.

Marai, Sandor, *Memoir of Hungary, 1944–1948*, trans. Albert Tezla (New York: Corvina, 1996).

Matthäus, Jürgen et al., 'Review Forum: Donald Bloxham, *The Final Solution: A Genocide*', *Journal of Genocide Research* 13:1–2 (2011), 107–52.

Matthews, Sean and Sebastian Groes (eds.), *Kasuo Ishiguro: Contemporary Critical Perspectives* (London: Continuum, 2009).

Mazower, Mark, *Dark Continent* (London: Penguin, 1998).

Mazower, Mark, *Hitler's Empire* (London: Penguin, 2009).

Miller, J. Hillis, '"Heart of Darkness" Revisited', in *Heart of Darkness: Case Studies in Contemporary Criticism*, ed. Ross C. Murfin (New York: Bedford Books of St. Martin's Press, 1996), 206–20.

Miller, J. Hillis, *The Conflagration of Community: Fiction before and after Auschwitz* (Chicago: University of Chicago Press, 2011).

Mommsen, Hans, 'What Did the Germans Know About the Genocide of the Jews?', in *November 1938: From 'Reichskristallnacht' to Genocide*, ed. Walter H. Pehle, trans. William Templer (New York/Oxford: Berg, 1990).

Moore, A. W., *The Evolution of Modern Metaphysics: Making Sense of Things* (Cambridge: Cambridge University Press, 2012).

Morel, E. D., *Affairs of West Africa* (London: William Heinemann, 1902).

Morel, E. D., *The British Case in the French Congo* (London: William Heinemann, 1903).

Morel, E. D., *The Congo Slave State* (Liverpool: John Richardson and Sons, 1903).

Morel, E. D., *King Leopold's Rule in Africa* (London: W. Heinemann, 1904).

Morpurgo, Michael, *The Mozart Question* (London: Walker Books, 2006).

Moses, Dirk, 'Conceptual Blockages and Definitional Dilemmas in the "Racial Century": Genocides of Indigenous Peoples and the Holocaust', *Patterns of Prejudice* 36:4 (2002), 7–36.

Moses, Dirk, *Genocide and Settler Society: Frontier Violence and Stolen Indigenous Children in Australian History* (Oxford: Berghahn, 2004).

Moses, Dirk, 'The Holocaust and Genocide', in Dan Stone (ed.), *The Historiography of the Holocaust* (London: Palgrave Macmillan, 2004), 533–55.

Moses, Dirk, '*Das römische Gespräch* in a New Key: Hannah Arendt, Genocide, and the Defence of Republican Civilization', *Journal of Modern History* 85:4 (2013), 967–13.

Mullan, John, 'On First Reading *Never Let Me Go*', in *Kazuo Ishiguro*, ed. Sean Matthews and Sebastian Groes (London: Continuum 2009), 104–13.

Myant, Maureen, *The Search* (London: Alma Books, 2009).

Naipaul, V. S., *A Congo Diary* (Los Angeles: Sylvester and Orpharos, 1980).

Nelson, Samuel, *Colonialism in the Congo Basin, 1880–1940* (Ohio: Ohio State University Centre of International Studies, 1994).

Ngai, Sianne, *Our Aesthetic Categories: Zany, Cute, Interesting* (Harvard: Harvard University Press, 2012).

Nixon, Rob, *Slow Violence and the Environmentalism of the Poor* (Cambridge, MA: Harvard University Press, 2011).

Norridge, Zoe, *Perceiving Pain in African Literature* (Basingstoke: Palgrave Macmillan, 2012).

Nzongola-Ntalaja, Georges, *The Congo: From Leopold to Kabila* (London: Zed Books, 2002).

Olusoga, David and Casper W. Erichsen, *The Kaiser's Holocaust: Germany's Forgotten Genocide and the Colonial Roots of Nazism* (London: Faber and Faber, 2010).

Pakenham, Thomas, *The Scramble for Africa* (London: Abacus, 1991).

Parry, Benita, *Conrad and Imperialism* (London: Macmillan, 1983).

Pearce, Andy, *Holocaust Consciousness in Contemporary Britain* (London: Routledge, 2014).

Popkin, Jeremy, 'Holocaust Memories, Historians' Memoirs: First-Person Narrative and the Memory of the Holocaust', *History and Memory* 15 (2003), 49–84.

Prager, Brad, 'The Good German as Narrator: On W. G. Sebald and the Risks of Holocaust Writing', *New German Critique* 96 (2005), 75–102.

Radstone, Susannah, *The Sexual Politics of Time: Confession, Nostalgia, Memory* (London: Routledge, 2007).

Radstone, Susannah and B. Schwarz (eds.), *Memory: Histories, Theories, Debates* (New York: Fordham University Press, 2007).

Rapport, Frances with Anka Bergman, Terry Farago, and Edith Salter, *Fragments: Transcribing the Holocaust* (Swansea: Hafan Books, 2013).

Rawlinson, Mark, 'This Other War: British Culture and the Holocaust', *Cambridge Quarterly* 25:1 (1996), 1–25.

Reich, Tova, *My Holocaust* (New York: HarperCollins, 2007).

Reiter, Andrea, *Narrating the Holocaust*, trans. Patrick Camiler (London: Continuum, 2000).

Rensmann, Lars and Samir Gandesha (eds.), *Arendt and Adorno: Political and Philosophical Investigations* (Stanford: Stanford University Press, 2012).

Lewis, Roger and Jean Stengers (eds.), *E. D. Morel's History of the Congo Reform Movement* (Oxford: Clarendon Press, 1968).

Rose, Gillian, *Mourning Becomes the Law* (Cambridge: Cambridge University Press, 1996).

Rosen, Alan, 'Autobiography from the Other Side: The Reading of Nazi Memoirs and Confessional Ambiguity', *Biography* 24:3 (2001), 555–69.

Rosenthal, Norman, *Apocalypse: Beauty and Horror in Contemporary Art: Catalogue* (London: Royal Academy of Arts, 2000).

Rothberg, Michael, 'Between Auschwitz and Algeria: Multidirectional Memory and the Counterpublic Witness', *Critical Inquiry* 33:1 (2006), 158–84.

Rothberg, Michael, *Multidirectional Memory: Remembering the Holocaust in the Age of Decolonisation* (Stanford: Stanford University Press, 2009).

Rothberg, Michael, 'From Gaza to Warsaw: Mapping Multidirectional Memory', *Criticism* 53:4 (2011), 523–48.

Rothberg, Michael, 'Beyond Tancred and Clorinda: Trauma Studies for Implicated Subjects', in *The Future of Trauma Theory: Contemporary Literary and Cultural Criticism*, ed. Gert Buelens, Samuel Durrant, and Robert Eaglestone (London: Routledge, 2013), xi–xviii.

Rothberg, Michael, 'Multidirectional Memory and the Implicated Subject: On Sebald and Kentridge', in Liedeke Plate and Anneke Smelik (eds.), *Performing Memory in Art and Popular Culture* (London: Routledge, 2013), 39–58.

Rusesabagina, Paul, *An Ordinary Man* (London: Bloomsbury, 2006).

Said, Edward, *Joseph Conrad and the Fiction of Autobiography* (Harvard: Harvard University Press, 1966).

Saltzman, Lisa, 'Avant-Garde and Kitsch Revisited', in *Mirroring Evil: Nazi Imagery/Recent Art*, ed. Norman Kleeblatt (New York: The Jewish Museum and New Brunswick: Rutgers University Press, 2001), 53–64.

Samvin, William J., *The Black Man's Burden: African Colonial Labour on the Congo and Ubangi Rivers 1880–1900* (London: Westview Press, 1989).

Santner, Eric, *On Creaturely Life* (Chicago: University of Chicago Press, 2006).

Sanyal, Debarati, 'Reading Nazi Memory in Jonathan Littell's *Les Bienveillantes*', *L'Esprit Créateur* 50:4 (2010), 47–66.

Sanyal, Debarati, *Memory and Complicity: Migrations of Holocaust Remembrance* (New York: Fordham University Press, 2015).

Scherrer, Christian P., 'Towards a Theory of Modern Genocide. Comparative Genocide Research: Definitions, Criteria, Typologies, Cases, Key Elements, Patterns and Voids', *Journal of Genocide Research* 1:1 (1999), 13–23.

Schlant, Ernestine, *The Language of Silence* (London: Routledge, 1999).

Schlink, Bernhard, *Guilt about the Past* (London: Beautiful Books, 2010).

Sebald, W. G., *The Emigrants*, trans. Michael Hulse (London: Harvill Press, 1996).

Selbald, W. G., *The Rings of Saturn*, trans. Michael Hulse (London: Harvill Press, 1999).

Sebald, W. G., *Vertigo*, trans. Michael Hulse (New York: New Directions, 1999).

Sebald, W. G., *On the Natural History of Destruction*, trans Anthea Bell (London: Hamish Hamilton, 2003).

Sebald, W. G., *Campo Santo*, ed. Sven Meyer, trans. Anthea Bell (London: Penguin, 2006).

Sebald, W. G., *Austerlitz*, trans. Anthea Bell (London: Penguin Books, 2011).

Semprun, Jorge, *The Long Voyage*, trans. Richard Seaver (London: Penguin, 1997).

Sem-Sandberg, Steve, *The Emperor of Lies*, trans. Sarah Death (London: Faber and Faber, 2009).

Sereny, Gitta, *Into that Darkness: From Mercy Killing to Mass Murder* (London: Pimlico, 1974).

Sereny, Gitta, *Albert Speer: His Battle with Truth* (London: Picador, 1995).

Sheehan, Paul, 'A History of Smoke: W. G. Sebald and the Memory of Fire', *Textual Practice* 26:4 (2012), 729–45.

Sher, Antony, *Primo Time* (London; Nick Hern Books, 2005).

Sherry, Norman, *Conrad's Western World* (Cambridge: Cambridge University Press, 1971).

Silverman, Max, 'Interconnected Histories: Holocaust and Empire in the Cultural Imaginary', *French Studies* 72:4 (2008), 417–28.

Silverman, Max, *Palimpsestic Memory: The Holocaust and Colonialism in French and Francophone Fiction and Film* (Oxford: Berghahn, 2013).

Singh, Frances B., 'The Colonialistic Bias of *Heart of Darkness*', *Conradania* 10:1 (1978), 41–54.

Snyder, Timothy, *Bloodlands: Europe Between Hitler and Stalin* (New York: Basic Books, 2010).

Snyder, Timothy, *Black Earth: The Holocaust as History and Warning* (New York: Tim Duggan Books, 2015).

Soggot, David, *Nambia: The Violent Heritage* (London: Rex Collings, 1986).

Spark, Muriel, *The Prime of Miss Jean Brodie* (London: Penguin, 2000).

Speer, Albert, *Inside the Third Reich*, trans. Richard and Clara Winston (London: Phoenix, 1995).

Spivak, Gayatri, *A Critique of Postcolonial Reason* (Cambridge, MA: Harvard University Press, 1999).

Stangneth, Bettina, *Eichmann before Jerusalem*, trans. Ruth Martin (London: Bodley Head, 2014).

Stargardt, Nicholas, 'Speaking in Public about the Murder of the Jews', in *Years of Persecution, Years of Extermination: Saul Friedlander and the Future of Holocaust Studies*, ed. Christian Wiese and Paul Betts (London: Continuum, 2010), 133–56.

Steele, Meile, *Hiding From History: Politics and the Public Imagination* (Ithaca: Cornell University Press, 2005).

Stern, Frank, *The Whitewashing of the Yellow Badge: Anti-Semitism and Philose-mitism in Postwar Germany*, trans. William Templer (Oxford: Pergamon, 1992).

Stone, Dan, 'The Historiography of Genocide: Beyond Uniqueness and Ethnic Competition', *Rethinking History* 8:1 (2004), 127–42.

Stone, Dan, *History, Memory and Mass Atrocity: Essays on the Holocaust and Genocide* (London: Vallentine Mitchell, 2006).

Stone, Dan, *Histories of the Holocaust* (Oxford: Oxford University Press, 2010).

Stone, Dan, *Goodbye to All That?* (Oxford: Oxford University Press, 2014).

Stone, Dan and Dirk Moses (eds.), *Colonialism and Genocide* (London: Routledge, 2007).

Stonebridge, Lyndsey, *The Judicial Imagination: Writing After Nuremberg* (Edinburgh: Edinburgh University Press, 2011).

Straus, Nina Pelikan, 'The Exclusion of the Intended from Secret Sharing in Conrad's "Heart of Darkness"', *Novel* 20:2 (1987), 123–37.

Suleiman, Susan Rubin, 'When the Perpetrator becomes a Reliable Witness of the Holocaust: On Jonathan Littell's *Les bienveillants*', *New German Critique* 36:1 (2009), 1–19.

Tabner, Stuart, 'German Literature and the Holocaust', in Alan Rosen (ed.), *Literature of the Holocaust* (Cambridge: Cambridge University Press, 2013).

Taussig, Michael T., *Defacement: Public Secrecy and the Labor of the Negative* (Stanford: Stanford University Press, 1999).

Thornton, John K., *The Kingdom of Kongo: Civil Wars and Transition* (Madison: University of Wisconsin Press, 1983).

Torgovnick, Marianna, *Gone Primitive: Savage Intellects, Modern Lives* (Chicago: University of Chicago Press, 1990).

Torgovnick, Marianna, *The War Complex* (Chicago: University of Chicago Press, 2005).

Trezise, Thomas, 'Unspeakable', *The Yale Journal of Criticism* 14:1 (2001), 39–66.

Twain, Mark, *King Leopold's Soliloquy* (London: T. Fisher Unwin, 1907).

Unger, Michael, *Reassessment of the Image of Mordercai Chaim Rumkowski* (Jerusalem: Yad Vashem, 2004).

Vidal-Naquet, Pierre, *Assassins of Memory*, trans. Jeffrey Mehlman (New York: Columbia University Press, 1993).

Wainaina, Binyavanga, 'How to Write about Africa' (London: Granta 92, 2006).

Warin, François, 'Phillipe's Lessons of Darkness', trans. Nidesh Lawtoo, in Nidesh Lawtoo (ed.), *Conrad's Heart of Darkness and Contemporary Thought* (London: Bloomsbury, 2012), 123–42.

Watt, Ian, *Conrad in the Nineteenth Century* (London: Chatto and Windus, 1979).

Webber, Jonathan and Chris Schwarz, *Rediscovering Traces of Memory: The Jewish Heritage of Polish Galicia*, Littman Library of Jewish Civilisation (Bloomington: Indiana University Press, 2009).

White, Andrea, *Joseph Conrad and the Adventure Tradition: Constructing and Deconstructing the Imperial Subject* (Cambridge: Cambridge University Press, 1993).

Whitehead, Anne, 'Writing With Care: Kazuo Ishiguro's *Never Let Me Go*', *Contemporary Literature* 52:1 (2011), 54–83.

Williams, Raymond, *Keywords* (London: Fontana Press, 1988).

Wollaeger, Mark, *Joseph Conrad and the Language of Scepticism* (Stanford: Stanford University Press, 1990).

Woolley, Agnes, *Contemporary Asylum Narratives: Representing Refugees in the Twenty-First Century* (Basingstoke: Palgrave Macmillan, 2014).

Young, Robert, *Postcolonialism: An Historical Introduction* (Oxford: Blackwell, 2001).

Young, Tim, *Travellers in Africa: British Travelogues, 1850–1900* (Manchester: Manchester University Press, 1994).

Zilcosky, John, 'Lost and Found: Disorientation, Nostalgia, and Holocaust Melodrama in Sebald's *Austerlitz*', *MLN* 121:3 (2006), 679–98.

Zimmerer, Jürgen, 'The Birth of the "Ostland" out of the Spirit of Colonialism: A Postcolonial Perspective on Nazi Policy of Conquest and Extermination', *Patterns of Prejudice* 39:2 (2005), 197–219.

Index